FROM POLITICS TO PRISON

SCRIPTOR HOUSE
The Epitome of Greatness

L A R R Y   B A R T O N

Scriptor House LLC

2810 N Church St Wilmington, Delaware, 19802

www.scriptorhouse.com

Phone: +1302-205-2043

Published by Scriptor House LLC

Paperback ISBN: 979-8-88692-148-9

eBook ISBN: 979-8-88692-149-6

Acknowledgments

In writing this book, I was assisted by several people, including Bill Horner, Delane Barton, and M. M. Jones. However, without the involvement and support of my life-long friend, Miss Charlotte Staples, *FROM POLITICS TO PRISON* would never have been finished.

Working long hours every night and weekends for many weeks, Charlotte took a rough draft manuscript that was full of errors and with her expertise in typing and editing turned out a completed book of which I am proud.

Table of Contents

Foreword

Americans believe they have more personal freedom than any other people in the world. But do they? Or is personal freedom slipping away under the pretense of law and order?

Like most of you, I've been bewildered and frightened by the escalating crime rate. We cry out for harsher laws and find that the majority of politicians respond with tough campaign rhetoric lock 'em up. Throw away the key. Make 'em serve all their ne!"—a blanket solution for everyone convicted of crimes. sounds terrific, doesn't it? A quick solution for a nasty problem—it there's a catch.

The average person has no idea how easy it is to be dicted, convicted, and sent to prison. It's frighteningly simple for prosecutor to get what is known as a "Bologna sandwich dictment," a term, which means that it is so easy for a prosecutor get an indictment, they could indict a bologna sandwich. Or, put other way, it's fairly easy to convince a jury that defendants are lilty or they wouldn't be on trial in the first place.

This practice is surprisingly common among some members of law enforcement agencies being pressured to boost arrest quotas. nd there's certainly no shortage of federal statutes, which can be led to charge the accused. Once charged and indicted, those accused are pressured and badgered into pleading guilty to avoid sing to trial. How is this done? Simple. Promise the accused a sser sentence for pleading guilty, whether the individual is guilty not. At the same time, threaten the accused by implying that by leading innocent, there is a much greater risk of going to trial and letting a longer or even maximum sentence. That's essentially what happened to me. I was hurt, angry, and disillusioned because the whole process was so unbelievable to me. How could my country's judicial system be so totally based on political maneuvering?

Such practices, which coerce a surprisingly large number of nocent people into pleading guilty, greatly increase the strain on already overloaded prison system. According to statistics leased by the Justice Department in January, 1998, the number of state and federal prison inmates had climbed to 1.8 million. That's almost triple the 1998 figure!

The same report noted that for several years the United States has been locking up a greater number of its citizens than almost any other nation in the world. In 1996, an incredible 615 out of every 100,000 Americans were in prison. And that figure doesn't include the 518,492 people who were in local jails, awaiting trial or serving short terms. Currently, only Russia incarcerates slightly more of its citizens, imprisoning them at a rate of 690/100,000, compared to the United States number of 615/100,000 (The News Herald, Monday, June 23, 1997, p. 11A).

Many authorities see no beneficial results from the practice of locking them up and throwing away the key." This is especially true of first-time offenders who are charged with white-collar crimes.

"Inmate populations have quadrupled in the last 20 years," says Marc Mauer, assistant director of "The Sentencing Project" and author of the study, Americans Behind Bars, "but I don't know anyone who feels safer than 20 years ago… prison growth has been a waste of money."

Professor Alfred Blumstein of Carnegie-Mellon University puts it another way: "Suddenly, we've gone wild on incarceration, but there is no clear impact on crime rates."

It is not my intent to slander or embarrass anyone who was involved with my investigation and trial or any of their family, but I was prohibited from presenting evidence that would more than likely have exonerated me. In view of this, I decided to share what my testimony would have been. My family and friends know I was "set up," but on the other hand, even if God or His angels testified that I was not guilty of the charges, my enemies would still not accept the truth

Most of the material included in "my story," From Politics to Prison, is documented either by signed statements or tape, recorded conversations.

You will find it hard to find a stopping place as you laugh, cry, and feel anger.

JAMIE GRACE AND JERRY JACKSON

It was the first week in November of 1991, and I had been back in office for a month. Jamie Grace, Chief of Talladega County United Narcotic Office (UNO) and a former Talladega city employee, came to see me to express her concern about the drug problem that existed in Talladega and the surrounding cities.

Jamie had been placed in charge because of her ability, honesty, and tenacity in getting things accomplished. She was also a perfectionist and a workaholic who would investigate ANYONE.

"Larry," she said, "you supported me and good law enforcement during your other term as mayor, and I appreciate it more than you know. But now I need your support even more because of the huge increase in drug activity over the last few years."

"Jamie, I think you already know you have my full support. I have every confidence in you, and I'll be available to you if you need me." Having hired Jamie in 1985 during my second term as mayor, I knew how dedicated she was. As we continued our conversation, Jamie shared with me that one of her biggest concerns was the way things had allegedly gotten out of hand while George Montgomery served as mayor and Jake Montgomery served as city attorney.

"During George's administration, it seemed like he did everything he could to prevent good law enforcement, and his brother, Jake, was in a perfect position, as a city attorney, to tie our hands at every turn."

Jamie wasn't the only one who believed the Montgomerys tried to hamper law enforcement. When police captain (now chief)

Joe Hare made his bid for mayor in 1991, he ran newspaper ads depicting the bound hands of the police, and his ads alluded to the fact that "Under the Montgomery brothers' administration, the police had their hands tied." Naturally, the Montgomerys denied this

On November 19, 1991, Jamie came to see me with a man she introduced as Jerry Jackson.

"I'd like you to hire Jerry. I need him to work undercover for me. Of course, I'd be his supervisor."

How many hours, and what kind of pay are we talking about? Have you talked with the D.A. (District Attorney Robert Rumsey) about this?" I asked.

"No. I wanted to see how you felt about it first," Jamie said.

"I don't think it would be a good idea to hire him without going through civil service," I said.

"Could we hire him as a contract laborer?"

Jerry looked at me and said, "It just so happens that I'm a professional tree surgeon. I've seen hundreds of stumps around here. Removing those stumps would be a good cover for me, and it would benefit the city, too."

Jerry was right about the need for stump removal. Over the past few years, several storms and tornadoes had come through Talladega and had blown down hundreds of trees. Rescue squads and city crews used chainsaws to cut broken trees as low as possible, but there were still more than 2,000 stumps throughout the city. Not only were they unsightly, but being the home of Alabama Institute for Deaf and Blind, I knew. we had untold number of visually impaired individuals who walk the sidewalks on a regular basis. If for any reason they were to get off the sidewalk, they could stumble over these stumps and injure themselves.

Having remembered my earlier promise of support to Jamie, I agreed to hire Jerry as a contract laborer at $100 per day. For that amount, Jerry was to provide his own equipment and most of the labor. I agreed to have city crews clean up the chips and sawdust. I informed Jamie and Jerry that I wanted Jerry to report to me weekly and let me know how much work had been done and what area of town he was working in, but for security reasons, I did not want to be involved in any undercover work.

"Jamie, you're to be in charge of Jerry as far as investigative work, and I don't want any of the city employees to Know he is working with you."

An agreement was drawn up for our signatures. A copy is placed in each council member's mailbox at City Hall, and Jamie took a copy to give to the D.A. From the time he was hired to February, 1992, Jerry kson stayed busy. The only time I saw him was if I went out to ob site or when he came by City Hall to pick up his paycheck. nie kept me informed about progress on the undercover work he is doing for her. She was quite pleased with the information he is providing. I never questioned Jamie about who she was ilding files on. I didn't want to know. I didn't want to be cused of tipping off anyone.

The second week of February, 1992, Jamie came by the office. She was visibly upset. I asked my administrative assistant, trolyn Ricks, to hold all my calls.

"Mayor, Jerry told me some things that has me concerned, and I'm not sure where it will lead. He's shared with me that he is reason to believe several law enforcement officers, one or more employees in the D.A.'s office, a city council member and the son a council member, as well as a city attorney, are involved in gal activity and drug trafficking."

I had already heard these rumors around town, so the information didn't come as a complete surprise.

"Jamie, have you shared this info with Mr. Rumsey?" 1 quired.

"Only bits and pieces, but he thinks it might be bogus "information," she replied.

"You need to make sure Jerry is not being fed erroneous formation and that his informants are reliable and not just using n for their benefit," I said.

During my recent campaign for mayor, I had heard that a formerworker with Jamie when she was a city investigator had her raped or tried to rape her. I began to wonder if he could be le of the police officers who were alleged to be involved with illegal activity. After Jamie left my office, I phoned Edyth Sims, a back schoolteacher and second-term Talladega councilwoman, and inquired if she was aware of the rumor concerning Jamie and the officer.

"Well," she said, "Jamie filed a verbal complaint with me while George Montgomery was mayor. I met with Mayor Montgomery and Police Chief Mike Hamlin on several occasions.

I also talked to Mr. Rumsey about what Jamie had shared with me. They all refused to become involved, claiming it was Jamie's word against the officer. According to Jamie, the officer came to her apartment late one night and pounded so loud on her door that he woke up several of the residents. Jamie said she opened the door and let him in, not realizing he was either drunk or on drugs. She was already dressed for bed and had a bathrobe on over her nightclothes. Jamie said that after a few minutes he asked her to have sex with him and gave her a sob story about no home life. He kept after her, and she finally ordered him to leave immediately. Apparently, that's when he tried to force himself on her. Mayor, you know Jamie is 5'6" tall and only weighs about 125 pounds, but on the other hand, the officer is more than 6' tall and weighs a good 230 pounds. So it wouldn't be too hard for him to shove her on the bed and take off her clothes. Jamie said she struggled with him, and when he started trying to undo his pants, she hit him pretty hard, and when he fell on the floor, that gave her time to grab her gun that was on the nightstand. Jamie told him to get out, or she would kill him. 'I guess that gun got through to him because he finally left,' Jamie told me. I asked Jamie to file a written complaint with the police chief or the D.A., but she said, 'I'm afraid to. He is pretty heavy into drugs and alcohol and is capable of doing anything. On top of that, he wants my job and will do anything he can to discredit me so he will be appointed.'"

It was close to five in the afternoon several days later afer talking with Councilwoman Sims. City hall employees were beginning to leave for the day. Just as I was finishing up, my phone rang. It was Jamie.

"Mayor, I need to come by the office and talk. If I come now, do you have time to talk with me?"

"Sure, Jamie. Come on over," I said.

It was not unusual for me to be working late. Many nights I le in a police car with one of the officers. Being a former ice officer myself, I enjoyed the opportunity to see what was ng on around town. This also provided an opportunity to make st of street lights that were out or see what streets needed paving patching.

Jamie arrived shortly. She seemed agitated, and even before ing down, she said, "Mayor, something has got to be done about former co-worker."

I had never seen Jamie so upset. She was a very beautiful k woman who was in her mid-thirties, educated, intelligent, and rays composed. BUT NOT TODAY!

Trying to give her time to calm down, I said, "Why don't 1 sit down, Jamie, and I'll get you a cup of coffee."

I walked over to the kitchen in City Hall, poured Jamie a of coffee, returned to the office, and began to make small talk about Jerry and if she was satisfied with his work.

"Jerry's fine," she said. "He's still providing me with some usable information." She sipped her coffee, took a couple of p breaths, and said, "One of Jerry's sources said that my former worker is trying to sabotage my operation. I know he resents and is doing everything in his power to make me look bad. I re reason to believe he has found out who some of our rmants are, and he is calling them in for questioning about om they are buying drugs from under our supervision. Once he the names of those whom we are investigating, he contacts the g dealers and tips them off that they are being investigated. If is true, Mayor, it won't be the first time he's hindered an estigation. It's common knowledge in the D.A's office that he referred with a rape case. We had a taped confession, and the e was destroyed. He even warned the suspect that we were on him. The suspect just happened to be a snitch for him," Jamie continued

Jamie, are you sure the D. A knows about this?" I asked.

"Yes, he knows about it, but he hasn't taken any action"

"Jamie, there seems to be some bad feelings between you and your former co-worker," I remarked. "Would you like to share with me what the problem is?"

Jamie shared with me essentially the same story I'd heard earlier from Councilwoman Sims, so I asked, "Why didn't you file a formal written complaint?"

I could hear the pain and disappointment in her voice a she responded with, "I talked to the D.A. about doing that, but he was hesitant to get involved. He indicated it would just be m word against his, and since I am black and he is white, it would be better to just let it drop. "

"I think we should call in an outside agency and report this incident—maybe the justice department. What do you think?" Jamie said, "Maybe you are right, but I am doing some investigating of some possible illegal activity in the D.A.'s office and I don't need to do anything that would hamper my investigation. If I can prove what I think I can, we don't have to worry about him, or anyone in the D.A.'s office. I will give you written report soon. "

After about an hour of conversation, the intercom buzzed and my assistant, Carolyn, who also was working late, said, 'TI sorry to bother you, but Jamie has a call." I handed the phone t Jamie, and she spoke briefly to the caller, and as she hung up, she said, "It's Jerry, and he has a drug deal going down. I have got to meet him. Thanks for letting me cry on your shoulder. "

Not long after my meeting with Jamie, I requested a meeting with D.A. Robert Rumsey, his investigator Denni Surrett, Police Chief Mike Hamlin, Captain Willard Pee Wee Hurst, and detectives Eugene Jacks and Tom Bowerman. Jack and Bowerman were the investigators handling the rape case that Jamie had referred to during our meeting. Earlier, the rape victim and her husband had come to my office and filed a form complaint, so I also invited them to be a part of this meeting They were obviously upset and very vocal about how poorly the case was being handled.

Prior to the meeting beginning, I had a chance to speak with the D.A. and inquired about the alleged rape incident involving Jamie and this former co-worker. "

"Jamie and Councilwoman Sims came to see me about it, and I instructed Jamie to file a formal written complaint. To my knowledge, she never did. Under Alabama law, she still has plenty of time to file one if she wishes to," he said.

During the meeting with the rape victim and her husband, accusations flew about the inept handling of the investigation.

Captain Hurst tried to explain away the fiasco of the evidence being lost or misplaced as misunderstanding and unavoidable errors. He admitted that someone had accidentally taped over the confession, and some of the physical evidence had gotten lost in the lab.

However, nothing was really resolved, and the animosity was thick as the meeting came to a close.

For the next several weeks, Jerry kept in touch with me on a regular basis, but I had not seen Jamie. Jerry said he had not seen her either, but was under the impression that she was out of town. I was not concerned if Jamie was out of town. I assumed she was working on a case. Jamie would follow a lead wherever it took her.

On the morning of July 31, 1992, I was awaken from my sleep by the ringing of the telephone. I glanced at the lighted digital clock that was located on the nightstand next to the telephone. It was 2:13 a.m. It was not unusual for me to receive calls during the night. Being accessible 24 hours a day and returning phone calls had been one of my campaign promises, so my first thought was that someone had been arrested and wanted to complain to the mayor. Was I wrong!

"Mayor, I've got a problem. The D.A., Dennis and Ann are threatening me!" It was Jamie, and she was sobbing. Her speech sounded slurred, but I had no knowledge that she drank alcoholic beverages, and I knew she hated drugs —legal and illegal.

"What are you talking about, Jamie?"

"There are confiscated drugs and money missing from the

D.A's office, and they're trying to blame me. Only Robert (D.A.),

Ann, Dennis, and I know the combinations, " she said.

Circumstances had made it necessary for me to fire Dennis

Surrett, former chief of detectives, during my term as mayor in 1991, but the city council had placed him back on the payroll. However, Dennis eventually resigned, and the D,A. had hired him as chief investigator. Ann Wallace White also worked for the D.A. as a sort of girl Friday—investigator, secretary, bookkeeper, or whatever else the D.A. required of her.

"Jamie, why do you think Robert, Dennis, or Ann would want to blame you? It's hard to believe they would actually try to harm you."

"You don't know them!" she fired back. "I work with them almost everyday, and they are vicious, especially Ann. She's jealous of me and does anything she can to discredit me. She wants the D.A. to remove me and place Dennis in my position. I know what they have going on in the D.A.'s office. I have it all in a file, and when I complete my investigation, I will share it with you, and then we can go to the FBI or the justice department."

I was somewhat taken back. Even though Jamie had alluded something being amiss in the D.A.'s office, this was the first time I had heard her really speak negative of Mr. Rumsey. I knew she was really upset about something.

"Where are you calling from, Jamie?"

"I am at a friend's house. I can't go home. Ann has already beat me up and threatened my life. If I go home, I'm afraid she will come back to my house and kill me."

Jamie and I talked until almost 3:30 a.m. Jamie had calmed down with her speech much clearer, and she began to sound more rational.

"Mayor, I appreciate all the support you've given me.. you're a good man," she said.

"Are you going to be OK?" I asked and listened carefully for any hesitation or agitation in her voice.

"Yes, I think so. I feel a lot better. Goodnight," she said and hung up.

I had no way of knowing this would be my last conversation with Jamie, but as I lay back down, I had a strange feeling. Some of Jamie's remarks sounded almost like a farewell message. *Had Ann really beat her up and threatened her?* I knew Dennis and Ann were arrogant and had very few friends, but I had been under the impression that Jamie was able to work well with them. *Were drugs and money really missing from the vault in the D.A.'s office? What could Jamie know that would warrant calling in the FBI or the Justice Dept?*

I work with them and they are vicious. Jamie's words kept running through my mind. Something wasn't right. As her words kept running through my mind, unable to go back to sleep, I crawled out of bed and decided that I would try to contact Jamie later in the morning and invite her to lunch or supper and maybe get some answers.

By mid-morning, unable to locate Jamie, I reasoned that she had probably settled down, and if not, she would contact me; she always did. Jamie had indicated that she was with a friend, so she could have been calling from out of town. I still could not shake a bad feeling about some of the things that she had shared with me.

On Friday afternoon, Jerry came by the office around 5:30 p.m. to pick up his payroll check. Not having the authority to sign checks, I followed normal procedure by submitting a written request to payroll. Payroll personnel were responsible for typing all the checks, having them co-signed by two council members, and returning them to my office. Carolyn Ricks, my assistant, would place them on my desk, and I always had them ready to give to Terry when he came by.

As Jerry entered my office, he asked, "Have you heard the rumors that Ann jumped on Jamie, beat her up, and threatened her with a gun?"

My thoughts immediately turned to some of the things Jamie had alluded to in her conversation earlier. I grabbed up the telephone receiver, dialed her number, and after several rings with 1o answer, I slammed the receiver down and told Jerry to come with me. I pushed the speed limit getting to Jamie's apartment, only to find her gone. A couple of her neighbors told me they had not seen her that day, but she had been home for a little while yesterday.

"Some white lady and black lady was with her, and they left with some clothes," one of the ladies remarked. "That woman from the D.A.'s office had also been out there for awhile." the lady continued.

Our next stop was the D.A.'s office located in the Judicial Building. All the cars were gone, and it was obvious everyone had left for the weekend. Jerry and I hurried back to the city car I was driving and drove to city hall where I talked to the police dispatcher

"Have you heard from Jamie or had any radio contact with her, or has she left a telephone number where she can be reached?" I asked.

"Jamie's not on the air, but someone left a message that she would be off for a few days."

Frustrated, I turned to Jerry and said, "Maybe the rumor was just that—a rumor. Maybe Jamie decided to get away from the rat race for a while."

On Monday, August 3rd, around 1:00 in the afternoon,

Carolvn buzzed me and said that my daughter-in-law, Becky, needed to talk with me. At that time, Becky was news director for a local radio station. When I answered the phone, Becky asked, "Have you heard anything about Jamie?"

"Like what?" I responded. At this time, I had not shared anything with anyone other than Jerry about Jamie.

"You mean you haven't heard that she's dead? The police haven't informed you?"

"Talk to you later," I said, slamming the phone down and practically running to the other side of city hall where the police department is located.

"Do you know anything about Jamie?" I asked Judy

Williams, Police Chief Mike Hamlin's secretary.

"All, I know is that the chief got a call and left in a hurry for Jamie's house." she responded.

Rushing back to my office, I made a quick call to Becky, sharing with her what little I knew and told Carolyn that I would be gone for awhile. I quickly drove to Jamie's residence.

As I parked on the street in, front of the apartment complex located directly across from Talladega High School, the front door to Jamie's apartment was open. I could see several individuals just inside the room. As I approached the apartment and entered the front doorway, I immediately recognized D.A. Robert Rumsey, Investigator Dennis Surreft, T.P.D. narcotics investigator Leon Thomas, Police Chief Mike Hamlin, Talladega County Deputy Coroner Clarence Haynes (who is now Talladega County Circuit Clerk), along with one or two other individuals I did not recognize.

"What happened, Robert?" I asked D.A. Rumsey.

"Jamie committed suicide," he responded.

A sick feeling collected in the pit of my stomach as I walked through Jamie's small apartment to her bedroom. Her body was in a sitting position on the bed. Her hair was in curlers, and she was dressed only in her nightgown. There appeared to be blood on her temple. She looked like she was sleeping or unconscious—not dead. Could Jamie really have killed herself? In my experience, I had noticed that black people rarely kill themselves...nor did devout Catholics. Jamie was both.

My thoughts turned to what Jamie had shared with me during our recent visit and then what Jerry had told me later on.

Did Jamie really have a fight with Ann which ended up eventually with Ann's going back to Jamie's apartment and killing her? Did someone else from the D.A's office kill Jamie because of what Jamie had apparently stumbled on with her investigation? Was the former co-worker concerned that Jamie might be planning on filing a complaint against him for the alleged rape, and he became frightened and killed her? Jamie's words kept ringing in my ears, *"I work with them and they are vicious, especially Ann."* Knowing some of the things that Jamie had uncovered and was continuing with her investigation, I couldn't help but wonder if someone would try to harm me if they were aware of what Jamie had shared with me. I then thought about Jamie's investigation of several prominent people who were allegedly involved in the cocaine ring.

Had they found out and maybe had someone kill her and make it look like suicide?

According to rumors coming out of the police department, the gun Jamie allegedly used to commit suicide was not her regular revolver, if indeed it was hers. I wondered where this weapon had come from. Her regular service revolver was not found at her house.

As I reflected back to the scene where Jamie was in bed, it looked like she had been sitting up in bed reading, but if so, the impact of the bullet should have knocked her over... unless she had been killed and then placed in a sitting position. Something was definitely wrong with this scenario. I wondered how they had entered Jamie's house to know she was dead. Who tipped off the police or whomever to tell them Jamie was dead? Did someone else have a key to Jamie's house? Who would Jamie have entrusted with a key? I had not been able to locate Jamie, so who would have known she was at home, and how long had she been dead? Why was the D.A. notified before the police chief or me? As I left Jamie's apartment with all these thoughts and questions ringing in my head, I wondered if the D.A. would hold a press conference or issue some kind of statement, sharing with the citizens what he wanted them to know about this alleged suicide?

I wondered if there would be an autopsy. Later on in the afternoon, Mr. Rumsey and Chief Hamlin called a press conference and issued a brief statement alleging that Jamie had failed to report to work, and Detective Leon Thomas had been asked to check her apartment to see if she might be at home. When Leon entered the apartment, he found Jamie dead, according to Mr. Rumsey.

As I listened to Mr. Rumsey and Chief Hamlin issue this brief statement to the media and others who were in attendance at the press conference, I began to realize their statements made no more sense than Jamie's death. *Why had Leon Thomas, who allegedly was several miles away from town, been dispatched to check on Jamie when any police officer could have checked her apartment. Why wasn't Chief Hamlin notified and asked to check on Jamie? Did Leon have a key to the apartment? Did Mr.*

Rumsey dispatch a police officer to check on each employee who might not show up for work? For whatever reason, I had a hard time swallowing the statement that was being released to the media.

Something wasn't right about any of this. Jamie's mother and several other relatives lived in Anniston, Alabama, a city located 25 miles north of Talladega, so the funeral services and interment was held there. The church was packed. I knew Jamie was well respected and -had a lot of friends, but I was awed by the scope of her circle of friends. It appeared that every law enforcement officer in the state was in attendance. She had been a beautiful, honest person, and obviously well liked. I knew her as a dedicated employee to the citizens of Talladega.

As I approached the casket to view the body, I was shocked to see that the casket was closed. Why should it be? I wondered.

Jamie's face hadn't shown any damage. I wondered if Jamie or her family had requested a closed casket funeral. A crazy, weird thought flashed through my mind. Was Jamie really in the casket?

Was she really dead? There was no word of any autopsy report and no news coming from the D.A.'s office. Why was everything being kept so quiet?

As Sister Veronica from St. Francis of Assisi Catholic

Church in Talladega gave the eulogy, a few of her comments gave me reason to believe that she and Jamie had discussed some of Jamie's fears and concerns in relation to her job. I wondered if Sister Veronica or the family had seen Jamie's body?

A few days had passed since Jamie's death, and the only information given out by the D.A. was that Jamie had committed suicide. Case closed. But where was the autopsy report, and why had the results not been released to the media? And no mention had been made of the murder weapon, the mysterious gun. What about the money and drugs that were supposed to have been missing from the D.A.'s vault? If they were, why wasn't the media informed? Why were the mayors who were participating in the county-wide drug program not notified? Most important, if Jamie was truly dead, did someone make her murder look like suicide?

In view of the fact that Jamie's death had been hushed up, rumors began circulating among the blacks and the drug crowd that Jamie wasn't dead. There was speculation that she had been placed in a witness protection program because of numerous death threats, and she was in hiding. Rumors, rumors, rumors, rumors, rumors. but no concrete facts anywhere. *If Jamie was in a witness protection program, why hadn't she contacted me? She knew I was her friend and could trust me.*

Jamie's brother, a respected, high-profile attorney in Texas, had shared with me by phone that D.A. Rumsey had assured him he would share a copy of the autopsy report as soon as he received it. Her brother indicated he never received his

About a week after Jamie's funeral, Jerry was in my office.

I shared with him that in view of Jamie's death, I was going to terminate his employment with the city. I shared with him some of my concerns about Jamie's bizarre, questionable death and that I was having a tough time accepting all the explanations coming from the D.A.

"Mayor, there are some things you need to know. First of all, there is no way, Jamie committed suicide. If she is really dead, then someone killed her, and made it look like suicide. Jamie had too much going for her— a good income, nice car, decent apartment, almost anything else she needed, and above all, she loved her job. Jamie was respected by most of her fellow officers in this county and by people all around the state. If that isn't enough reasons that she would not have killed herself, her family loved her, and they depended on her. Jamie loved them, too. I hope you will keep me on the payroll a little while longer and let me see if I can tie some loose ends together."

"Have you ever talked to Leon, Dennis, Ann or the D.A.? I questioned.

No, but the D.A. knows who I am. Jamie told me she had shared this information with him and what I was involved in," Jerry said.

"Do you know anything about confiscated drugs and money missing from the D.A.'s evidence vault?" I asked.

"Yes, Jamie was investigating some illegal activity in the D.A.'s office, but all she had shared with me was that Ann and Dennis were living way above their income and were constantly in need of additional money. Jamie told me that some of the money, cocaine, and marijuana confiscated from drug arrests had come up missing after the cases were disposed of. She was sure that Dennis or Ann or maybe both of them were taking them. I recall her saying on one occasion, that if the citizens of Talladega County only knew what went on in the D.A's office, there would be a housecleaning like you have never seen before, and someone would go to jail.

When I first started working for Jamie, she thought the sun rose and set on Robert Rumsey, but something happened, and one night we were on a drug stakeout, and Jamie made a comment that the D.A. isn't what, people think he is ... "he's probably the most dangerous man in the state of Alabama."

"Did Jamie tell you what she meant by this remark?" I asked

"No, that was probably the only time I ever heard her say anything bad about the D.A. Jamie was pretty closed mouthed."

As Jerry revealed these things, I tried to decide if what he was saying was true, or was he just making up things in an attempt to keep his job. I quickly brushed this thought from my mind because Jerry had talked with me just a few weeks prior to Jamie's death about another job offer he had in another state. Besides, most of what Jerry was sharing with me fit with what Jamie had told me.

"If you'll let me stay on and work for the city, I'll finish grinding the remaining stumps, and maybe I can find out what really happened to Jamie. By the way, did I tell you that on the night before Jamie was found dead the next day that three individuals from the D.A.'s office and a fourth person I could not recognize were at Jamie's apartment?"

"Do you know that for sure?" I asked.

"Yes. I was parked in the high school parking lot across from her apartment around 9:30 p.m., waiting for a drug buy to go down when I saw this car drive up and park, and four people got out of the car and went to Jamie's apartment. In a matter of seconds, they entered the apartment. I assumed they were there to talk about some cases that were coming up in court.

"How long did they stay?" I asked

"I left around 11:00 p.m., and they had not left the apartment," Jerry said.

Did Jamie know about the drug buy and that you were watching her apartment?" I asked

"I wasn't watching her apartment. Like I said, I just happened to be there for a drug buy. Jamie would not have known about the drug buy because I had not seen her for several days. I did not know that she was home. I don't know how these individuals got into the apartment. I never did see Jamie at the door."

Those remarks really got my mind in a whirl. *What were these four individuals doing at Jamie's apartment the night before she was found dead? Is it possible Jamie was killed that night and then the D.A. sent Leon down the next day to find her? Is it possible that Deputy Coroner Clarence Haynes could have been that fourth person? Having worked in a funeral home for more than 20 years, Clarence would certainly know how to make murder look like suicide. Clarence is a close friend of the D.A.'s, and it was no secret that he and Ann were spending a lot of days and nights together. There could be a connection.*

"OK, Jerry, I'll keep you on a week-to-week basis. I expect you to bring me up to date on everything you and Jamie have been investigating. You have to keep me informed. I've got to know the truth about Jamie," I said.

"Mayor, that's just what I intend on doing. I've got some tapes and videos of things in this town that will blow your socks off. It's shocking what goes on in Talladega, but I don't know if my material can be used in court," Jerry said

"Whether I can use the material in court or not, Jerry, I want a copy of everything you have relating to you, Jamie, and what you two were working on."

"Most of the material is at my house in Douglasville, Georgia, but I can get it to you," he said.

Several weeks had passed since Jamie's death when the

D.A. asked me to set up a meeting in the city hall auditorium with Police Chief Hamlin, Captain Joe Hare, Captain W. E. (Pee Wee)

Hurst, Investigator Dennis Surrett, and the Talladega County mayors who were members of the U.N.O. task force. Mr. Rumsey had indicated to me that he wanted to discuss the future of the drug task force that had been headed up by Jamie.

After his opening remarks, it became apparent the D.A. wanted to place Dennis Surrett in the director's position. Captain Hurst was vehemently opposed because he believed he should have the job. As I listened to the pros and cons of why Dennis should have the job and the comments made by Capt. Hurst of why he should have the job, my thoughts turned back to what Jamie had shared with me several months prior. *Dennis wants my job, and Ann and Dennis are trying to make me look bad so Dennis will be placed in my position.* It was very obvious to me that Jamie had shared with me the truth.

The discussion was becoming very heated when the D.A broke it off with the statement, "If Dennis doesn't get placed in this position, then my office won't have any more to do with the program." So much for open debate.

Based on what Jamie had shared with me about money and drugs missing from the D.A.'s office and what Jerry had shared with me about the night before Jamie's death, I became highly suspicious of the D.A.'s adamant support for Dennis.

The meeting abruptly came to an end, and for the first time, I felt uneasy around the D.A. He had changed, and the very air around him felt out of tune. I made up my mind that I had to make a recommendation to the city council—one that Mr. Rumsey would not like

Shortly after the D.A's meeting, I met with Chief Hamlin and several other officers and detectives. We agreed that I would speak to the city council and recommend that no more money be appropriated for the county-wide task force. Instead, the city could create it's own program, concentrating on Talladega. The council approved my recommendation at a council meeting, and it was made a part of the minutes

In mid-October, Jerry came by the office and brought me up to date. He shared with me that several individuals were working for a council member at his place of business, but no records were being kept of their employment, and no taxes or social security was being withheld. Jerry went on to say that a former drug dealer who had served time was now working for this council member and allegedly was the main man for this council member and a city attorney involved in trafficking of cocaine. As Jerry shared with me information he and Jamie had obtained about illegal activity involving council members, a city attorney, law enforcement officers, a bank official and other prominent citizens, I asked, "Can you prove any of this?"

"I have much of it on film and or audio, and some of the conversations I have on cassette tape is worse than the other material. You will see when I provide you a copy of all the material I have," Jerry said.

At a council meeting in March, 1993, one of the council members asked me who Jerry Jackson was and what was he doing for the city. The question came as a surprise because each council member had received a copy of the agreement signed by Jamie, Jerry, and me. Furthermore, the council had been approving Jerry's paycheck each week for more than a year. Apparently this council member had forgotten about the contract or either they had found out that Jamie and Jerry were investigating them. I had been informed that this council member had several teenagers in the community stealing everything from jewelry to clothes, and this council member was paying the teenagers a few dollars for this expensive merchandise

Jerry remained on the payroll until the first Friday of May,

1993. Near the end of April, he had shared with me about two job offers —one in Mississippi and one in Georgia, and he felt it was time to move on.

"Mayor, I've taken out every stump in the city, and even though I feel sure Jamie didn't kill herself, I don't know what else I can do to prove it. The D.A. has done a good job of covering up this murder. No one is willing to challenge him, and with the coroner and state investigators backing them up, who is willing to take them on?" Jerry said. "All the tapes and videos are at my place in Douglasville. I hope you will be able to use them at some point. As soon as I have made copies, I will call you, but in the meantime, if you would like to see all the material Jamie and I collected, I will let you know when I will have time to get with you," he said.

Without a doubt Jerry had done an outstanding job. More than two thousand stumps had been removed, and he had also been instrumental in gathering an incredible amount of information While Jamie was alive, and even now, Jerry and I had maintained a good working relationship. He had fulfilled his contract. and more.

As a life-long resident of Talladega, I was aware of the many skeletons in the closet of many prominent citizens, but Jerry had provided information that would cause divorce and create panic if this information were leaked to the citizens or carried before a grand jury for indictments. Remembering that Jerry had not taken a job he had been offered earlier in the year, I was curious if Jerry had seen threatened by someone whom he had been investigating, and this was the cause of him leaving at this time.

On Sunday, two days after Jerry had resigned his job, I received a phone call from him at 3:00 p.m. He wanted to know if could drive to Douglasville, Georgia, and view all the tapes and videos he had taken. I agreed to meet him at Shoney's just off the (-20 Douglasville exit

As I approached the exit designated by Jerry, I spotted the Shoney's sign, and Jerry's motor home was parked in a gas station not across from Shoney's. I pulled my car in beside his motor 1ome, and he told me to follow him. We drove about two miles to 1 subdivision of relatively new homes and parked in the drive of one of them. We went into the house, and Jerry introduced me to a woman named Jeanetta but did not indicate their relationship, if any. Jeanetta had a pot of coffee boiling hot and served it to us in the den with a tray of cookies. Jerry had a tape player and VCR ready, and for the next hour or so, I listened to portions of tapes and watched parts of videos, all the while taking notes on pertinent information

One incident on video concerned a former superintendent of Talladega City Schools. The video showed the superintendent coming out of a store which Jerry said was located in a city this side of Atlanta. This former superintendent was shown carrying several boxes of goods to a city-owned car and placing the items inside.

"What store is that, and why did you record him carrying the boxes?" I asked.

"I was on my way home one day," Jerry continued, "and recognized the superintendent's car in front of me. I was curious about where he was going, so I followed him. Jamie and I had received information that he was using his city car, and maybe city money, to promote his private business of assembling golf clubs and selling them.

As the videos rolled on, I saw a council member's son giving small plastic packets to teenagers, and they were handing the council member's son money. This kid is heavy into drugs," Jerry said

"Recognize that man?" Jerry asked, as a council member appeared on the screen, entering what looked like a motel room.

"Watch this," he continued. A young, attractive, white woman, the daughter of a prominent family in Talladega, got out of a car parked in front of the door to the room. As she exited her auto, she looked around and went into the room which the council member had just entered. I recognized the council member, and it was well known in the black community that he is a lady's man.

Mayor, that woman that just entered the motel room is heavy into cocaine and a personal friend of a city attorney. The sound on the video is distorted, but you can hear enough that not only is this a drug deal but a sexual encounter," Jerry said.

As the door of the motel room continued to be displayed on the screen, from the sounds coming through the speakers, there was no doubt that there was more than a drug deal going down.

"Jerry, how in the world did you get the sound of what's going on in the room on video?" I asked.

"Wait until you hear some of the tapes I made of conversations and action that went on inside of this council member's office," he responded.

"How did you get these recordings without your being in the room?" I asked

Jerry laughed and said, "I own an interest in a detective agency, and we have means to listen in on almost anybody, anytime, anywhere without them knowing," he said.

Jerry stopped the video, placed a cassette in the recorder, turned it back on, and asked, "Recognize those voices?"

After listening for a few seconds, I said, "It sounds like the president of a bank and a Talladega County attorney."

"It is," Jerry said.

As I continued listening to the tape, it was obvious they were discussing the estate of an influential senior citizen who had passed away recently. The gist of the conversation was that the bank president and attorney were going to pick out the items of furniture and antiques they wanted for themselves and sell the rest at an auction. The tape ended, and Jerry inserted another one.

"Can you recognize that voice?" he asked.

The quality was not the best, but it sounded like Jamie talking to someone. It appeared she was emotional and concerned about her welfare and what was happening concerning her job. The following is the conversation transcribed from the tape.

"Hi Joanne. This is Jamie. I have just got to talk to somebody. My whole life's falling apart (pause). Well, it's like this, you know who my co-worker is. He has broken in my house, tried to rape me, and I'm afraid that something's going to happen.

The D.A. and Dennis both have hit on me to go with them, and I don't know what to do about that because my job is in jeopardy, but I'm afraid at this point my life may be in jeopardy (pause) because they have told me if any of this ever gets out, I will be sorry (pause). I am afraid they are going to do something_to me and make it look like suicide. If anything happens to me, make sure it's investigated because no matter how scared or depressed I am. I would never commit suicide. There are a lot of powerful people involved in this —the mayor and Chief Hamlin both know all about the rape (pause). Yes, I've taken a 10 mg Valium, but that's not much, but Sandra gave it to me because I was so upset. I just don't know what to do! (pause) Ann is even involved in this, and she is really after me. (crying) I'm sorry, I didn't mean to cry. If anything happens to me, please get in touch with my brother, the lawyer, and he'll know how to make sure it isn't covered up and made to look like something it isn't."

As the tape ended, Jerry remarked, "This tape was made a few days prior to Jamie's death, but I was reluctant to tell you about it."

"Why?" I asked.

"Because I didnt record it myself, and I am unable to verify where it was made or who Jamie was talking to. The woman who gave me this tape didn't want anyone to have it. She was afraid for her life.

"This is almost unbelievable, Jerry. My first thought would be to get this material before a grand jury for their consideration, but I can't trust the D.A. I also could go to the newspaper and force the D.A. to present these things to a grand jury, and if anyone wanted to file a civil suit, then I certainly could introduce all this information plus subpoena the various people involved. I guess I could get the bank examiners and auditors involved and examine records and various documents. But at this point, I don't know who to trust."

"You're right about not trusting the D.A. It looks like he is right in the middle of things," Jerry remarked.

"It's getting late Jerry, and I need to be heading back to Talladega. I would like to take all this material back with me," I said.

"I haven't had a chance to make a copy of all the documents, etc., but you can keep the duplicate of what I do have, and I will either mail you the rest of the material or bring it to you, but before you go, let me show you a part of two more videos," Jerry said.

As the images appeared on the screen, Jerry quipped,

"Here comes the judge with two bodyguards."

I couldn't believe what I was seeing. A Talladega County Judge, a Talladega County Commissioner's wife, and a city detective's wife made a hugging threesome as they walked toward a motel room. The judge was in the middle of these two women, and it looked like they were having to hold him up. It was apparent tey had been to a party somewhere and did not seem too concerned that someone would see them. They were all laughing and staggering toward the motel room door.

The next scene showed three individuals connected with the A's office and a fourth person, walking up to Jamie's apartment. After a few seconds, her door opened, and they all went in. The fourth person was partially hid behind one of the individuals from he D.A's office, and it was impossible to identify him. The fourth person was a lot shorter than the person they were walking beside. [made this on the Sunday night before Jamie was found dead on Monday," Jerry remarked. This is what I was telling you about in our office when I asked you to let me stay on a little longer. Do ou remember?"

I not only remembered this conversation, but I remembered Il the other things that Jamie and Jerry had shared with me. As I departed the house and started my trip back to Talladega, I purposed in my mind to contact the Alabama Attorney General and hare with him what I had learned.

The next day, Monday morning, I contacted Mr. Jimmy vans, the Attorney General, and discussed my misgivings about re alleged suicide of Jamie Grace. Making him aware of the various tapes, videos and documents that were available, he promised he would have one of his investigators contact me. He ever did. As the days turned into weeks, I began to inquire about Ar. Evans and learned that he and D.A. Rumsey were very good riends. I had no proof, but I was sure Mr. Evans made contact with Mr. Rumsey, and he sold him a bill of goods.

On May 18, 1993, a few days after my conversation with Ar. Evans, I received an anonymous telephone call that I was being investigated about what Jerry Jackson was doing for his pay.

"How do you know I am being investigated?" I asked the caller.

"I have a scanner that can pick up certain type portable telephone conversation, and I happened to scan in on a conversation between the personnel director Sue Horn and Fire

Chief Roy Johnson. Sue Horn was talking a hundred miles an hour and was telling the chief all about how council member Rip Williams had signed a complaint on the insistence of detective Ken Sisk. Sue told Roy that Detective Sisk said they needed a complaint signed so it wouldn't look like a witch hunt," the caller continued.

"How do I know if you are telling me the truth?" I asked the caller.

"I have a tape player connected to my scanner, and when I realized what the conversation was, I turned on my player and recorded the conversation. Not only was Sue running her mouth about you to the chief, but as soon as she quit talking to him, she called several other individuals and shared the same information," he said.

"Would you like to have a copy of the tapes?"

"Yes. I would!" I responded.

"I will see that you get a copy."

In view of the news from the mystery caller, I buzzed

Chief Hamlin on the intercom and requested that he come to my office. Within a few seconds, the chief was in my office, and I asked him if he or someone with the police department was conducting an investigation on me about anything. The chief denied having any knowledge of any investigation.

The next day, Chief Hamlin came back to my office and informed me that he had been made aware that council member Rip Williams had signed a complaint alleging that he did not know who Jerry Jackson was

"Now that Rip has filed a complaint, there will have to be an investigation," the Chief said.

"Do what you have to, Mike, but I'd rather you'd call in an outside agency, and not get the police department involved in a political squabble." I said.

For whatever reason, Mike did not call in an outside agency. Instead, he assigned Detective Ken Sisk to investigate me. *Great choice,* I thought. Ken is a police officer who was reduced in rank for conduct unbecoming to an employee. Chief Hamlin also assigned Capt. "Pee Wee" Hurst to assist Det. Sisk.

Suddenly, it felt as though I were becoming hopelessly entangled in a mesh of political intrigue and contradictions. The irony was that Rip was one of the of the council members who had approved all of Jerry's paychecks, and he even authorized two nore of Jerry's checks after filing the complaint which stated that he didn't know who Jerry was. A cold lump formed in my stomach.

What in Sam Hill was going on? Why did Rip wait until Terry left to make it known about the questions in the complaint? He was one of the people Jamie and Jerry had been investigating. What if Rip found out, got to Jerry and threatened him or paid him to get out of town? Was Rip somehow involved in Jamie's death? Was that why Jerry had suddenly decided to leave town?

On May 19th, Capt. Hurst and Det. Sisk came by my office and asked if I would talk to them about the investigation. I agreed to tell them what I knew. During the subsequent taped interview, I answered all their questions and explained Jerry's overall functions or the city, how he had been hired on Jamie's recommendation, and about my meeting with Jerry in Douglasville, Georgia to review he tapes and videos.

"Would you go to Douglasville with us sometime soon?"

Det. Sisk asked.

"I'd be glad to," I answered.

At one point in the interview, I told them about the taped conversation of Jamie crying and stating that the DA and Dennis were trying to date her and that she was afraid for her life.

"Did you hear that tape?" Pee Wee asked.

"Yes, I heard it, and before Jamie died she told me a former co-worker got drunk one night, then came over to her apartment, and tried to rape her. She told me the only reason she didn't press charges is because she was afraid he'd try to kill her."

"She said that he tried to rape her? — not that he did," Pee Wee asked.

"That's what I said— that he tried to."

Det. Sisk interrupted, "I can't think of anything else we need to ask you."

"I can't either," Pee Wee said. "I think we covered everything we need to."

The tape recorder was still on, and they were gathering up their notes, pads and other things.

"Did the D.A. know about Jerry? Jamie said she told him about Jerry working with her," I asked.

"Not to my knowledge, she didn't. I don't think the D.A.

wants to know who our informants are," said Pee Wee.

They left, and I thought about the interesting fact that Pee Wee didn't deny that the co-worker tried to rape Jamie.

Wonder if the co-worker was the fourth person at Jamie's apartment the night before she was found dead?

On July 30, 1993, I dictated the following letter to my administrative assistant, Carolyn Ricks, and she typed it for my signature:

CITY OF TALLADEGA

Post Office Box 498

Talladega, Alabama 35160

July 30, 1993

Robert Rumsey, District Attorney

48 N East Street, Rm 107

Talladega, Alabama 35160

Dear Robert:

For the last few weeks the rumors have been rampart as usual in

Talladega concerning the alleged grand jury investigation surrounding myself and possibly others at City Hall. Even though our conversation of approximately two months ago where you informed me that your office was not investigating myself, the rumors still exist.

The only people that know the trith about the Jerry Jackson issue and the other employees that were utilized on contract labor are myself, Jerry Jackson, Jamie Grace, and God. Jamie is deceased, Jerry is out of state, and I have no way of knowing if you and the investigators have been in touch with God lately concerning this issue.

Therefore, that leaves me that knows the whole story, and I am readily available to talk with you and/or the grand jury. If a grand jury is empanelled to consider allegations or improprieties at City Hall, I respectfully request the opportunity to appear before the grand jury and answer any and all questions.

There are other matters concerning the alleged cover up of Jamie

Grace's death and the alleged attempted rape of Jamie by a city of Talladega police officer that need to be discussed

Thank you for your consideration in this matter.

Sincerely,

Larry Barton
Mayor

LB/cr

Weeks went by and turned into months. Det. Sisk, Capt. Hurst, and two D.A. investigators, Dennis Surrett and Ann White Wallace, who had also been assigned to the investigation, were busy reviewing city hall records of paychecks and correspondence.

All that time and effort to try proving Jerry Jackson never existed.

Strangely, the D.A. kept telling me I wasn't being investigated. But his team continued working around the clock on my case. I gave them my complete cooperation, even giving them permission to search my house and office without a warrant. I had nothing to hide.

From May through December, 1993, 1993, council members increasingly smelled blood—my blood. Council president, Donald

Hubbard, and council member, Rip Williams, both craved to be mayor. They knew that if I were forced out they would have a shot at it. They teamed up with another council member, Horace Patterson, and got legal help from attorney, Jake Montgomery. This ambitious group looked for every ordinance on the books which could be used to strip away all my power as mayor, from petty things like removing one of my office phones to relieving me of the power to hire and fire employees, and prohibiting my use of the city car traditionally assigned to the mayor for official business.

One humorous headline came out during the investigation. When I learned that the council had stripped me of the use of the city car, which was a Dodge Dynasty, my mother offered the use of her 1969 Plymouth Fury III. I accepted the offer and Mary drove me to mother's to pick up the Plymouth. When I arrived back at city hall, the media was there and picked up on the fact that I was going to be driving mother's Fury III. The next day the headline of the news article about my being deprived of the use of the city's Dodge Dynasty and going to be driving mother's Plymouth Fury III read, *"BARTON LOSES DYNASTY LEAVES IN A FURY!"*

Almost every week they came up with something else, and made sure it leaked to the local newspaper, the Daily Home. Even though I had not been charged or indicted, there was almost nothing they didn't try in order to get a headline to discredit me or make me look guilty of some unnamed charge.

While the council and the D.A.'s team were busy spreading gossip, I was busy contacting individuals whose names had been given to me by Jerry. In the event they were able to get an indictment, I felt it imperative that I be prepared to present the evidence Jerry and Jamie had been working on.

One person Jerry had mentioned was a deputy sheriff in Andalusia, Alabama. The deputy happened to be a black female, and Jamie's long-time friend. I was finally able to contact her by phone. The deputy said she had talked to Jamie shortly before her death, and Jamie told her that she was very concerned about certain aspects of her job and her continued employment.

"Jamie didn't explain everything," the deputy said, "but she told me enough so I could tell how scared she was. After she calmed down some, she said she was engaged to be married and wanted me to attend the wedding. It. was supposed be in a couple of months. Who in the world would commit suicide when they had all that going for them?"

Next, I contacted three other people Jerry told me about. gave me names of their family members who had worked for a cil member at his business but were never paid by check. They le hired them and always paid in cash; no money was withheld xes or social security benefits.

One day while I was trying to gather evidence, Sandra tt, Dennis Surrett's wife, came by my office and wanted to

"Mayor," she said, "Dennis left me and has filed for divorce. coroner (Clarence Haynes) moved out of Ann's house, and is has moved in. He and Ann are planning to get married. And I's not bad enough, they're stalking me."

"Stalking you?"

"Yes. I'm here to get a warrant for their arrest. They park driveway and watch the house for hours on end, and they've aken things from the house. I'm going to try getting them for of property, too.

"Do you know anything about what went on when Jamie

"I asked, and told her some of the things I had found out.

"How do you know about the fight between Ann and Jamie hese individuals from the D.A's office being there the night e she was found dead?"

I explained Jerry Jackson's involvement, and as we talked, a verified many things Jerry had said.

"After Jamie's death, Dennis got hooked on medication. He used to take any kind of medicine, but when he got involved Ann and Jamie's death, he told his doctors he was very ed out and having a lot of trouble sleeping. He managed to lot of drugs. Our medical bills were astronomical. By the I don't believe Jamie committed suicide, but if she did, she pressured into it by Robert (D.A.), Dennis and Ann," Sandra

"She couldn't have used her gun," Sandra continued, use I had it in my possession at my house. After Ann jumped mic at her house and knocked her down in the floor, I took to my house, and she stayed with me for several nights."

Once again thoughts begin running through my mind. *Was? murdered and someone made it look like suicide? You don't know them ... they are vicious ... especially Ann. Had someone who was being investigated by Jamie killed her? A lot of prominent people were being investigated.*

"Sandra, did Jamie ever indicate to you that she wanted to or had considered suicide?" I asked.

"Something happened...I was in Huntsville working once and something happened. It was during AEA, and next thing I knew, Dennis called to say Jamie tried to commit suicide. They brought her right up to Huntsville where I worked... where there is a hospital, and they logged that she was on vacation... but she was in the hospital."

"In Huntsville?"

"In Huntsville."

"I wonder if she was admitted in her name," I continued.

I don't now what name they put her under, but Dennis told me what hospital they put her in...I'd have to look at the phone book and check the name."

"Sandra, the word got back to me that Jamie had gotten pregnant by an individual in the D.A.'s office. Now, I don't know whether this is true...I mean this is second-hand talk. This is what Jerry told me that he had found out that the rumor was... but not knowing anything about Jamie's sexual activities, etc...but she did tell me that a police officer tried to rape her."

"All I know is that whcn Jamie and Dennis would go off looking for the guy they called Rambo, he would introduce her as Jamie Surrett, his wife. I don't know how they stayed in the motel...if they stayed in one room or two rooms, but I would imagine if she presented herself as his wife...that you could possibly check the records and find out how many rooms they paid for. I don't know how they registered in the motel, but it was a joke that they told people her name was Jamie Surrett, and people called back asking the District Attorney's office for Jamie Surrett. Now if they posed as man and wife, did they have two rooms or one?"

"Sandra, do you know whether Jamie ever had an

abortion?"

 "I heard that she had."

"Yeah. Well, see, that's what Jerry Jackson kept telling me, at Jamie told him that an individual in the D.A's office got her egnant. You know, that's all, I can't prove it. Jamie is no longer ith me. I know she called me at one point..

 "That was before they put her in the hospital the first time. ut that's all Dennis said... all that was on her mind...she had an ortion before. Ann said that Dennis swore he didn't know who e father was, that there was the question of who the father was, id it had not happened... it had just happened before they put her the Huntsville hospital."

 "But you don't know where she had the abortion?"

 "Seems like...I only halfway remember...seems like she went to Atlanta to have the abortion... but I don't know how much

 What some of these truths are... because Dennis apparently has en lying.

 "But she did tell you she had an abortion?"

 "No, she didn't. Dennis told me that."

"Dennis told you that. Well, no wonder Dennis and Ann were upset when they found out I had information about that."

"And the autopsy that was done at her death was only done

1 the head. They, did not do a full-body autopsy. and Dennis was ying.. told me they owed that to Jamie."

"Owed Jamie, or owed Dennis and Robert?"

"I'll tell you, Dennis went berserk. He actually went berserk, and he was on antide-pressants from Craddock Clinic. And know he stayed on them from the time Jamie killed herself until January when the last insurance thing had come through, but he had ten back to Craddock Clinic there in Sylacauga to get more pills."

"Well, Sandra, you need to be careful. If Dennis gets desperate, he will do anything, and right now they are desperate. hey don't know what I know, they don't know what kind of tapes have got...they are running scared right now.

Sandra, does

Robert (D.A.) know about the abortion...I mean the breakdown cause of the abortion?"

Yes, both of them know.

"OK, but Robert didn't know that Jamie stayed with you three nights before she died?"

"No."

"Does Robert know about them going in there and saying and doing the things they did to Jamie that Thursday night before she was found dead on Monday?"

"You talking about at the motel?"

"I am talking about the apartment."

"OK, where Ann knocked her around?"

"Yes."

" Yeah. and they threatened her job... they threatened her...they did not have a right to threaten Jamie?"

"The D.A. knows about this?"

"No, they lied and then covered up...they called me crazy...and they said nobody would listen to me if I told about it."

"Well, she says on the tape that Jerry gave to me that she is afraid of losing her job and that she is scared for her life... that a co-worker had already tried to rape her... and that Dennis and Robert were hitting on her... whatever she meant by that, and she said that Ann Wallace was right in the middle of all this."

"True. I told Pee Wee about all this when I was going through my divorce, but he didn't see fit to investigate. I talked to Leon about this. Dennis turned on Leon."

"Did he? Robert got completely upset with me about the city not continuing to be a part of the county drug force after Jamie's death, and when Robert wanted to put Dennis in control and after the county unit fell apart, Robert apparently placed Dennis and Ann in control of what was left of the program."

"That's exactly right. They took over Jamie's job well before she killed herself."

"If she killed herself."

"True. Jamie was put under a lot of pressure at the D.A.'s office. She was under a tremendous amount of pressure that last weekend. They put the pressure to her about her job and that she was not producing enough."

"Sandra, do you not think you need to go public with this?

The people need...I mean... Dennis will do…"

"Nobody has ever questioned me...nobody cares...and I have already been told that everybody thinks I am crazy anyway, and

"But Sandra, you have just told me some stuff in the last ten minutes that I have already got on tape."

"Let me tell you, Carol (not real name), her black friend, was there that Thursday night when Ann beat up Jamie and knows what went on, and Dennis and Ann claim that Carol hates whites, and they covered up what Carol knew."

"This Carol was at Jamie's house on Thursday night when the fight took place?"

"She was there when I got there."

"And they have not interviewed her?"

"They would not interview her...Ann kept calling, wanting to know...calling Leon's wife...wanting to know what Carol was going to tell them... they were real uneasy on what was being told happened... they claimed Carol hates whites, and as far as I know.. nobody never talked to Carol...and the FBI never tried to talk to Carol either. This whole thing is scary...and I know an awful lot...I know a lot about the District Attorney's office...and they... I'm sitting in a real bad situation."

"No, you are sitting in the driver's seat."

"No, I' not."

"Hey, the D.A. is not above the law himself."

"Ann told me today that she could harass me the rest of my life, she was smarter than me...and I couldn't prove nothing on her. nobody could prove nothing on her. and I've been threatened by Dennis today...he told me if I tried to have him arrested for all he is doing to me or report any of this, it would be the worst thing I ever did in my life..

"Sandra, do you recall Jamie ever sharing with you that a person by the name of Jerry Jackson was working with or for her?"

"No, because I really wasn't that close to Jamie. The only way I really got in on the last few days of her life was Ann Wallace...went into her apartment that night...they had it out...and Ann called her an alcoholic...and told her that the men didn't want to work with her...got her upset...started to the bedroom...ran and knocked her down in the hall."

"Knocked Ann down?"

"Ann knocked Jamie down...Ann was knocking Jamie around...Ann was knocking Jamie around...Ann got scared and called Dennis...Dennis went up there...Carol came in up there...her black friend, Carol...Jamie got upset...they couldn't control her...she told them to call me...if I would get Ann out of the house...to get Ann out of the house..just get her out...that's when I took Jamie to my house and kept her three days. While Jamie as at my house, she talked to me about the pressure she was under. Her conscience was bothering her about the abortion... she was Catholic, and they did not believe in that... but she was Catholic when she committed suicide, and that bothers me.”

“But, Sandra, you are positive they put her in a hospital in Huntsville?”

“It was in Huntsville is what I was told at the time because I thought it was strange that I was sitting right there at Huntsville working...and they brought her to Huntsville... now why not Birmingham? But they were hiding her from the city and told her that if Pee Wee or anybody found out... she would lose her job.”

“Sandra, I need you to get me the name of the hospital in Huntsville and anything else you can think of.

“You need to talk to Carol...she was there when I got there... she knows more than I do... what happened before I came in... She was Jamie’s best friend.”

“If you can think of anything, Sandra, that I need to know……..”

“There is no telling what I might could think of if I could just bring my mind back and relive those days...’ cause I mean it was down and dirty and ugly... and Clarence Haynes was in on the autopsy... supposedly to preserve Jamie’s reputation.”

“Sandra, would Dennis have had the capability of killing her or having her killed then figuring out a way to get out of that room?”

“It was supposedly to have happened on Sunday night. The best I can recall, Dennis was here on Sunday night. I’ve seen him fork on things when he was supposed to go on vacation. We were going to the FBI conference to register my child down there. We are going to leave on Monday. Dennis went in to work...not planning on it. He called me back around two o’clock and said, Ride by Jamie’s and see if both cars are there. She didn't show up or work...but don't go in the apartment...don't go up to the door.. don't go in!'""

"Sandra, you need to report this to someone.. you cannot afford to run.

"Part of what was bothering Jamie when I was with er...Greg, another friend of hers, does know...Greg knows... she talked to Greg and Carol."

"Sandra, do you think Jamie would have shared with them if co-worker had gotten her pregnant?"

"She would not have shared it with Greg, but she might ave with Carol... Greg knows a lot of what happened with her co-vorker and the police department... He knows a lot...'

As Sandra and I ended our conversation, I knew now why Jennis, Ann, and Robert were investigating me day and night in an tempt to have me charged with something in order to try and liscredit anything I might say concerning their alleged activities.

Before Sandra left city hall, she signed a warrant for the rrest of Dennis, but no action was ever taken it was swept under the rug. No surprise since Dennis was the D.A's right hand man, nd he would soon be the same for Ann, if he weren't already. handra finally gave up and moved to another city to get away from them.

The investigation continued, and the city council fired Diane Gardner, a twenty-year employee; Janice Ford, a thirty-year employee; Roy Bean, a ten-year employee; and Becky Ashley who lad been employed for about two years. They were all accused of overing for me about. Jerry Jackson and failing to inform council members. These four people had never known what Jerry was doing. Their only crime was being my friends. And for this, they were fired.

As the investigation was coming to a close, several people who had been questioned by one or more of the investigators, told me they were being pressured to remember things they knew nothing about. They were led to believe they could be prosecuted if they didn't testify against me and help convict me of my yet uncharged crimes. I told each of them just to tell the truth and not to worry about me.

On December 28, 1993, my attorney, Rod Giddens, told me I had been indicted by a federal grand jury in Birmingham, and was being charged with one count of fraud and twenty-six counts of money laundering of $5,925.

"Larry, I was notified by the federal officials that you have been indicted, and one of the investigators has led the FBI to believe that you are a dangerous person, and when they come to arrest you, there is no telling what you might do. The FBI wants to come to your office, serve the indictment warrant, handcuff and leg chain you, and make a media event out of it. I have shared with the authorities that you are not dangerous, nor a threat to anyone, that you are a family man, who is involved in church and civic activities. The court has agreed to let me bring you to Birmingham and process you in. I told them we would be there within an hour," Rod said. I immediately left my office, walked to my car, and drove to where Rod was waiting for me. Upon arriving at the federal building in Birmingham, Alabama, I was photographed, fingerprinted, and appeared before the magistrate.

Having my indictment read to me and my entering a "NOT GUILTY" plea, I was permitted to sign a $500 signature bond and Rod and I returned to Talladega. My trial had been set for March 2, 1994. Since I was charged with a federal statute, Rod recommended I retain Bill Dawson, a Birmingham attorney with federal court experience.

I was certainly upset about the indictment but not yet really concerned. I knew all the stump work had been done, and it was not against the law for Jerry to work as an informant.

Then, about the 19th of January, 1994, I received the following letter in the mail:

January 17, 1994

Dear Mayor Barton,

 I have just read about you being indicted because of Jerry. I cannot believe what I am reading. It looks like you have got some stupid crazy people in Talladega.

I am really shocked about that Williams councilman. Jerry said

Williams found out that he was working undercover and threatened to pose him if he didn't give him and Jerry Wilson a cut of the tree work. That is one of the reasons Jerry started to leave Talladega in March. hey was shaking him down pretty bad. They found out Jerry was a ex-con. Jerry is wanted in another state and he was afraid they would find out and have to go back to prison. I can't give you my address because the federal agents will track him. We live in constant fear that he will be caught. He is too sick to go back to prison. I believe he would die. Jamie knew Jerry had been in prison and was a good family friend. Jerry told me about some of the undercover work with Jamie. You need to bring this out in court. Jamie didn't commit suicide. A policeman raped her and somebody name suret and Ramsey made her sleep with them. She got pregnant and had a abortion.

They were at her house the night before they found her the next ry. Some woman with them. Jerry was parked at the school lot across om the house. They stayed real late. I am so upset I know I am writing crazy, but what they are doing you just wrong. I have to figure someway to help you out and not get Jerry in jail.

Jamie gave Jerry some of her drug files and said someone in her office stole money and drugs. Jamie was killed before she could tell about it. You man not recognize my name but I'm the woman you met in Douglasville, Ga. when you listened to the tapes and looked at the videos. Jerry was supposed to mail you a copy of them. He is going to e real upset when he finds out about your problem because of him.

 I don't know if you know or not, but he's got throat cancer and in Florida with Uncle Wylie since November. He is getting treatment own there. I am going to send him this newspaper article.

My sister still lives in Anniston. Maybe I can get a message to her and let her contact you. I'm afraid to call you. I don't know if they're listening to your calls.

This whole thing is crazy. I don't believe the police knows the whole story. I hope you sue everyone. Will get in touch with you someway,

Jeanetta

I immediately turned the letter over to the investigators. In spite of the contents of the letter, during my week-long trial in Birmingham, I learned that the prosecution was going to try proving Jerry Jackson didn't exist and that this was only a scheme of mine to defraud the city. About the third day of the trial, I was offered a short sentence to plead guilty. Since I wasn't guilty and believed in the judicial system, I refused the offer.

The prosecution then produced several witnesses who had apparently been coached on their answers to the prosecutor's questions. Two of them, Jerry Wilson and Thomas Green were both ex-cons and testified they were professional tree surgeons.

They said they had removed approximately fifty stumps from the city for pay, however, Mr. Green said he loved the city of Talladega so much, he had removed the other two thousand or so stumps for free. Interestingly, when my attorney cross examined him, he was unable to recall where they were located.

Mr. Green had billed the city for more than forty stumps he claimed to have removed from in front of the Talladega Bible Methodist Church. But I had refused to pay the invoice at the time, believing that no work had been done at this location.

Indeed, Jimmy Wilcox, the church clerk, was subpoenaed and testified that no work had been done. Mr. Green had lied.

Two witnesses for the defense, Charles Amason and Jay Shirley, were both tree surgeons. They testified that they had met and talked to Jerry Jackson, and he told them he was employed by the city of Talladega to remove stumps. However, several other defense witnesses, J. W. Baker, Viva Cooley, civil defense director Buddy Holcomb, Mary Nelson, Jim Perley and James Swinford all testified that although they knew the tree work had been done in their communities, they never knew the person who did the work. Listening to these witnesses made me realize that only Amason and Shirley had actually met Jerry, and my attorney had been instructed by the court that Jerry's tapes and videos could not be introduced as evidence unless Jerry was there to verify their validity. Unfortunately, I had no way to find Jerry, and although Dennis and "PeeWee" had implied they would go to Jerry's house in Douglasville, Georgia, even asking me if I would be willing to go along, they never seemed able to find time for the trip.

At some point, I made a request to D.A. Investigator Dennis Surrett to have a composite drawing made in order to show it to the employees and see if they would not recognize Jerry.

Dennis replied, "You have the best working on this case. If he is out there, I will find him."

As the trial came to a close, I tried to put myself in the jurors place and figure how they might be perceiving the testimony. I realized that even though the evidence showed that the work had been done, without Jerry's testimony, it looked bad. In his closing remarks to the jury, the federal prosecutor, Assistant Attorney Bill Barnett even admitted that the work had been done but said he didn't believe that anyone named Jerry Jackson had done it. He told jurors that Jerry was only a figment of my imagination and that I was Jerry Jackson.

I don't even know how to crank a stump grinder, much less run one, I thought.

It was very obvious Mr. Barnett was doing an excellent job of swaying the jury, but I still held on to that thread of hope that they would see through his smoke screen. So many outstanding citizens of the town had testified that all the work had been done, including the prosecutor himself admitting to the fact. As Mr.

Barnett closed his remarks to the juror, I still didn't understand why I was even being tried.

Mr. Barnett had already convinced a federal grand jury that the work had not been done, but then in court he admitted that all the work had been done. If the work had been done, and it had, then there was no crime.

The trial lasted a week, including one and a half days for jury deliberation. I simply couldn't believe what I was hearing when the foreman read the verdict. I may have been guilty of the way I handled the hiring of Jerry, but I knew I was not guilty of the charges. I had always believed in the judicial process. Judge Edwin Nelson allowed me to remain free on a $500 signature bond and set April 22, 1994, as my sentencing date.

Ironically, on March 11, 1994, four days after my trial ended and too late to help, the following letter came in the mail:

Mr Barton,

In the spring of 1990, around April, a friend and I, Jennette Harrold had gone to the Alabama Showpalace in Anniston. We danced and talked with Mr. Jackson. He was from the Houston, Texas area and so was I. He told us he was in Alabama to clean up some of the damaged trees from the storm. He asked how far to Munford and Talladega. We told him, then he met us for breakfast and asked if we would show him where both towns were. We did and Jennette asked me to take her back to my house in Sylacauga. He rode to town with us and I had to be in Anniston later that morning and he rode back to Anniston with me. He was staying at the Holiday Inn in Oxford.

He was around six foot tall, dark hair and had a dark tan for that time of year. When I said something about it, he said he worked outside all the time and he was part Indian. He drove a red pick-up and had a trailer with some type of equipment on the trailer.

Hopefully this will help. If I can be of further assistance, please let me know. I try and visit my family in Childersburg, Alabama at least once a month.

Sincerely,

Suzanne

On April 220d I stood before Judge Nelson with my attorneys, Rod Giddens and Bill Dawson. The judge informed me that for the $5,925 conviction, the penalty could be up to forty-five years in prison and $1 million in fines. At that moment, I was just thankful the death penalty was not an option! Murderers, rapists, bank robbers, and child molesters aren't subject to such harsh penalties, I thought.

Judge Nelson sentenced me to 51 months in prison, two years of supervised release, and a $1,350 court assessment. He wished me good luck.

Before we left, my attorney filed notice with the court that an appeal would be forthcoming. In Alabama, when you're an elected official convicted of a felony, you're required to vacate office immediately.

LEAVING HOME

It was Friday morning, May 27, 1994. I woke up about 4:00 a.m. I had chased sleep until after midnight and was still tired and groggy. I climbed out of my sleep fog, and the dismal thought hit me like a dash of ice water... *Today is the day I have to report to Eglin Federal Prison Camp by noon.*

Comfortable, everyday sounds and smells from the kitchen brought me back to the present. Sadly, I realized that my wife, Mary, was fixing what would be our last breakfast at home for many months. I looked at the familiar surroundings of our bedroom. My eyes came to rest on the grocery sack Mary had filled with the only personal belongings I was allowed to bring with me to Eglin. So few worldly possessions one shirt, one pair of slacks which I would wear on the trip, five tee shirts, five pairs of shorts, five pairs of socks, one handkerchief, toothbrush and toothpaste, one container of deodorant, one razor with blades, and a Bible. My throat ached with unshed tears. So, I've been reduced to this.

With a resigned sigh, I quickly showered, shaved and dressed, and went to the kitchen. Mary and I strained silently through breakfast, unable to make our usual small talk and break the poignant silence. Mary was still in shock, though I knew a righteous anger was just below the surface of her forced outward calm. The tears she tried to hold back slipped down her cheek, reminding me of how worried she was about the possibility of losing the house, the car and everything else we owned.

I've always been proud of my excellent credit, and we both feared that the sudden loss of my $40,000 annual income would destroy the good credit we had worked so hard to build. I thought about our years together, and a deep sadness filled me to realize I'd be in prison for our 38th wedding anniversary on December 14th. Our marriage has been like a lot of other people's some years full of bumps, bruises, and hard knocks-others full of good times that I wouldn't trade for anything. But through all those years, Mary was the stabilizing force and the special glue that held our marriage together.

While at Eglin, many inmates shared with me that their wives asked for a divorce when they were sentenced to prison or soon after they got there.

Apparently, the wife was too embarrassed or lacked the inner strength to weather the circumstances. Some found the financial strain too great, and others discovered that the long wait is a very lonely situation, and sought out other relationships. Not Mary. Although the circumstances of my imprisonment were both emotionally and financially traumatic for her, she stuck with me through the whole arduous ordeal. She visited and I phoned as often as possible, and we wrote regularly to help keep us in touch with the life to which I longed to return.

At 6:00 a.m., my son, Delane, arrived with his wife, Becky, and daughter, Jessica. Delane had insisted on driving me to Eglin and reminded me that it was almost time to go. Just then, I was deeply grateful for Delane's strength and ability to roll with the punches because as my glance traveled from one sad, tense face to another, my own strength seemed to be draining away.

My daughter-in-law, Becky, appeared to be holding up well, but I worried about my 11- year-old granddaughter, Jessica. She didn't entirely grasp the implications of what was happening, but she was victim to the sarcastic and even cruel remarks made by her classmates. Public figures like mayors are the object of intense media coverage.

Just prior to leaving for Eglin, our Pastor, Rev. Lee Brasher, was also at our house, and we all joined hands as Pastor Brasher prayed that God would give a special touch to our hearts and lives and give us sustaining strength through the situation.

After the prayer, I made a quick call to my 82-year-old mother, Ruby, to reassure her that I was going to be fine. Then I picked up the grocery sack of meager belongings and said painful good-byes to the rest of my family.

As Delane and I walked down the front steps, I saw Bill Kimber, a reporter from our local paper, the Daily Home. I had agreed to his request to make the trip with us and do an interview for the newspaper.

A television reporter had also arrived at the house, apparently hoping to record my eleventh-hour comments for posterity. The TV interview was over all too soon, and with a final glimpse of my home and everything dear to me, I climbed into the car with Delane and Bill.

Once underway, I felt an odd sense of relief. Delane joked my sagging spirits out of the hole they'd been trying to sink into. I was filled with great pride in this man, my son. Refreshed by the healing effects of Delane's jokes, I was able to answer.

Bill's questions with wry humor to disguise my inner turmoil.

Gradually, I felt better and recovered my old determination. In spite of being grievously disappointed by the way the judicial system had handled my case, I was determined my enemies were not going to break me mentally or emotionally.

Part of my philosophy is: If you can't take the heat, get out of the kitchen. Eleven years in politics had been excellent training for learning to take the heat. Besides, I still had high hopes for the appeal filed by my lawyer, Bill Dawson.

MEANWHILE BACK HOME

I learned later, after I had left, that our eleven-year-old granddaughter, Jessica, could not understand why I was having to leave and not be able to attend her graduation party from elementary school.

To help keep her spirit up, Mary and the family members kept Jessica busy and went on with the planned party. As the activties came to a close, Mary returned home, all alone. In Mary's own words, the following is the scenario of what took place that night.

"As I was preparing myself for bed, I had cut out the bathroom light and staring down the hallway into the living room and kitchen, there was something that grasped my heart... just like a vise... and I said, 'Lord, if you don't help me through this, I'll never make it.'

"Larry had changed shirts prior to his leaving the house, and as I walked into the bedroom, his shirt was hanging on the back of the chair. I picked the shirt up and buried my head in it... that's all I had left.. was the shirt and the scent of his cologne on the shirt. I held on to that shirt and carried it to bed with me that night... that's all I had left... the fragrance of his clothes.

"The next day, Jessica came to visit me, and she saw the shirt and smelled of it and said, 'This smells like PaPa.. MaMa Bart, since PaPa's gone, I'm going to stay with you, and I'll take care of you.' I told Jessica that she could come and stay as long as she wanted to.

"As the days went by, the fragrance of Larry's shirt begin to fade away. Jessica would say, 'MaMa Bart, we can't let PaPa go.' Jessica would go in to where the cologne was on the shelf and get Larry's cologne and spray it on the shirt and say, 'We can't let PaPa go.'

"As the days turned into weeks and weeks into months, I would come in from my job at Alabama Power Company and my thoughts would turn to a bill coming due, and I would remind God, 'God, I've lived for you since I was fifteen years old, and you told me in your word that you would do such and such, now here I am, Lord.' One night, I crawled on my hands and knees into the bedroom, and I buried my face into the carpet, and I said, 'God, you've got to give me strength" and he did.

"Every week when I would get paid, I would put my hand on my check and say, 'God, stretch this money.' He did. I was able to meet my house, car, and insurance payment, food on the table, and my tithe was always first. God did what I asked him to do:

FIRST DAY AT EGLIN

Delane stopped the car in front of the Receiving and Discharge building of Eglin Federal Prison Camp about 11:30 a.m. I pushed my reluctant six-foot frame out of the car and said a last painful goodbye to my son. As I climbed the steps of the two-story white frame building. I barely noticed the beautifully kept grounds and well-maintained facilities. Even if I had, it wouldn't have surprised me.

In December, 1979, during my first term as mayor of Talladega, a similar federal prison opened there. Ironically, as mayor of the city, I was invited to tour the facility many times. It's hard to forget good political habits no matter where you are, and I took time to shake hands with the inmates during the tour. My good friend, Bill Key, who was a prison employee and had come along on the tour, noticed what I was unconsciously doing. He laughed and said, "Larry, these guys can't vote for you."

I was in the Talladega facility many times after that for the regular meetings and visits as a part of my mayoral duties.

CHECKING IN

Upon reaching the door of the receiving building, I entered a large room which was divided into sections by glass-enclosed cubicles. An attractive female officer of about thirty with brown shoulder-length hair checked me in. The white shirt and gray pants of her prison uniform were neat, crisp and clean.

She was all business, but not sarcastic or severe.

"Please take all items out of your bag, and spread them on the table," she said. She noted all my belongings on an inventory list form, then instructed me to sign it, verifying the list as correct.

She took my driver's license and social security card, placed them in my personnel file and informed me they would be returned when I was released from prison.

"You can put your things back in the bag now. When you're done, go over there and strip off your clothes," she said, pointing to a cubicle across the room which contained a sink and commode and was solid up to waist level for partial privacy. "A male security officer will be here in a few minutes to search you."

He arrived shortly, and the female officer left the room. At least I don't have to do this in front of 50 other guys like I did for my Army physical.

It doesn't take long to search a naked body, but to me, it seemed a humiliating eternity. When it was over, the security officer handed me a pair of undershorts, a tee shirt, a pair of baggy Air Force-blue trousers, and short-sleeve shirt.

"Get dressed." he said. "The Physician's assistant (P.A.) is coming to interview you."

P.A. Hernandez was a 35-year-old Puerto Rican with light copper skin and carefully groomed, jet-black hair. The interview was brief. Just a lot of routine questions about my medical, dental, mental and emotional status. Throughout the interview, he treated me with respect, and I recognized in him caring and compassion.

"All inmates are required to have a complete physical", he said. "Later, you'll be tested for AIDS, TB, and every other the condition known to man. By the way, everyone calls me Doc! "Questions completed, he took me to a 12 X 12 holding cell in the office area where I had to wait for my assigned counselor, Mr. Farmer, to escort me to my new home away from home--Dorm Five.

I looked around the bare cell and saw that it was immaculate. No one would have been afraid to eat off of the spotless floor. Soon bored with cell inspection, my thoughts turned inward. *Pretty funny. I am assigned to a camp with no fences, no armed guards. I could just walk off if I really wanted to, and they place me in a holding cell to wait ten minutes for a counselor. Maybe it's supposed to be a psychological thing... wonder what my family is doing right now.*

Oh, Mary, I never thought I'd miss you so much. So soon The first time I saw Mary, I was thirteen years old and playing piano for the Spring St. Church of God. It didn't take us long to get acquainted and we started sitting together during services and going to various church events. We dated for almost three years and decided to get married in December of 1956. By then, Mary was eighteen and had just finished high school. She was a clerk at the textile mill in town, making $1.25 an hour. I was sixteen, still in high school, and working part-time for Kwik-Chek grocery, making 50 cents an hour.

Being poor wasn't new to me. I was raised in a cotton mill village in Talladega where my parents were employed by the Bemis Bag Company. My sister and brother, Edith and Charles, and I never went hungry, but our parents weren't paid much, and we were lucky to have clothes to wear. Most of them were patched and darned many times.

I had one dress suit. It had been presented to me by the church members in appreciation for the many hours, since age 10, I had spent playing piano for them. I wasn't ungrateful for the suit but despised wearing it because its 100% wool material irritated my skin. That was still my only suit when Mary and I set our wedding date. As fate would have it, the weather turned unseasonably warm that week in December. Wool is irritating enough in cold weather, but in hot weather it's unbearable. "What am I going to do?" I wondered frantically.

Desperation, like necessity, is the mother of invention. I decided to wear a pair of well-worn cotton pajama bottoms under the suit pants. Instant relief. The suit didn't scratch a bit as I stood before the justice of the peace and nervously uttered, "I do." Mary has never let me forget that I was married in my pajamas.

Ten minutes after I'd been put in the holding cell, a security officer jerked my thoughts back to the present when he unlocked the door and led me to the linen room. He told me to pick up two blankets, two sheets, a pillow and pillowcase. As soon as I had everything, he turned me over to my counselor, Mr.

Farmer, who had just come in, looking for us. Juggling my grocery sack and armload of bed linen, I followed him out of the receiving building and onto the compound with as much dignity as my baggy pants would allow.

CLUB FED

Eglin belongs to an elite group of over 90 institutions, which make up the prison system. Its 28-acre compound is maintained under contract by Elgin Air Force Base. It is one of the most beautifully landscaped pieces of property in the world. Tall trees, lovely shrubs, and a variety of colorful flowers cover the grounds, giving the appearance of a luxuriant Garden of Eden.

At the back of the compound is a large five-acre lake teeming with bass, trout, red fish, mullet, and brim. There's no fence around the compound and no armed guards. Since the inmate population consists of individuals who commit non-violent white-collar crimes, presumably they require little supervision and present minimal risk to the community. The facility is designed as a short-term facility with five years as the average sentence served. But there are also some long-term inmates more about them later.

QUICK TOUR

Mr. Farmer took me on a quick tour of the grounds, pointing out the various buildings which housed the barbershop, commissary, Vocational Tech School (VTS) and chapel. We finally arrived at Dorm Five, located at the end of the compound on the north side of the lake. It's the most conveniently located dorm in close proximity to everything.

Later, I found out that Dorm Three was built especially to house those convicted during the Watergate conspiracy hearings. The cubes in Dorm Three were a spacious 10 x 10 compared to the 6 x 8 cubes assigned to most inmates, perhaps in deference to the former status of the Watergate criminals.

DORMS, RECREATION, AND TAXPAYER COSTS

Eglin Federal Prison Compound has five air-conditioned dorms, each with a capacity of 192 inmates. Dorms consist of four sections, A, B, C, and D. Each section has 24 cubes. A cube is a six by eight-foot space, containing a bunkbed, two small lockers, and a tiny area used for writing letters, etc. Two inmates share this very limited space.

Sounds pretty much like a prison, so far, doesn't it? Ah, but wait. how would you like to have clothes, well-prepared nutritionally-balanced meals, and excellent medical and dental care, ill at no cost? Or a private tennis court, softball and baseball field, and another court for handball, basketball, and volleyball? Or how about a special area with thousands of dollars worth of exercise equipment, a large wide-screen TV, one of the best law libraries in he world, and a very respectable regular library? Inmates have all of these things and more.

It doesn't take a Philadelphia lawyer to figure out that regardless of how many crime bills are passed by Congress, crime won't be appreciably deterred if criminals know they stand a good chance of being sent on an all-expense-paid vacation, compliments of the taxpayer. One can only speculate that if the homeless, estimated at more than seven million nationwide, ever found out about "Club Fed" (the nickname given to Eglin Federal Prison Compound by inmates because of its country club atmosphere), here would be a rash of crime, just so the homeless could reap all these benefits. Granted, inmates are away from their families and solated from regular society, but to a great extent, so is anyone serving in the armed forces, Peace Corps, and similar organizations.

And they, too, must comply with rules and regulations. The average annual cost of each inmate's stay at facilities like Club Fed s estimated at $20-30,000 annually.

DORM FIVE

Several inmates greeted me as I followed Mr. Farmer into Dorm Five. "Are you the mayor?" one asked. *News travels fast in prison, especially with the help of TV.*

"Yes," I replied as my counselor led me through the dorm.

We finally came to my assigned area. Each small living space is called, appropriately, a cube and I was given #20-up. (Up refers to the upper bunk.) A man sat hunched over the cube's tiny writing area. He turned around, and the clean-shaven, olive skin of his face crinkled into a smile. He was about 5'10" and 170 pounds. His black, neatly trimmed hair was peppered with gray.

"This is Pat, your bunkee, " said Mr. Farmer. (Bunkee is the nickname for the person with whom you share the bunkbed in your cube.) "I'll leave you two to get acquainted."

While I put my belongings in the cramped locker designated for the top bunk and made my bed, Pat told me he was an Italian originally from New York City but had moved to Florida 30 years ago. "But we can talk more about personal things later," he said. "Right now, we'd better take a little trip around the compound. You need to know where all the yellow boundary lines are. Crossing them is big trouble. If you do, they charge you with attempted escape and send you to a facility with higher level security. Worst of all, you get time added to your sentence."

Pat gave me a fast, but informative tour, and when we got back to the dorm, I asked him the question that had been on my mind all day.

"Pat, what's the best way to get through this thing?"

"Larry," he said, "the best advice I can give you is to do one day at a time. Be careful whom you talk to, keep a low profile, and don't owe anybody any money. They could turn out to be snitches, keeping the guards informed about everything. In return for this service, they get everything from small favors for information on small-time inmates to sentence reductions for obtaining information and testifying on big-name inmates."

"Thanks, Pat. That helps. It sounds like good advice."

Pat finished the tour by showing me the dorm's general layout. There were two bath areas, each consisting of 16 shower talls, 16 sinks, 8 commodes, 8 urinals, 3 water fountains, and 2 pacemakers all shared by the dorm's 175-190 inmates. A regulation-size pool table dominated the large common area, and here were several tables for playing cards or board games.

It turned out to be one of my favorite places because mail all was held there. The big-screen TV was in a separate room.

Outside at the rear of the dorm was the most surprising thing to me a small outdoor theater with a giant screen. Up to wo hundred inmates could sit on benches bolted to the ground and watch movies or other special presentations.

I thought, "I don't have all this at home!" Home. The word hit me with unexpected pain. I stared at scenes inside my lead for a few moments and looked up to see Pat watching me with understanding in his eyes.

Sensing my sudden need to be alone, he asked, "Would you like to walk around the grounds on your own for a while?"

"Yes, I would. Thanks for everything, Pat. I'm glad you're my bunkee."

THE CHAPEL

The place I wanted to go. needed to go…was the chapel. I'd seen the new, modern building during Pat's guided tour. He told me the auditorium was large enough for about 200 people and fully equipped with a piano, organ, and an electronic keyboard. It was the presence of those instruments drawing me to the chapel that day. I've been involved in church work and music most of my life, and music never fails to comfort and inspire me. In spite of Pat's help and encouragement, I was beginning to have a "pity party" for myself. I needed all the comfort and inspiration I could find.

The silence and soft light coming through the chapel windows seemed to embrace me the moment I walked through the door. I sat down at the piano and started playing softly, "Oh, How I Love Jesus", and then, "God Is So Good." Without warning, tears coursed down my cheeks, and I realized just how heartbroken I was about having to go to prison for charges I was not guilty of. Loss of income and how Mary and I would meet financial obligations worried me. I sat there playing and crying, and suddenly a prayer, wrenched from my very soul, formed in my mind.

"Lord, I don't understand why all this has happened or why You haven't answered the prayers of all those who are praying for me, but I still believe in Romans 8.28, and I do love you, Lord."

I'm not sure how long I'd been playing to my private pain and grief when I heard a voice ask, "Are you all right?"

All my life I've been told that God sometimes speaks to people in an audible voice, but I was astounded just the same.

Cautiously, I turned my head toward the sound of the voice and saw, not God, but a tall, middle-aged, black man who had quietly entered the chapel while I was playing.

"I'm Isadore," he said. Those words marked the beginning of a friendship I'll cherish for the rest of my life.

ENLIGHTENMENT AT EGLIN

During my stay at Eglin FPC (Federal Prison Compound), I met and became friends with many inmates and heard the stories of how they had wound up in prison. The more I heard about their experiences and the more court transcripts and P.S.I's (pre-sentence investigative reports) I read, the more obvious it became that many of them were victims of the same system of unjust wheeling and dealing which had convicted me.

I've always been pro law and order and slow to anger, but as inmates described injustice after injustice, my anger and disillusionment grew. Even though I had been railroaded, it was still too incredible for me to believe that what I heard and read was actually happening to so many ordinary people in America. The injustices were no respecter of age, status, race, creed, or color.

Inmates ranged from 20 to 80 years of age, from indigents to millionaires. Some were snatched from highly productive working situations, and others were retirees, receiving retirement checks from all types of employment, including government jobs. There were whites, blacks, Hispanics, Haitians, Cubans, Puerto Ricans, Mexicans, Indians, and many more in the racial and cultural mix of inmates.

Eglin FPC, like many other prisons of its kind, was built to contain inmates who commit non-violent, white-collar crimes. Most of the prison population is made up of people who formerly worked as professionals bankers, lawyers, dentists, doctors, druggists, politicians, ministers, C.P.A's, judges, prosecutors, teachers and many other professions and trades. Some are guilty, many are not. In the following chapters are some of their stories.

ISADORE'S STORY

"Larry," Isadore said, after I got over the shock and realized his voice wasn't God's, "I've been praying for a piano player, and it looks like my prayers have been answered."

"I sure wish God had consulted me before sending me to this particular location to play the piano, " I said.

We both laughed, and somehow, I began to feel better. Isadore told me there was a Protestant service every afternoon, a regular Sunday morning service, and a business-men's worship service on Saturdays. Our friendship grew with every passing day. We worked out a number of songs, which became a regular part of the various services and talked as often as we could.

Isadore, an ordained Baptist minister, was an excellent singer, and a member of the prison Chaplain's Protestant Council He was serving a 15-month sentence for alleged business tax violation. His wife had also been charged, and had served a sentence at the women's prison in Marianna, Florida. She was released in March, 1994. Isadore, a former pastor and pillar of the community, said he took the fall for a man who was his silent business partner in an apartment complex operation. The man was a prominent figure in the community and the person the government was really trying to convict. Apparently, there wasn't enough evidence against the man.

"The government tried to get me to testify against my partner," Isadore said. "They told me if I'd do it, my wife and I would get probation. I'm no snitch, Larry, and I refused to testify. So, they sent me and my wife to prison. Lucky for us, our kids are grown and living away from home. without that extra worry. It's been hard enough Isadore's release date was scheduled for early September 1994. In July, he resigned from the Protestant Council and recommended that I take his place. I was surprised and humbled when the inmates voted unanimously to elect me to the council.

Just before Isadore got up to sing *"My God is Real"* at his last Sunday service, I presented him with a bookmark engraved with a poem I had written in tribute to my friend

ISADORE

Over the years, I've made friends,

And each day meet many more,

But never, in all those many years

Has there been one like you, Isadore.

Of all the places to meet a man

In prison on my arrival

Soon, I knew how vital you were

To the matter of my survival.

A few short weeks, so little time

To pray, sing, and talk

But time enough to know for sure

That Isadore "walks the walk."

Too soon, next Tuesday, I'll say goodbye

Your time is done–you're out the door,

But through my tears, I still thank God

For a friend like you–Isadore.

Larry Barton

September 6, 1994

After Isadore said his last word and sang his last song, there wasn't a dry eye in the chapel. All the inmates came to their feet and gave him a standing ovation.

ORIENTATION

When inmates first arrive at Eglin, they're assigned to odd jobs like raking leaves, emptying trash, and picking up cigarette butts. These chores take about an hour. The rest of the day can be spent eating, sleeping, shooting pool, playing cards or whatever. During this initial orientation period, each inmate receives a complete physical and is examined by a dentist and optometrist.

Not long after I started my orientation, Joey, one of the inmates, approached me and asked, "Are you really the mayor of Talladega, Alabama?"

"Yes, for the past eleven years," I answered.

"Well" Joey continued, "my boss is a racing nut, and he wants to meet you. He goes to the car races at Talladega every year." I assured Joey that I would make it a point to meet his boss.

That night at mealtime, one of the inmates whom I had become acquainted with approached me at the table where I was eating

"Why doesn't the captain like you?" he asked

"I don't know the captain," I responded. "Why do you ask?"

"He was visiting our job site today and your name came up about another politician being in camp. The captain remarked he would have you "bustin' rock" for the next four years."

While we were eating, the captain came into the chow hall and when I saw him, I recognized him as being a former employee at F.C.I. in Talladega while I served as mayor, and I knew he was a personal friend of one of my enemies. I understood why he would make such a remark.

The next day, I walked over to the vocational tech school (VIS) where Joey was chief clerk. He introduced me to his boss, Frank, and two of the instructors, John B. and John M. who were civilians employed by the government.

Talladega, Alabama, known as "The Racing City", has the largest auto racing track in the United States. Because of my connection as mayor of Talladega, Frank and I hit it off immediately, and he talked non-stop for over an hour about auto racing. Frank shared with me that he was a racecar owner and driver, and knew all the drivers, their records, their standing in the polls and the kinds of cars they drive. He's the only man I've ever met who loves and knows auto racing as well as my friend Don Naman, director of the Motor Sports Hall of Fame in Talladega, Alabama

Finally, Frank stopped talking auto racing long enough to ask, "Have you been assigned to a permanent job?"

"Not yet," I responded.

"I need a tool and supply room clerk. How would you like to work for me here at V.T.S.? You'd have an air-conditioned office and work about six hours a day, Monday through Friday.

"Sounds good to me," I said, "but will the captain have to approve my assignment?" I explained to Frank why I was asking.

"Don't worry about the captain. He is being transferred."

I accepted the job offer and gave thanks to God for working things out. I remained with V. T. S. until April 1995 at which time I was assigned to work in the prison barbershop.

DINING HALL SCHEDULE

Long before going to prison, I watched enough James Cagney prison movies to fear I might be fed bread and water with a little meat gruel thrown in on Sundays and holidays. What a pleasant surprise when I first saw the weekly menu posted on the dorm bulletin board!

The menu included a generous variety of foods at each meal, a coffee hour from 5:30 to 7:00 a.m. for early risers, and brunch for those who sleep in on Saturdays, Sundays, and holidays. Far from being a bread and water diet, it was a menu to put many households and restaurants to shame.

K.P. DUTY AND THE WASTE FACTOR

I was assigned to work in the kitchen for several days during the second week of my orientation period. Kitchen chores lasted from 8:00 a.m. to 5:00 p.m. It was the only job I had during orientation which took more than one hour a day. Regular workers are on one day and off two. Inmates like working there. It allows them lots of time off to read, exercise, and play ball. On warm days, they lie out by the lake and get a tan that would be envied on the Riviera.

The dining hall is set up cafeteria-style. Inmates serve themselves and are responsible for taking their dirty dishes to the sink area when finished. Small signs are placed in front of certain items, indicating only one serving is allowed usually bacon, sausage links, and cake items. The sign seldom stops those wanting seconds, but if they're caught, technically they could be sent to the county jail or given extra duty. Usually if they're caught, all that happens is that they have to put the extra food back. If caught several times, they're given extra duty.

My job was to help clean up the king-size pots and pans and mop the floor after each meal. The work area allowed a bird's-eye view of the entire kitchen, and I couldn't believe what went on in that view. Many racks nearly full of bread were rolled out at the end of each day and thrown into the garbage dumpster. Large quantities of leftover food were ground in the garbage disposal and washed down the drain. It looked like enough food to feed several hundred extra people a day.

When I asked one of the permanent workers about the incredible waste, he said, "This goes on every day.

"Why isn't it reported?" I asked.

"This is just a drop in the bucket to what goes on in a month's time," he replied. "If you want to stay at Eglin, you'd better keep your mouth shut »

"A few months ago, more than $10,000 worth of butter, chickens, turkeys, steaks, bacon that kind of stuff came up missing."

"But where did it all go?"

"Straight to a restaurant near here where one of the govemment employees is a silent partner," he said, raising his eyebrows in a knowing look.

While he talked, my brain was busy dipping into its store of facts and figures, and I recalled statistics as appalling as what he was telling me.

More than seven million homeless and those on welfare or fixed incomes go to bed hungry more often than not. They can't afford even the essentials for survival. There's a terrible inequity here somewhere. If this kind of waste is going on in every prison, people are suffering needless hunger, and the taxpayers are really being ripped off.

SICK CALL

I'd been at Eglin a little over a month when I developed a persistent cough, which gradually got worse. After two weeks of coughing nonstop and being plagued with chills and fever, I finally gave up and went on sick call.

I knew it was serious because when P.A. Hernandez examined me, he immediately scheduled an x-ray appointment for the next morning at the nearby Air Force hospital.

Picture me at 7:30 a.m., the next day, in the X-ray room wearing one of those ICU (I-see-you) gowns. For 30 minutes, I was turned every way but loose while lying on a cold, hard, tilt-a-whirl x-ray table. When they finally did turn me loose, I was told to report back to camp, and they would call the results to the P.A.

Rain, like my cough, had been nonstop for two days, and the compound was ankle deep in water. Somehow, I managed to wade back to the dorm. No sooner had I gotten to my cube and started taking off my waterlogged shoes, when an announcement came over the loudspeaker: "Inmate, Larry Barton, report to the base hospital immediately."

Having no dry shoes, I pulled the soaked shoes back on and slogged back across the compound to the hospital. It was only about 300 feet, but with the fever, chills, soaked clothes, and rain still coming down, it seemed like miles. I practically crawled up the hospital steps and into the hospital. The receptionist told me P.A Hernandez was waiting for me. I shuffled into his office and stood there shivering and dripping water.

"Barton," he said, "X-ray called and said you have pneumonia."

"Doc, I didn't know what I had, but I've sure felt terrible for the past few days," I said between coughing spasms.

As I waited for P.A. Hernandez to make notations on my medical chart, 1 said a silent prayer for God to give Doc the wisdom to treat me with the right medicine. I didn't want to die in prison.

Hernandez finished writing, looked up and said, "Larry, I'm putting you on a three-day convalescent leave and giving you enough penicillin to take two tablets every six hours for ten days."

He gave me a bottle of penicillin with the directions written on the label. I thanked him and reluctantly trudged back through the ankle-deep water to the dorm. Shaking, shivering and sloshing in the rain, I thought, *If this weather kills me, I won't have to worry about pneumonia or serving the rest of my time.*

With the last of my strength, I showered and managed to struggle into some dry clothes and pull myself up to the top bunk.

I Literally collapsed and immediately fell asleep.

Several hours later I awoke. My fever and chills were gone, my cough had subsided and other than still being weak, I was feeling much better. In a couple of days, I was nearly my old self again. When I finished the penicillin, Doc sent me back to the hospital for a follow-up x-ray. The results my lungs were clear. I said a prayer of thanks for my amazingly fast recovery. Even though I had taken the medicine, I felt in my heart that God had lent a healing hand.

FATHER'S DAY - JUNE, 1994

Days piled on look-alike days, and I often sought mental and spiritual refuge in the special garden area behind Dorm Five. specially designed as a place for meditation, it is resplendent with flowering shrubs, graceful old trees and a colorful array of flowers Lining the winding paths.

Just before Father's Day, I was sitting on one of the garden's concrete benches reading my Bible. I badly needed the peace and inspiration I often find in its pages. Thoughts of being away from my son on Father's Day, and the pain of my own father's recent death haunted me.

The depression I usually managed to hold at bay gripped me. Tears filled my eyes, blurring the words I'd been trying to read.

From somewhere amid the anguish, words and sentences found their way into that painful jumble of thoughts. I'm no poet, but was inspired to write the following poem.

Father's Day in Jail

Father's Day is special

A day that's really swell

But let me share a story

About Father's Day in jail

All my life I went to church

And tried to do what's right

But there were just a few, who

Fought me with all their might

They couldn't beat me at the polls

And found me "not for sale"

So, they trumped up bogus charges

Now, it's Father's Day in jail

I eat and sleep and do my job

While I wait and pray for bail

But while I wait and wait and wait

I'll spend Father's Day in jail

Inmates are from all professions

And just to name a few

Doctors, lawyers, politicians

And several preachers, too

We share our tales of sorrow

As we wait and wait for bail

But I and a million others

Will spend Father's Day in jail

So, as you daily go your way

Please pray with us for bail

Then, maybe we won't have to spend

Next Father's Day in jail.

Larry Barton

June, 1994

When I returned to my dorm, I set down and wrote one of the closest, dearest friends I have, a letter. Max Morris, formerly a resident of Talladega, Alabama, now residing in Cleveland, Tennessee, had made it a point to call and write regular through my indictment and trial. Max, a national evangelist, pianist and singer had been raised up in the Church of God in Talladega, and served as pianist until he left for college. Max's mother, Dessie, and my mother sang in the church choir and trio for many years and Max played the piano. While I was at Eglin, Max and another good friend, P. D. Wesson drove over 800 miles roundtrip to visit. Max also shared my story with all his worldwide prayer partners (WWPP) and the congregations wherever he preached, received thousands of letters from all over the world. If there was return address, I always responded.

The following is the letter to Max:

Dear Max,

Thank you for your letter and packet of material. Always good to hear from you. Also good to talk with you by phone.

I am receiving letters, from individuals, from different churches ou are visiting. Even though I don't know them, it lifts me up to know lat people still care and are keeping us in their prayers.

So many good things are taking place, and I wanted to share ith you and the prayer partners. First, I was elected by the inmates to erve on the Protestant Council. My primary function will be to select re different inmates to sing, read the devotion, take prayer requests and ther things for the Sunday Morning service. I am honored to have been elected to this position. I will still be assistant pianist.

Secondly, I am still enjoying my job. With my involvement with re church, I could not have gotten a better job assignment.

Lastly and most important, is the way God is blessing at Eglin. When I arrived here, May 27th, the attendance for the weekday service as very small. The same for the Saturday night Full Gospel Men's fellowship and Sunday morning service. In the past six weeks, we have organized a gospel choir, and started promoting the special singing, to help get the inmates involved. This past Saturday, four inmates were baptized, and at the Saturday night service, one of the inmates, that is a Pentecostal preacher, brought the message after all the special music. At he close of the service an old fashion altar call was given and seven of he inmates were saved. Our attendance for all services has doubled, nd this morning, we had 147 in church. God is really blessing. If this continues, we will not be able to get the men in the chapel.

Max, I do not consider me being in prison, as a valley in my life but just changing mountaintops. The government may take me away from my family and friends. but they cannot take God away from me or me from God.

My 82-year-old mother came to visit, and one of the hardest things that I have ever had to do was say good-bye. At her age, and the distance from where she lives, I never know if I will get to see her again. But one consolation, I know she is heaven bound; of course you know that.

Max, I appreciate and love you and proud of the work you are doing. Keep on keeping on and keep me, my family and the inmates in your prayers. May God Bless You.

Larry

VISITATION

My sister is a worrier. Edith worries about everything. If there's nothing to worry about, she worries about that. She's the kind of person who calls to share a secret and whispers into the shone because she worries that someone will overhear. But wonderful worrier, Edith, was one of my biggest supporters while I was in prison. She wrote faithfully every week, visited as often as possible and probably gave me a lot more financial support than she could afford.

Edith's first prison visit was memorable. Like me, she'd seen too many prison movies about how prisoners are supposedly created, and I could tell she had something on her mind while I tried to bring her up to date about prison life. Finally, she asked the question that's a great concern to many inmate families

"Are there any homosexuals in your dorm?"

Before answering, I glanced at the curious, expectant expressions on the faces around the table in the visiting room--Edith, her husband, Elvin, her son, Glen, Diane, his wife, and my mother, Ruby. I drew my chair up closer to the table, leaned over toward them and said softly,

"I don't know if there are any homosexuals here or not, but occasionally, late at night, it's not unusual to see two or three men taking showers together."

"What? What!"

"Did you hear what he said?"

"Does anyone do anything about it?"

"Who all knows about this?'

Everyone was getting excited, Edith most of all. I thought it was time to set their minds at rest.

"Edith, I'm just teasing. If something like that happened and was discovered, the inmates involved would be shipped out immediately to another facility."

There was a lot of relieved laughter. We all relaxed and enjoyed the rest of the visit. Too soon, it was time for them to go.

Good-byes are one of the hardest things about prison life. You want with all your heart to go with them, back to the things you know and love. But you have to watch them walk away, time after time.

My 82-year-old mother hugged me and said, "I love you,

Son. I'm trying not to cry."

Tears stung my own eyes as I said, "Go ahead and cry,

Mother, it's all right."

There were about a hundred other inmates going through the same painful farewells. Everyone was doing fairly well until a beautiful two-year-old girl in her daddy's arms said, "Daddy, please go home with me. I don't want to leave you.

FOURTH OF JULY, 1994

In the weeks after Father's Day, I had become pretty well adjusted to prison life and was looking forward to the July 4th holiday. Inmates who had served a lot of time told me that it would be a really special day a big cookout, singing groups, ball games and lots of other activities.

The day dawned with perfect weather. I spent the early part of the morning walking, working out with weights and getting a tan down by the lake. By noon, over 850 inmates had gathered around the picnic tables and begun filling plates with grilled hamburgers, hot dogs and barbecued ribs. There was old-fashioned lemonade to drink and watermelon for dessert.

Many servings later, we were almost too full to walk over to the softball field where the different bands and singing groups were set up to perform. Some inmates weren't into the music, but there was something for almost everyone in the other sports areas.

Baseball, horseshoes, softball, etc. As the day wound down, I was surprised to realize it had been a thoroughly enjoyable day. Yet, that night, as I lay awake thinking about it, a part of me wondered how our government could justify that kind of wining and dining of so-called criminals.

If we are truly criminals, it seems we should be treated in a way that is more of a real punishment for crimes committed. If not, it makes little sense for us to be here at all, costing taxpayers an average of $25,000 a year per inmate, when we could be doing productive community service while working and paying taxes ourselves. There must be an alternative.

Feelings about what I'd seen that day kept churning inside me, and I couldn't sleep until I put it on paper. Remembering the new crime bill pending in Congress, I decided to write a letter to Senator Joseph Biden, Chairman of the Judiciary Committee, expressing my views of the waste of taxpayers' money where alternative programs would be more practical. Needless to say, never received a reply from the senator.

PAULA

A couple of months after I came to Eglin, a long-time friend came to visit. It was such a beautiful Sunday afternoon in July, I invited my visitor to sit with me at one of the concrete picnic tables just outside the visiting room. There were 50 other inmates and their families and friends who had the same idea.

A couple of tables away I noticed "Flex," an inmate who lived in my dorm. He worked as a prison barber and was serving five years for a drug charge. He was talking to a young woman, so beautiful she could have been a movie star. I thought that maybe it was his wife. I assumed the elderly lady sitting at the table with them was his mother or mother-in-law.

Flex got his nickname from fellow inmates because they so often found him in front of the restroom mirrors, flexing and admiring his muscles. He spent all his spare time working out with weights and jogging. I found out later that he had worked as a male stripper before coming to prison, and probably wanted to keep his figure so he could return to his occupation.

My friend and I were deep in conversation about who was serving time, what kind of people they were, and prison life in general, when I saw Flex heading toward our table with the lovely young woman on his arm. We made mutual introductions. When Flex introduced the woman as Paula, his sister, something tickled the back of my mind. She looked very familiar, but it still didn't register that this was the same Paula who had shown up at a party with O.J. Simpson on the night prior to the death of Simpson's wife and friend

Flex told Paula I'd been mayor of Talladega, and she wanted to introduce me to their mother. Flex headed toward the soft drink machines, and Paula, my friend, and I walked over to their table to meet her mother. During the 10 minutes or so we talked, it was inevitable that the subject of O.J. should come up. At that time, it had only been about one month since the murders had occurred, and it was still big news.

"I'm surprised to see you here." I said.

"Well, I made a short visit to see my parents in Panama City. It's only about an hour's drive from here, and I wanted to see my brother before I fly back to California to be close to 0.J.

"Do you think he murdered his wife and her boyfriend?" I

asked.

"Ive been a close friend of O.J.'s for a long time," she said, "and I just can't believe he's guilty of murder. I think I know him well enough to know he's innocent."

Paula visited her brother regularly until his release in September 1994. I happened to run into Flex a few days before he left.

Hi, Larry," he said. "Listen, I've been wondering about the best way to get an interview with the media."

Flex knew I'd been in politics and had dealt with the media on many occasions. "It depends on what kind of information you've got and whether anyone thinks it's newsworthy," I said.

"Well, here it is, Larry. Paula's making a fool of herself or letting O.J. make a fool of her, depending on how you look at it.

Deep down, Paula believes O.J. killed those two, but she's sticking by him anyway."

"But Flex, that day I met Paula she told me she believed O.J. was innocent."

Flex laughed and said, "Sure, that's what she tells everybody. She's so obsessed with O.J., she's willing to sacrifice everything for him, including her movie and modeling career. She's even done a nude session for one of those skin magazines-Penthouse, I think, just to get some money. The thing is, I know if O.J. beats the murder rap, he won't wipe his feet on her.

"I don't like my sister being played for a fool. It really makes me mad. What I can't figure out is why she's so obsessed with him. She could have almost any man she wanted, and I believe she could be a famous movie star and very rich, if she'd only concentrate on her career."

"I think maybe the tabloids might be your best bet," I said.

"Why don't you try calling the Enquirer, the Star or the Globe?

Tell them who you are, and what you've been telling me just now. One of them would probably be interested."

"Thanks for the advice, Larry. I'll do that as soon as get out next week."

Flex's fears about how OJ. would treat Paula after his release on Oct. 3, 1995, were apparently justified.

According to an article by Peter Burt in the Oct. 31, 1995 issue of the Star, "O.J. Simpson is already two-timing Paula Barbieri, the beauty who stood by him during his murder trial.

Pals say he's hot and heavy with sexy ex-cheerleader, Gretchen Stockdale... Meanwhile, Paula is waiting for O.J. at her home in Panama City."

Yet on the same day, the Oct. 31, 1995 issue of the Globe reported that a "close pal" stated: "O.J. said, 'Baby, please come to Los Angeles. I need you at my side. I want to marry you.' According to the article, O.J. flew to Florida to be with Paula on "the day before Sydney's (his daughter] birthday."

Whatever the truth, an Associated Press report in the Nov. 11, 1995 edition of the Tampa Tribune reported that after Simpson's release Paula said, ... it was a realization for me that he was going to [continue to] live there [Los Angeles] in that lifestyle." "Barbieri, 28, refused to say how she told Simpson their three-year relationship was over: I think that's really private. *

On November 14, 1995, I saw an article in the Globe which quoted Flex as having said: "My sister is brokenhearted, but she's dumped O.J., and I hope this time it's for good."

Flex says Paula is especially hurt because she remained faithful to O.J. for the 15 months he was locked up. "She always believed in his innocence.

When he was released, she thought they'd live happily ever after."

PHILLIP'S STORY

Working as a clerk in the tool and supply room, I had a chance to meet each inmate who enrolled in the classes offered there. I had met Phillip before while playing piano for the inmate choir, and encouraged him to enroll in the small engine class. One night, during his 15-minute break, he came to my office. He was obviously depressed.

"Phillip, what's wrong? Is there anything I can do?" I asked.

"Oh, Larry, I don't think there's anything anybody can do.

I've got a wife and four children, and they're having a terrible time trying to make ends meet. Without my income, they're having to live on food stamps and welfare in one of those run down government housing projects. My oldest kid is only seven years old."

"How did all this happen, Phillip?"

"I lost my job several years ago. Like most people, we pretty much lived from paycheck to paycheck, and had almost nothing to fall back on. It didn't take long for finances to get really desperate. Some guys I knew told me about a man who owned a big ship and needed laborers, and I was able to get on with him. I worked the first day loading big wooden crates on the ship. They paid me $200 for the day's work.

"As I was leaving for home, one of the guys who had worked there a long time told me that there was heroin in those crates. Lord knows, I needed work, but I didn't want to be part of a drug operation. So, I quit.

"Three years later, the ship's owner was arrested and charged with smuggling drugs. The prosecutor offered the ship owner probation if he would give the authorities a list naming everyone who'd ever worked for him.

"I was indicted, along with 53 others. They told me that if

I'd plead guilty, I'd only get ten years. If not, I'd probably get 25 years or more. I couldn't really afford a decent defense attorney.

And even if I could have, there was no guarantee I'd be found innocent. So, I pled guilty."

If Phillip has to serve the full ten years for one day of unknowingly loading crates of heroin aboard the ship, it will cost taxpayers over $250,000 dollars plus whatever welfare benefits his family is able to get while he's in prison. Due to his financial problems and the distance involved, Phillip won't get to see his family during the entire ten years.

This man was convicted, separated from his family and sent to prison because he was trying to make a living. The owner of the ship who was actually running drugs received probation.

This certainly says something about the American justice system.

And it isn't good.

DIETING

For the first few weeks at Eglin, I was lonely and had far too much free time on my hands. Those of you plagued with weight problems won't be surprised to learn that I was eating every time the dining hall doors opened, not to mention all the times I went back for seconds, especially for milk and desserts. Ample food in general, milk and desserts in particular, do interesting things to the waistline. After a week or so of making a hog of myself, I noticed my pants were getting a little tight. "Must be the detergent making them shrink," I told my bunkee.

When I could no longer fool myself or anyone else, I decided to go on a diet. I struggled through a few days of dieting, and on July 23rd, after many false starts, expressed my frustration in a poem.

NOT FAT-JUST FLUFFY

I reported to prison a little bit heavy

But still ate three meals each day

I ate all I could cookies, meat and gravy

I gorged like a horse bolting hay.

Why not go on a diet, I thought

Imagine how trim you can be

But after few hours of doing without

I wondered if losing weight was for me.

I came to my senses one day in the shower

Standing there all in the buffy

Without much effort, I convinced myself

I wasn't really fat- just fluffy!

Larry Barton

July, 1994

It was fine to joke about my growing fat rolls, but by the first of August, I had gained so much that I weighed 230 lbs. It was time to get serious. I attacked weight loss with a vengeance. I walked, jogged, used the exercise equipment, and stuck to a diet that would have starved a bird. Within two months I lost 25 pounds. My waist size went from 40 to 36". I was very proud of myself.

ERNIE

Washing clothes is not my favorite thing, especially in the prison laundry, but it has to be done. The trick is when to do it. The laundry was open from 5:30 a.m. to. 9:30 p.m. seven days a week. But with only twelve washing machines and twenty dryers for over 850 men, choosing the right time requires clever maneuvering to avoid spending hours waiting for empty machines. I quickly learned to go as soon as the doors opened or as late as possible at night.

One morning in August, I picked the 5:30 a.m. time to beat the heat and the crowd. Since wash cycles take 25-30 minutes, I put my clothes in the washer and went to get a newspaper to read while I waited. At that hour it was still dark, but not too dark to notice Ernie, a young, black man, sitting on the steps of the hobby shop building.

"Hi, Ernie," I said as I passed by. My steps faltered. Something told me to go back and see if something was wrong. "Are you okay, Ernie? Do you need anything?"

"I was just praying for an orange. Do you have one you could give me?"

Sure, there are a couple of oranges in my locker, but if I give them to Ernie, I won't be able to buy anymore until payday.… and only then if there's enough in my account, I reasoned.

This may sound selfish, but I only made 29 cents an hour.

Out of that I had to buy laundry detergent, deodorant and other personal items before I could even consider luxury items like fruit and candy. Small things take on great importance when they're hard to come by. It felt like I was battling the Devil. To share or not to share--that was the question.

After a few moments of mental struggle, I said, "Yes, Ernie, I have an orange. Wait here. I'll go get it for you."

I walked back to the dorm, opened my locker, and considered the two plump oranges and one juicy apple sitting on the shelf. Hesitating only slightly, I grabbed both oranges and took them back to where Ernie sat waiting. His eyes lit up as he took the oranges.

As he walked away, I heard Ernie murmuring, "Thank you, Jesus, thank you Jesus. Thank you for the oranges."

Later in the week, I ran into Ernie's friend, Willie. I told him about the incident with the oranges and asked, "Willie, would you mind telling me a little about Ernie's background?"

"Well," Willie said, "it ain't too good. His daddy left when he was just a kid, and his mamma wasn't real concerned about where he was or what he did. He was mostly raised on the streets. He only made it through the eighth grade, and then he got into the drug scene. That's what he's serving time for--a drug charge. The only income he's got is the eleven cents an hour he makes from his prison job. (Inmates are paid according to their level of education and job assignment.)

After Willie left, I thanked God that I'd been able to overcome the desire to keep the oranges for myself. They had only cost me thirty cents each, but their value to Ernie had been immeasurably greater. Just a few days later, a friend sent me a $20.00 money order, and I was able to buy all the fruit I wanted.

God works in mysterious ways.

VANESSA (FORMER MISS AMERICA) WILLIAMS

"My clothes are in there." I said to the inmate who was opening the door of the dryer when I returned with my paper. "I'm just tryin' to find my own clothes," he said, scowling at me. I sighed towardly and thought, *He's probably one of those who put his clothes in the first available washer and leaves the laundry to watch TV or whatever.*

It was already getting hot, and the heat had scorched my patience. The washer/dryer thing was a sore spot with me, anyway. since so many men had to use so few washers and dryers, the rule las that everyone was supposed to stay with their clothes, getting dem in and out as quickly as possible. Inmates who left their clothes knew someone else would have to take their clothes out before being able to use the washer, and would probably put the clothes in a dryer.

A sweet deal for them. They got part of their laundry done by someone else and didn't have to stop watching a ball game or taking nap. I hated doing my own laundry and sure wasn't thrilled about going someone else's. There aren't many things that irritate me, but that was one of them.

"If you'd stay with your clothes like you're supposed to, you wouldn't have to hunt for them," I said, scowling back at him.

There was a sneer on his young, black face as he said, "They told me you was prejudiced and racist."

I could feel my face flushing, not from embarrassment, but from anger at his absurd remark. Race had absolutely nothing to do with my laundry, and I would have said the same thing to any inmate.

If he only knew. My enemies in Talladega called me "nigger lover" because I insisted on focusing attention to the concerns of all my constituents in Talladega, regardless of race. I had an excellent relationship with the black citizens and received a large black vote during elections.

"I know all about you," he said. "You're the one who took the key to the city away from Miss America just because she was black. You really think you're somethin', don't you? But you know what? You aint nothin'"

It was obvious he had heard about what happened in 1954, but it was equally obvious that he didnt know what really happened and was looking for a fight verbal or otherwise. In light of his arrogant attitude and ignorance of the faets, my first impulse was to help educate him. Instead, I took a deep breath and told myself there was no use getting into trouble over a punk.

I began to wonder who he was, where he came from, and how he knew about my experience with Vanessa Wanis, Winner of the Miss America pageant in 198.

Listen, young man," I said, "I don't know who you are or where you came from, but you're sure confused about what happened between Vanessa Williams and me. If you'd like to know what really happened, I'm an authority on the subject."

I was surprised to hear him reply, "Yeah, I'd like to hear your version. And by the way, my name's Eric, not young man"

"Okay, Eric. Come over and sit down, and I'll tell you how it was."

By then, Eric had found his clothes in another dryer. He shook them out ready for folding and joined me on the row of chairs along the wall

"One of the first things I did after being elected mayor of Talladega." I told him, "was to take a stand against pornography. 1 convinced the city council to pass an ordinance, regulating the sale of pornographic material.

"Attorney, Jake Montgomery, was my most vehement opponent on the pornography issue. He objected strenuously. The merchants who sold it weren't enthusiastic either. The ordinance required them to pay a $2,000 license fee just to sell pornographic material. On top of that, each magazine had to be individually wrapped in opaque plastic and stored under the counter or in a closed cabinet. Finally, the ordinance prohibited anyone under eighteen from doing business at a place where books and magazines were sold.

"In spite of Attorney Montgomery's protests, the ordinance passed. After that, no legitimate businesses in the city sold any material which could be called pornographic —from magazines like *Playboy* on up to hard-core stuff. Some time later, the attorney ,general of Alabama took a tough stand on pornography throughout the whole state. I like to think he was influenced by our success in 'Talladega.

"Vanessa Williams, Miss America in 1983, was invited to be grand marshal of the Talladega Christmas parade. She agreed to do it, and as a part of the ceremonies, was presented with the key to the city. The following summer the news media announced that *Penthouse* magazine had obtained pictures from a freelance Photographer, depicting Vanessa Williams posing with someone Ise in simulated sex acts. Allegedly, these pictures had been made several years earlier. When I heard the news, my first impression was that someone was trying to make a fast buck off of Vanessa because of her Miss America status, and I was inclined to ignore the publicity, hoping it would go away. But over the next few days 11 the media ran stories on Vanessa, and the local radio talk show made a big deal out of the fact that she had been presented with a key to the city. Soon, everyone in the city was talking about it. The handwriting was on the wall, and I knew that as the mayor responsible for pushing through our new pornography ordinance,

I'd get lots of pressure to take some kind of action. Before doing anything, I felt I had to find out if the pictures were as graphic as they were alleged to be. Since there were no stores in Talladega selling *Penthouse* due to the pornography ordinance, I bought a copy in Birmingham a few days later. The pictures were pretty much as the media had described them, and I knew there was no escaping some kind of action on my part.

"After several days of mind-wrestling the problem, I decided that if Vanessa had been up front with pageant officials concerning her past endeavors, she wouldn't have been permitted to enter the Miss America contest. Then she wouldn't have been chosen Miss America for 1983 and subsequently invited to serve as grand marshal. Certainly, she wouldn't have been presented with a key to the city. Even though it was only a brass key mounted on wooden plaque, it symbolized that the city was honored to have the recipient represent Talladega.

"I finally decided to write to Ms. Williams, explaining the stand I'd taken against pornography and about the resulting ordinance in Talladega. I described my disappointment and regret that something like this had happened and told her that if I'd known about her past connections with pornographic publications, I wouldn't have presented the key to the city in the first place.

"I went on to say, that in view of the city's ordinance and my own personal convictions, I felt that I had to request that she return the key to the city.

"And that's what I did, requested that she return the key.

There was nothing in the tone of letter, which could have been construed as a demand."

"Man, this don't sound nothin' like the version I heard."

Eric said, shaking his head. "Did she answer your letter?"

"No, but a couple of weeks later, I received a very nice letter from her mother. In a nutshell it said, 'Even though Vanessa made a mistake in the past by posing for those pictures, it is in the past, and we'll keep the key.' As far as I was concerned, that was the end of it. But I was in for big a surprise. About the same time I wrote the letter to Vanessa, my good friend, Willard McDonald, invited me to speak at an anti-pornography rally in Ashland, Alabama. He wanted me to describe the actions we had taken against pornography in Talladega and explain how well they'd worked

"Afterward, there was a question-and-answer session, and someone asked about the Miss America situation. I told them about the letter, requesting that Ms. Williams return the key to the city and the reasons for feeling it necessary to take such a step.

"They applauded my answer, and once again, I thought that was the end of the matter. Once again, I was wrong.

"August Lehe, a reporter for the Sylacauga Advance and a long-time friend was in the audience, He's one of the few reporters I know who does honest, factual reporting, and he knew I felt the public had a right to the news, good or bad. His article about Vanessa and the key to the city appeared in the weekend edition of the Sylacauga, Alabama paper. It was straightforward news reporting and a fair account of what had happened.

Unfortunately, it was picked up by the national wire services. When I arrived at the office on Monday, the story had broken loose everywhere. My excited secretary told me all the national news services were looking for me, and even the BBC wanted an interview. After that grueling day finally ended, it seemed every news outfit in the world had contacted me, wanting the juicy' details of the Miss America incident. It even made the *London Times*. By the time the different media had put their particular spin on the story, they had me demanding that the key be returned to the city.

"The next few weeks were as close to a political nightmare as I ever want to get. I received hundreds of phone calls, letters, and cards from all over the world. Some were complimentary, and some were vulgar. Two letters were outright threatening. It was my first experience with the national media and the way they could take a relatively low-key remark and turn it into a circus of sensationalism.

I know their responsibility is to sell papers or increase ratings, but I think they also have a moral responsibility to the public and the people about whom they report to practice the kind of honest, factual reporting done by my friend, August."

"Man, you got yourself in some kind of bind, didn't you?" Eric said.

"Yes, I'm afraid I was pretty dumb about how things worked on a national scale, and it made everything a lot harder. If 1 had it to do over, I'd handle a lot of things differently." first came in.

"Say, man, I'm sorry I talked so rough to you when you You know, Larry, you're the only white man who ever took time to talk to me like I was human. I ain't got no education, and everybody's always treated me like dirt. I'm in here because I couldn't get no job and didn't know what else to do except sell drugs for money to buy medicine and food for my mamma."

"It's okay, Eric. I think I understand how you must have felt. Why don't you come to our church service Sunday? If you like to sing, we could sure use you in the choir."

Eric's eyes lit up and he said, "I'd like that, especially if you sing some of them old gospels like my mamma was always hummin' around the house."

I laughed as we shook hands and said, "Gospels are my specialty. Ill make sure we sing a lot of them."

Eric did attend services. He became a Christian and sang in the choir until he was released.

DUCKY

Another popular area in the camp, is the recreation center.

This is where the inmates can go to play tennis, basketball, softball, lift weights or exercise on the various equipment available.

Lewis, nicknamed "Ducky," was riding the stationary bicycle when I arrived for my daily exercise hour. Just the two of us alone at this time of the morning. I asked Lewis how he acquired the name "Ducky."

According to Lewis, he was hunting on a federal game preserve and a game warden approached him and arrested him for shooting a "duck." Lewis said that he informed the game warden that he was not aware that he was on government land, and even if he was, he had not even fired his rifle. Lewis asked the game warden to show him the duck that he allegedly shot. The game warden said he could not find the duck, but he saw it fall' from the sky.

Lewis went to court but before trial was afforded an opportunity to plead guilty and serve 3 months at Eglin or go to trial, and if found guilty, be sentenced to 1-2 years.

Lewis, plead guilty. Ducky's community was made safer, and it only cost the taxpayers around $6,000 for his vacation.

DR. CHING

One particular Saturday morning, the sun was shining... no work and a perfect day to relax and get a tan.

The fish were jumping in the water, and the inmates were lying on the beach, listening to their radios.

Between the ocean and the "meditation garden" is a camp perimeter asphalt road. Many of the inmates utilize this road for walking or jogging, this beautiful morning, was no exception. From where I was sitting, I could see the men. As they passed by, most would wave or speak.

Dr. Ching, a 62-year-old Chinese doctor, who became an American citizen, stopped by to chat. A very fine Christian, who had enjoyed a very successful practice for over 30 years prior to coming to prison, is a family man and a pillar of the community.

According to Dr. Ching, he had received an application, in the mail, unsolicited, offering him a credit card, with a $20,000.00 limit. All he had to do was fill in the blanks, mail it back, and wait for final approval. This was done, and in a few days, Dr. Ching received a credit card.

Several months later, Dr. Ching went to the bank, secured a cash advance and deposited it to his account. Dr. Ching was never late with his payment and had reduced the outstanding balance considerable, when he was indicted.

The charge an attempt to defraud a federal bank and mail fraud. Dr. Ching had allegedly failed, unintentionally, to list a long term financial obligation on the credit application, and upon an annual audit of the bank issuing the credit card, Dr. Ching's loan was pulled to verify information on his application, for accuracy, and it was discovered he had failed to list this obligation.

Dr. Ching was permitted to plead guilty, receive a one-year sentence, and pay a fine. Dr. Ching lost his medical practice, his reputation and was separated from his wife, of 40 years.

Once again, justice served, the community made safer and it only cost the taxpayers approximately $25,000.00 for Dr. Chino's all-expense-paid vacation in beautiful Florida

BOB

Dr. Ching had only been gone about ten minutes, when Bob, a very dedicated Christian and choir member, stopped by.

Bob, a man in his sixties and very well respected by all the inmates, was serving a twenty year sentence. Bob was in his tenth year on July 24, 1994. He had been charged with conspiracy.

Bob, who was a relatively quiet individual, was noticeably disturbed. I asked him if he was feeling OK, and he responded that his son, who was 33 years of age, had passed away the day before.

I asked if he would be going to the funeral, and he said, "No. "

Bob went on to say that the warden would only grant him a one-day furlough, and there was no way he could go and come due to the distance. Bob's home is a 1600-mile round trip from Eglin.

"Larry, " Bob continued, "This is the hardest thing I have had to face, in the ten years I have been in prison. Being away from the family is tough, but at a time like this it is almost unbearable."

"However", he said, I had the privilege of seeing my son saved when he was a teen, and I know he is in a better place today". By now, tears were rolling down our faces.

Bob's son had been left paralyzed from an auto wreck in 1990. Through the weeks and months following Bob's time of sorrow, he never missed a Sunday singing in the choir.

BILLY

Billy, a young white male in his early twenties, weighing in excess of 400 pounds, was sentenced to six months at "Club Fed." He had pled guilty to conspiracy to defraud a bank.

Billy was a computer "Whiz" and knew everything from A-Z about computers. He could hack into any computer. Billy's trouble with the government started when he went to his local bank and applied for a loan. Billy's loan request was denied, and this upset him tremendously.

Upon returning home from the bank, Billy sat down at his computer and figured out how to gain access to the customers' accounts at this bank. Once he gained access, he proceeded to withdraw money from customers accounts that carried a large balance and deposited the money into customers' accounts that were overdrawn or carried a small balance. Total amount of money that was transferred, was $100,000.

Billy's stay at "Club Fed" cost the taxpayers more than $15,000. No question that Billy was wrong and should have been punished, but should the taxpayers be stuck with the tab? This being Billy's first offense, he could have been placed on probation and fined heavily. Then if he violated his probation, send him to prison.

BOULEVARD

Boulevard, a Brazilian, was without a doubt, the most outspoken inmate in camp when it came to Christianity. Short in statue, 5' 4", he made up for it when he witnessed for the Lord. Whether singing, "The Love of God", speaking in a Saturday night Full-Gospel Business Men's Fellowship Meeting, or just in a one-on-one conversation, there was no misunderstanding about Boulevard's commitment to God.

Prior to becoming a Christian, Boulevard was a semiprofessional soccer player. Becoming very popular with the fans, the fame, and nightlife scene overshadowed his thinking, and he became involved with cocaine. He was trying to keep pace with the so-called "in crowd" in the drug scene.

In 1989, Boulevard married a beautiful American lady, and a year later, they became the parents of a healthy baby girl. The birth of his daughter was the turning point for Boulevard. At the insistence of a teammate, Boulevard attended a revival at a Pentecostal church and was converted. His wife, an atheist, was visible upset.

In 1991, almost one year to the date of turning his life around and leaving the soccer team, Boulevard was indicted by a federal grand jury for conspiracy to distribute drugs. The offense for which he was indicted occurred prior to his becoming a born-again Christian. Prior to his court date, Boulevard's wife begged him to take her and their daughter, leave Miami, and go to Brazil.

She was confident that if they left the U.S., the government would not extradite him for a small drug charge.

Boulevard spent many days fasting and praying about leaving the country and keeping his family together or face up to what he had done and possibly go to prison and lose his family. He pled guilty and was sentenced to five (5) years in prison. His wife filed for divorce.

In August, 1994, Boulevard • was awakened around midnight, leg shackled, handcuffed, and taken to the county jail. No explanation was given at the time for this action. There is no cell on the compound at Eglin for long-time use. The county jail is known as "THE HOLE."

Upon arrival at the county jail, the jailer pushed a button, a buzzer sounded, and the locked gate to the main cell block opened, and Boulevard was led down the hall, past several other cells, where other prisoners were, to a large cell, sometimes referred to as the "Bull Pen." As Boulevard was being led down the corridor, he could hear the clanging of the gate as it slammed shut.

As Boulevard entered the "Bull Pen", the stench of sweat and filth was almost enough to make a person puke. Several other men were already in the cell

One prisoner, tall and unusually thin, with shaven head, was talking loud to himself in a language only he seemed to understand. An elderly, bearded man sitting on the floor paid no attention to him. He was busy combing the floor with his hands, hoping to find a cigarette butt. Having found one, he picked it up, lit it, and a sigh of contentment came from him.

Across the cell was a young Cuban, his shirt torn and covered with blood. He was gnawing on a stale piece of bread. At the end of the cell, a young, black, muscular-built man in tight black stretch pants got up from where he was sitting and came over to Boulevard and said, "Wanna get friendly, boy?" His mouth was smeared with bright red lipstick, and he flexed his arms, revealing his biceps. Before Boulevard could respond, the "he-she" moved back across the cell.

"I tried to sleep, but the old filthy mattress, on the floor, was covered with urine, vomit, and bugs," Boulevard said. "This cell must have been where they raised bed bugs.'

During the next several days of confinement, Boulevard read from a pocket Bible and told the prisoners who would listen that God loved them, and there was a better life. At first, they laughed and made fun of him, but after three days of praying, fasting and reading the Bible, the prisoners apparently realized that he was not putting on about a better life. Different cellmates begin to ask him about God and what they had to do to be saved. Boulevard shared and prayed with each one that asked him to.

After eight days in the county jail, Boulevard was informed that he would be going back to the camp. According to the information that he received, an inmate in the same dorm where Boulevard lived and one that he had thought was a friend, apparently had gotten upset about Boulevard'spraying and witnessing to the other inmates. Several weeks back, he had found an 8-foot dead snake under his pillow. At the time, no one could prove who placed the snake there.

Boulevard was further informed that the reason he had been locked up was that this same inmate had filed a report with the camp security officer, alleging that Boulevard was planning on escaping from the camp and fleeing to Brazil. Upon investigation, the officer realized this was not the case, therefore clearing Boulevard of any wrongdoing. This investigation also revealed that the same inmate had placed the snake under Boulevard's pillow.

The inmate who filed the false report was taken away in chains to another prison.

As Boulevard was escorted from the county jail, the prisoners asked him to have prayer with them. He was permitted to do so.

On Sunday following his return to camp, I asked Boulevard to sing in the Sunday moming service. He testified and shared what he had been through and then began to sing *"The Love of God."* When he went into the chorus, *"The love of God, how rich and pure, how measureless and strong, it shall forever more endure,"* tears were flowing from many of the inmates' eyes.

Upon his release, Boulevard plans to go into the full gospel ministry, possibly in Brazil.

COLUMBUS DAY WEEKEND OCTOBER, 1994

The warm days of summer gradually disappeared into the cool nights and crisp mornings of fall. Trees brought out their lovely reds and golds. Like the changing season, inmates who had done their time left for home, and a fresh batch came in on the prison bus almost every day.

The new prisoners were younger, mostly Caucasian, and I detected a more blatantly arrogant, know-it-all attitude in them.

They seemed to have no respect for authority, and though obviously street-smart, they had little education otherwise. It was probably lucky for them that they came just in time for the long holiday weekend before facing the harsh reality of how different their lives were going to be.

Except for a few in food service and the medical facility, all inmates were given a four-day weekend to celebrate the holiday. Old-timers looked forward to the big cookout planned for Saturday, and all the activities like softball and horseshoes to pass the time. Most people on the outside who have limited leisure time would consider four days with absolutely nothing to do except play, the good life. But on the inside where you have few responsibilities, it's often hard to fill the hours with anything that makes your life feel meaningful.

Saturday morning wasn't much different from all weekend mornings. Sweet rolls and coffee from 5:30 to 7:30 a.m. and breakfast at eight. After all that food, most of us needed the 4 1/2 hours until cookout time just to work up an appetite. Appetite or not, by 12:30 almost 900 men were lined up with mouths watering, just thinking about the surf and turf (shrimp and steak) or grilled hamburgers and hot dogs with all the trimmings.

Someone waiting in line said, "If the food was always this good, I'd be mighty tempted to renew my membership in Club Fed"

If we had a golf course, this would be a first-class country club or retirement home. I wondered how many people would love to have just the scraps from these meals? So many human beings, whose only crime is to be poor, are slowly starving to death while we, who are supposed to be a menace to society, are eating like upper-class citizens.

REPAIRS AT THE TOOTH AND BONE SHOPS

The Root Canal

A broken cap on one of my jaw teeth was the price I paid for all my gorging at the Columbus Day cookout. On top of that, I was having a lot of pain in the heel of my right foot. I went on emergency sick call and wound up with appointments on two consecutive days; the dentist on the 19th and the podiatrist on the 20th of October. Appointments, work schedules, etc., for all inmates are posted on the bulletin board in every dorm. Failure to keep appointments or report for work details is subject to disciplinary action.

As the day for my dental appointment loomed closer, I was tempted to risk disciplinary action. I kept having nightmares about what the dentist, Dr. David Liebetreas, told me when he gave me my appointment. He had examined my uncapped, naked tooth and described my options in frightening detail.

"You have two options," he said. "I can either pull what's left of your tooth or do a root canal. In a nutshell, a root canal involves killing the nerve, drilling a hole in the tooth stump, inserting a steel pin and building a new tooth on the pin."

I thanked him and practically ran out of his office.

Although I wanted to save my tooth, I was convinced that if I chose the root canal option, I would surely die. I watched the calendar with growing dread as the date for my appointment came nearer. Hoping to ease my mounting anxiety, I sought out a couple of old-timers and asked about their experiences with the dentist. One inmate, named Jack, told me the dentist had pulled his tooth and did a great job.

"I didn't even feel the Novocaine shots," he said. There was one little problem though."

"What?" I asked, expecting the worst.

"He pulled the wrong tooth." Jack's expression never changed as he delivered this piece of news which confirmed all my fears.

Another inmate, Pete, chimed in. "I had some work done earlier this year. The needle the dentist stuck into my gums went clear through to my brain. Never felt a thing."

After Pete's last remark, neither of them could keep a straight face. They burst into laughter, and I nervously joined in.

"Seriously," Pete said, "we've both had root canals done, and Dr. Liebetreas did a super job."

"He's a Public Health employee assigned to the camp, and knows all the latest procedures. He's supposed to be one of the best around," Jack said.

I felt a little better after talking to them, but was still not especially eager to keep my appointment. Nevertheless, after reluctantly deciding to have a root canal, I kept the dreaded appointment, and before I knew it, sat fidgeting in the dental chair, waiting for death. If it kills me, I can get out of prison early, I thought.

To divert thoughts of doom, I sent my eyes on a rapid trip around the room. My glance slid across the objects hanging on one wall, then jerked back and gave my brain the unwelcome information that a hammer, saw, screw driver, and several other tools were menacingly displayed in someone's hasty idea of an artful arrangement. I had a sudden urge to empty my bladder.

"What are those for?" I asked through a constricted throat and cotton-dry mouth.

Dr. Liebetreas looked where my trembling finger pointed, laughed and said, "Don't worry, Larry. Woodworking is my hobby and those are some of the tools I use." The bathroom urge subsided somewhat.

For the next two hours, I attempted to push my body down into the padding of the dental chair. Monica, the young, female dental assistant, used a device that worked like a vise in reverse. She inserted it to stretch my mouth open to a width that was just short of dislocating my jaw. The device wasn't necessarily meant to be an instrument of torture. Without it, twenty fingers, several pounds of gauze and a threatening array of instruments couldn't have been rammed into the limited space of my mouth while Dr.

Liebetreas' jackhammer drill beat a scary, whining rhythm on my hapless tooth. Actually, Jack and Pete were right. I didn't feel the injection and had no real pain. But my anticipatory anxiety level was extremely high, especially when they used the little blowtorch to kill the nerve in my tooth. At that moment, I was sure I'd be getting out of prison early—feet first. Finally, the torture was over, and Dr. Liebetreas told me to rinse my mouth.

Rinse what? After two hours flat on my back, swallowing I know not what and Monica with her little rubber suction hose which nearly took out my tongue and the lining of my mouth, there's wasn't much left to rinse. My dead tongue and lips tried valiantly to follow the rinsing instructions. I managed to slosh a small amount of water around my oral cavity, but the bulk of it sprayed in all directions, dribbling over my lifeless lips and down my chin. It occurred to me that if they would give me a bar of soap and a towel, I could take my shower now and save time.

I staggered out of the dental office, a beaten man. Gradually the Novocaine wore off, and I welcomed the discomfort in my mouth as a sign that I was still alive.

THE BONE SPUR

Barely recovered from my orthodontics ordeal, I reported to the camp hospital the next day. Since they have no Podiatrist there, the prison bus took me to Dr. Zi's office in downtown Ft. Walton, about three miles from Eglin.

Shortly after I arrived, they x-rayed my right foot, then took ne to an examining room to wait for the doctor. I felt pretty good bout seeing Dr. Zi. It was my first appointment with a foot doctor, but I'd never heard of anyone dying from being treated by me.

Fifteen minutes later Dr. Zi walked in carrying my x-rays. he examined my foot, studied the x-rays and said, "Larry, there's a bone spur in that foot. It's what's been causing you so much pain. "You have three options for your problem."

Having heard this option jargon the day before, I felt a small twinge of anxiety. "What are they?" I asked bravely.

"Well, we can operate and take out the bone spur, inject cortisone to clear up the inflammation, or do nothing."

My favorite was the do nothing option, but the Cortisone rection won out. If length can be measured by pain, the needle he stuck into the bottom of my foot was three feet long. The thought that I'd get out of prison early ran through my mind again, and the urge to go to the bathroom returned with a vengeance.

For all that, I survived and was quite satisfied with the treatment I received. Outside prison, a conservative estimate for ne cost of the medical and dental treatment I received would be about $700. Because I was an inmate, taxpayers paid the bill.

On the way back to Eglin, the bus driver stopped to pick up an inmate, Ed, from his appointment at another doctor's office. We arrived back at Eglin right at lunchtime. Ed and I headed to the dining hall and discussed our recent appointments over lunch. I mentioned what I thought my treatments had cost. Ed laughed and said, "Yours is just a drop in the bucket compared to what the government has spent on me. Over the past two years, I've had three surgeries for a hip replacement. The first two didn't take, but I guess the third time was a charm"

"That would have cost a bundle on the outside," I said.

"Yeah, it would, but that's not all. I had two liver surgeries to remove abscesses, a hernia repair, and a bad bout of pneumonia that put me in the hospital for a couple of weeks. On the outside, all that would probably have run over $350,000.

Ed had already served 24 months of an 84-month sentence for possession of a pound and a half of cocaine. Based on an average yearly cost of $25,000 just to house an inmate, and assuming he has no further medical costs, Ed's prison stay will end up costing the taxpayers over half a million dollars by the time he gets out.

JIM BAKER

"How well did you know Jim Baker," I asked Tony, as we were taking our morning walk.

Prior to being assigned to Eglin, Tony had been an inmate at Jessup, Georgia, and was there when former TV evangelist, Jim 3aker was transferred from a prison up north.

I had been a semi-TV fan of Jim, having watched the PTL program many times. I was still having mixed emotions about how the government can send a man to jail for spending money that legally was his. *If someone gives me a dollar, then I should be permitted to spend it without "Big Brother Government" looking over my shoulder. Former Governor Guy Hunt was treated the same way, with the exception that he did not have to serve any time. Have we become the land of the federal government and home of the convicted?* I thought.

As Tony and I continued our two-mile walk, we talked about the stories that had appeared in the various tabloids, concerning Jim and Tammy. Several articles had portrayed Jim as a homosexual—quite a change from his image of TV preacher.

Tony said, "Jim is not a homosexual. He was shy and maybe appeared effeminate and a little overweight when he came to Jessup, but the stories of him being queer was a bunch of garbage."

"After Jim arrived at Jessup, he began a regular exercise program. For several hours a day, he would work out with weights, exercise, and jog. He also spent a lot of time in the sun.

When Jim was released, in the summer of 1994, he was tan and in good physical shape."

As our morning walk ended, and we were approaching the form, Tony said, "Larry, for the five years that I have been in prison, you are the only inmate that I know, that receives about as much mail as Jim did. Most of the inmates do not receive any nail." Tony was right. I did have many friends, and they had stuck by me.

A few weeks later, another inmate transferred from where Jim Baker was first incarcerated. This inmate, weighing about 450 pounds, walked real slow but was nicknamed "Bullet"_ super nice personality but had a sleeping sickness. "Bullet" could be reading a book, sitting in a chair, talking or eating and just go to sleep. He was medically unassigned.

One day "Bullet" and I were talking and the subject of Jim Baker came up. "Bullet" was very complimentary of Jim. "Bullet" said, "Jim had a great sense of humor. When the tabloids would print stories that Jim was a homosexual, Jim would laugh and say, that he paid dear for his sexual encounter with Jessica Hahn."

SHERIEF LEE ROY

It was June, 1983. Sheriff Lee Roy Hobbs was near the end of an unprecedented third term as sheriff in north Harrelson County, Mississippi. He was in the middle of a re-election campaign, running for a fourth term and had been conducting an undercover drug operation in between campaign activities.

On June 16th, just as dawn was breaking, Sheriff LeRoy drove his black, county-owned Oldsmobile, and parked it near a farm on Hwy 67 in north Harrelson County, Mississippi. Several hours later, a prisoner in handcuffs, he was taken to the federal courthouse in Biloxi, Mississippi by federal agents who caught and arrested Lee Roy during their own sting operation.

Agents also arrested the sheriff's chief deputy and eight others, including Mississippi Gulf Coast crime figure, D. J. Venus Ill, and his two sons, who allegedly had Mafia connections, and were heavy into dealing drugs and promoting gambling activities All were charged with conspiring to import cocaine. Ironically, Sheriff LeRoy's chief deputy was innocent but was being used by the FBI to set up the sting operation. The deputy thought he was helping the sheriff.

The FBI built a very strong federal case against Sheriff Lee Roy. The case included strong allegations that he was a friend of D. J. Venus and reputed New Orleans Mafia leader, Carlos Marcello.

"What's really ironic," said Sheriff LeRoy, "is that I reported all my contacts with those same people to the FBI. You have to make contacts with them to find out things.

It's one of the many occupational hazards for law enforcement officers. I told the FBI a lot of stuff they didn't even know about those guys. Some thanks I got!"

Because of the strong case the FBI had built against him, Sheriff Lee Roy changed his plea from innocent to guilty of racketeering charges. He pleaded guilty to two charges: accepting kickbacks from a Gulfport bonding company and taking $29,500 for the release of two county prisoners.

"Want to hear another good one?" Sheriff LeRoy asked. "Albert Necaise, the former district attorney, had the exact same two charges against him, and they were dismissed a year later by Judge Barbour."

Sheriff Lee Roy made bond after his arrest and remained free until he pleaded guilty and subsequently self-surrendered. On May 29, 1984, he turned himself in to the federal authorities in Jackson, Mississippi, and began serving a 20-year sentence.

On Halloween night, 1994, Lee Roy and I were watching Monday night football on the large outdoor screen behind the dorm. During the commercials, our conversation inevitably turned to talk about how prison camps were a joke and a little-known, unnecessary burden on taxpayers.

"You know, Lee Roy," I said, "I'm human, and I usually enjoy steak and shrimp more than beans and cabbage. I like jogging around the beautiful grounds instead of doing calisthenics twice a day and all the other amenities like big screen TV. Still it seems to me that if you're sentenced to prison, especially if you're truly guilty, you should be doing 'hard time' so it's not so inviting to come back."

"I know what you mean, Larry," said Lee Roy. "A lot of inmates are living better than they could ever hope to live on the outside. The average person simply doesn't have all the benefits we have (free medical care, etc.), not to mention an income, small though it may be, with no expenses for food, shelter or clothing.”

“That’s exactly what I mean, I said, “and here at Eglin it’s even better than at the few other nice prison camps I know about.

They say it’s the Cadillac, even of the elite prison camps.”

“”That’s for sure,” said Lee Roy. “I’ve been places you wouldn’t believe with some of the most brutal, vicious convicts in the federal prison system. One guy I was in with had murdered six other inmates.”

“Sounds like you had a tough time, LeRoy.”

“You better believe it! I spent every day while I was in those other places, begging them to move me closer to home. Finally, after six years, they transferred me to Eglin in December of 1990.

“It was like being in hell right after I began my sentence. For the first ten days and eleven nights I was in Talladega Prison. They put me under a 23-hour a day lockdown.

“You know the kind one of those single-man cells.

Stripped down without even bedclothes … so I couldn’t hang myself, no doubt … leg and wrist restraints fastened to the bed, under 24-hour surveillance. Once a day, they traded the restraints for a pair of handcuffs, and one hour every other day, with my hands cuffed behind my back, I was allowed to stand in a a 6 x 10 chain link enclosure, ostensibly to get some sunlight, and they let me take a shower, while the guards watched, of course. I don’t know if you’ve ever had to be in a room like those single-man cells with total silence for ten days or not, but it’s truly horrible.”

"No, Lee Roy, I haven't," I said. "I guess I don't know what a real prison is like at all." In my heart, in spite of how I felt about the luxuries at Eglin, I hoped I would never be faced with that other extreme of prison life.

"I hope you never do, Larry. You know, my mother died several years ago while I was in LaTuna Prison, and they wouldn't let me go to her funeral. After I came to Eglin, I hoped it might be different, but when my stepfather and a brother-in-law died, I wasn't allowed to attend their funerals either."

I thought of my own mother and other loved ones and prayed I would get to see them before there were any funerals. It was hard for me to imagine what he'd gone through—not only in solitary but also as he described coming off of alcohol.

"While I was in the Talladega prison, I had a complete breakdown. It was partly because of the awful situation, but also I had suddenly been cut off from the alcohol I'd been drinking for so many years. With the stress of my drastic change of my status, the solitary confinement and the withdrawal, I went berserk.

They finally had to put me on a drug called Vistaril while I detoxed."

"What exactly does 'detox' mean, Lee Roy?"

"Well, Larry, very simply it means a period of time when you're trying to get any kind of toxic substances out of your system. Alcohol is just as toxic as any other drug like cocaine or heroin.

Since your body is used to having it and has become dependent on its effects, it protests pretty violently when the substance is suddenly cut off, of course, how badly it protests depends on how much and how long you've been giving it the toxic substance.

"I'd been using alcohol for a lot of years. At first, they didn't give me anything. But after I sweat, shook, puked, screamed and hallucinated, they put me in restraints and started giving me large doses of Vistaril. Most substance abuse recovery programs don't use that kind of treatment, but it's what I got. At first, I needed 450 mg. a day to keep me from being a problem to them, but when they moved me to New York they cut the dose in half. A couple of years later, I got off of it voluntarily."

"But wait a minute, Lee Roy, how come you got such a stiff sentence and such awful treatment? I thought you were doing undercover stuff"

"Larry, I just don't know for sure. I've gotten very bitter about the way the judicial system operates. Sometimes, sentencing and treatment seem to be the whim of whoever sits in the power seat at the time and whatever they may want for political reasons, or maybe who you know has a lot to do with it. Whatever the reason, I've already done twelve years in the federal prison system, and I know of almost a dozen convicted murderers who came in after I did and have already been released.

"You know, I can't understand these people."

"Did you ever read that article in the Miami Sun Herald where U.S. District Judge William Barbour called me down when I was sentenced?"

"No, LeRoy, I didn't. What did it say?"

"Well, I've got it memorized. It went like this: 'The court is unimpressed with the expressions of remorse attributed to you by your attorney. The court feels you still want to live the high life, and that you want to continue to associate with high rollers. It did not take you long to succumb to the temptations and become entwined in the crime which apparently has been rampant in that part of the state.'

" What I can't understand," Lee Roy said, "is why Judge Barbour gave me the 20 years for my charges, and a year later, turned around and dismissed those exact charges against the district attorney, Albert Necaise."

"What does Necaise have to do with you?" I asked.

"Well, that's another story, but in a nutshell, I knew a lot of dirt on Necaise, and they told me that if I would testify against him, they would help me get a sentence reduction. Need I say they lied? Then, adding insult to injury, the Bureau of Prisons Parole Board told me, 'After looking at the overall picture, we feel you should serve the whole 240-month sentence. Ive been before that parole commission three times, and they denied my release every one of those times. I tell you, Larry, it's been an unbelievable nightmare."

We both forgot about football as Lee Roy talked through the commercials and well into the fourth quarter of the game.

"I remember thinking, 'How can you be so stupid?' I had suspected all along it was a trap. Everything was too vague. I told D.J. (Venus) at the time he was crazy because it sounded like a trap. He said, 'No, a major drug cartel wants to start running drugs through here, and you can make the biggest legal case in history.'""

Lee Roy hopes to return to the Mississippi gulf coast.

"It's a great place to live, work and raise a family. I love the gulf and most of the people there," he said with a bitter laugh.

In the meantime, he spends his days at Eglin working in the safety office at twenty-nine cents an hour. He is responsible for checking fire extinguishers, preparing safety reports, etc. Ironically, Lee Roy replaced a former federal judge. The judge had the same job responsibilities until he was released from Eglin.

"I was the clerk for the associate warden when I left

LaTuna. My supervisor recommended me for a superior performance award, and I got it. You wouldn't believe what a beautiful prison record I've got ... for all the good it does me."

"It all sounds pretty grim to me, Lee Roy," I said

"It is, but there've been a few funny things along the way.

You know how they always try to keep former law enforcement officers away from any prisoners those officers put behind bars?

"Well, when I was in Phoenix a guy walked up to me and said, 'Did you ever know that little sheriff in Biloxi? I stuck up a bank on Pat Harrison Avenue there, and they put me in the Gulfport jail. That little sheriff came up there one time, and you look just like him.'"

"That's because I am. Small world."

WILL

Of all the inmates who came and went while I was as Eglin, Will was the one who made me feel the saddest. I found out that he was originally from Illinois but had lived in Alabama several years. He reported to camp a few days before Thanksgiving. A new face in the chow line caught my attention that day. His gray hair, stooped shoulders, and slow shuffle set him apart from the other inmates. I wondered why someone his age was at Eglin.

A few days later, I sat alone at a table close to the chow line. Will saw the vacant chairs at my table and shambled toward me like a man who wasn't sure he could put one foot in front of the other. He made it to the chair across from me, put his tray down, and leaned heavily on the edge of the table.

"Are you okay?" I asked.

He nodded affirmatively and stood there gripping the edge of the table for a while, not answering, gasping for breath. At last, breathing hard, he put his tray on the table and sat down. Still, several minutes passed before he was able to speak.

"I got emphysema real bad," he said between wheezes.

"They told me a few years ago I had emphysema, and it got a lot worse the past two or three years." He picked at his food without much interest, occasionally taking a small bite.

I knew about emphysema. My parents worked in a cotton mill over 40 years, and I had seen what breathing cotton lint had done to them.

"Did you ever work in a textile plant?" I asked.

"No," he said, "not in all my 70 years. Mostly I was a tractor-trailer operator. Drove my own rig all over the country."

We talked a while longer, and when he found out I was from Talladega, his eyes lit up

"I used to take the boys and girls at AIDB (Alabama

Institute for the Deaf and Blind) home for the holidays. I was a part-time driver for the transit system that had a contract with the state. I got a real kick out of driving those kids."

He chuckled at the memory. and immediately started his hacking, wheezy cough. The light went out of his eyes and a thin

film of sweat broke out on his face. Just when I thought he was about to bring up pieces of his lung, the cough slowed to an occasional spasm, and he was able to resume picking at his food.

As we finished eating, I realized he hadn't told me why he was in prison. In light of his difficulty breathing, I decided to find out later. Not long after that, I was in the TV room and happened to glance out the window. There was Will, shuffling slowly down the sidewalk with a cigarette hanging out the corner of his mouth. Considering his severe emphysema, it was shocking to see him smoking. I wondered again why this man was in prison and why I couldn't get him out of my mind.

Income tax evasion? Embezzlement? Drugs? Surely not drugs. A 70-year-old man half dead with lung disease involved with drugs? He just doesn't fit the profile of the drug dealers or even drug users I've met since I've been here.

Saturday morning two weeks later, Will wandered into the TV room and eased down several chairs away from me. He was breathing hard and began rocking back and forth in his chair. Shortly, he got up, looked around, sat back down, and rocked some more. He repeated this behavior several times. Suddenly, it hit me.

Why, he's got Alzheimer's! He acts like a former neighbor of mine that I used to visit at Talladega HealthCare Center.

After about fifteen minutes of rocking and getting up and down, Will left and went back outside. Through the window I saw him light up another cigarette.

"That man needs to be in a hospital or nursing home," said an inmate sitting next to me.

"Do you know him?" I asked.

"Not really, but I work in the office where all the inmates' records are kept, and according to his records, Will was busted for possession of crack. Supposedly, they confiscated about $500 worth of crack from him. They don't say he was a seller, just a user. He's doing time because he wouldn't give any names to the investigators. Rumor has it the drugs belonged to his son who lived with him at the time. Will wouldn't turn him in.

"He's been diagnosed with emphysema and the early stages of Alzheimer's. He's supposed to serve 30 months, but I'll be surprised if he lives that long. They're going to have to send him to a medical facility before long."

Here he is, sick and probably dying, with no one around who really loves or wants to take care of him. More justice. Somewhere there's a prosecutor and a judge who must feel really good, knowing they got this dangerous criminal off the streets Sure, it was illegal for Will to have any crack, but the real reason they convicted him was because he wouldn't give them any names.

A week before Christmas, they handcuffed Will, shackled his legs, and put him on a bus to a destination unknown by the inmates. The rumor was that he was being transferred to a medical facility at another prison.

As I watched the bus drive away, I wondered how long Will would live and what the total cost of his upkeep would be to taxpayers.

THANKSGIVING

Facing the first Thanksgiving away from home was almost too much for me. But the day dawned cold, clear and beautiful, perhaps God's way of reminding me that I still had a great deal to be thankful for. My health was good, my family was doing well... all things considered, and I was fairly well adjusted to my situation. If I had to be in prison, Eglin FPC was by no means the worst place to be.

Certainly, it was easier for me than for the fifty new inmates who had arrived a few days earlier. I imagined them feeling the almost overwhelming isolation and depression I experienced when I first got to Eglin. The Thanksgiving feast and a long weekend of tennis, volleyball, and other activities probably wouldn't have helped much then. It made me realize just how much progress I'd made toward adjusting to my situation.

But not quite as much progress as one of the old-timers who said, "If the B.O.P. (Bureau of Prisons) would just allow conjugal visits, I'd never want to leave!"

By now, I even found myself looking forward to some things-like old-fashioned turkey dinners and the special Thanksgiving services. During special services, we often shared spiritual experiences which had greatly changed our lives. There had been a lot of those services since my arrival and I thought I'd heard it all... until I heard Carlos.

CARLOS

Carlos was a 25-year-old Haitian, 6' 5" tall, weighing in at 295 pounds. He wore a size 14 shoe. Not surprisingly, his nickname was "Giant Man." His body unfolded into unbelievably large sections and towered above the podium as he got up to speak. He grabbed our attention with the very first sentence of his story and never let go.

"You may find this hard to believe, but I'm thankful to be at Eglin. I'm thankful just to be alive."

Soon, everyone was spellbound by the quiet intensity of his deep, bass voice as he revealed detail after gruesome detail of his experience.

"I was born in Haiti and raised in the Catholic church. My parents were very strict. We attended mass every Sunday and often in between. They made sure I had plenty of religious instruction and wouldn't allow me to get involved in the witchcraft or Satan worship so prevalent then in Haiti.

"Just after my nineteenth birthday, my parents were killed during one of Haiti's "little disagreements." You know the kind.. wholesale slaughter of anyone who happens to be in the way .. just to show who's in charge."

There was bitterness in Carlos' voice, and I sensed it covered the deep pain of a young man who'd been forced to witness to destruction of all he knew and loved in a blood bath. My heart ached for that young man who stood before us with the courage to tell what had happened and what came after.

"I managed to get away," Carlos said, "and was able to reach Miami. A friend of mine from Haiti let me stay with him and got me a job in a fast-food place. I felt very lucky, but very guilty, too, when I got word that my sisters and brothers had been sent to an orphanage.

"I enrolled in college and made a lot of new friends.

Unfortunately, some of them were gang members involved in Satanic worship. The things they were into went against everything I'd been taught. Even so, slowly but surely, I became more and more involved with them. They made it so easy.

"Because of my size, I guess they were all a little atraid of me and wanted me to be with them instead of against them. For whatever reason, they nearly fell over each other to "take care of me." Drugs were mine for the asking, and before long they made. me their leader. I was a big man in more ways than one."

I detected a note of sarcasm when Carlos called himself a big man. Considering what happened to him later, he must still feel deep regret and not a little self-disgust for having been drawn into a situation so contrary to all he'd been taught.

"At first, I shied away from witchcraft and Satanism. But as I got more entrenched in the gang and the drug scene, my perceptions were dulled, and the occult became very tempting. After all, the gang members all participated. And I was their leader, wasn't I?

"Once I accepted this idea, I jumped into it with all the enthusiasm of a new convert. I read every book and magazine on the occult and related practices that I could buy, beg, steal or borrow. The material included information on sadism, sorcery, and real hard-core pornography, both heterosexual and homosexual

"As I became increasingly immersed in it, I often attended Satanic rituals held in an old barn out in the country. There were always several hundred people a mix of men and women, usually 18-30 years old, mostly white. There were salesmen, carpenters, teachers, students, college professors, clerks, housewives, truck drivers, preachers, a few priests, and a scattering of other professions and trades. Members were called witches or brothers, regardless of sex. Female witches were often utilized by the high priests or master counselors to run errands, deliver drugs, provide sex for the master counselors (almost all housewives were required to do this), and various other common tasks.

Many members specialized in a particular aspect of Satanism. Specializations included but weren't limited to demonology, the summoning of different demons, necromancy, a type of communication with the dead accomplished by conjuring up spirits, vampirism, belief in and practices of vampires and blood-sucking ghosts; and lycanthropy, assumption of the form and traits of a wolf by means of witchcraft.

"The High Priest of Satan sits on a throne and conducts the ceremony. A lot of the ceremony's ritual is designed to deliberately and viciously pervert sacred Christian tradition. At some point, it includes the ritual sacrifice of an animal, usually a young goat or calf. At the ceremonies I attended, the sacrificial altar was usually a granite slab supported on two sawhorses. It was placed in the center of a nine-foot circle inside the barn.

"Young boys or girls were used instead of goats or calves for several of the ceremonies I witnessed. The children sacrificed were run-aways, usually picked up by members at a bus station. The Satanists seemed to be able to find children no one cared about enough to even file a missing person report.

"During the ceremony, they have a container into which the priests have just urinated. They slit the child's throat, hold the container under the child's neck, and drain the blood into it. When the body fluids are thoroughly blended, this foul mixture is poured into a large chalice. The priest takes a drink, gives thanks to Satan, and passes it around for leaders and each member to share.

"After the ceremony, the child's body is discarded. Even if the mutilated body is found, if the child was never reported as missing, the police can't trace it and end up having to report an unsolved homicide. In the Miami area, there's such a high crime rate that police are often unable to do more than scratch the investigative surface of such cases."

Sacrificing children! A shudder of revulsion went through me. It was beyond comprehension. I glanced around and could tell by the expressions of my fellow inmates that they felt it, too. Those of us unfamiliar with Satanism could hardly believe what we were hearing. Even those who had heard of such rituals were appalled by the reality of hearing such a shockingly vivid firsthand account.

Carlos cleared his throat, took a long drink from the water glass beside the podium and continued his shocking story.

"I remember one ceremony in particular," he said. "It sticks in my memory because it was my first "Black Mass.' What blew my mind was realizing that all the traditional Christian rituals were reversed and deliberately profaned. Blasphemies took the place of prayers. A 'priest' read words attributed to Satan from a book called The Great Mother. It was placed in the center of a pentagram drawn on the stomach of the naked girl who was tied and unconscious on the altar. Smoke curling up from a crucible on the altar contained fumes of the drug, belladona, derived from the deadly nightshade family of plants. Belladona is used in medicine to reduce spasms of the digestive system, bladder, and urethra. But it has many side effects, including confusion, lightheartedness, blurred vision, rapid heartbeat, and even delirium. Inhaling the fumes apparently creates a state of controlled mindlessness desired by the priests as they intone passages from the book. Those who have grievances (prayer requests) speak that we may all bind together at this hour and direct the power of our father, Satan. As each grievance is expressed, the priest prays to Satan, asking that the request be granted. All those present encircle the priest, put their hands on him, and chant the request to Satan several times in unison.

"When they finished and everyone had resumed their places, the priest removed the book, grasped a knife, and spread his arms in an attitude of supplication above his head.

"Facing the pentagram on the girl's stomach, he said,

Master, we petition thee in the name of our lord, Satan, to send your messenger to answer our request.' Then, he plunged the knife into the heart of the girl on the altar, sacrificing her to appease and supplicate Satan."

Carlos stopped a moment, and in spite of his detached tone, it was obvious that telling the story was difficult for him. He wiped off the film of sweat, which had formed on his face and took another long drink of water before continuing.

"As the months went by, I was drawn deeper and deeper into the gang's dark practices. I became a sexual sadist. Some of you may not know that sexual sadists are people who get their kicks by inflicting pain and torture. They have strong fantasy lives. Most of them start out with sadomasochistic pornography, then graduate to sadomasochistic practices with a consenting partner. When that loses its kick for them, they find ways to use unwilling victims, turning them into 'sex slaves.'

"If you think this is rare, I have news for you. According to statistics, there are thousands of sadists, and they include some very influential people.

Your next door neighbor could easily be a sadist."

My next door neighbor? It's just not possible. Pictures of my neighbors scrolled down my mind's screen, and I eliminated them one by one. It was just too ludicrous to contemplate. Carlos's voice brought my attention back to what he was saying.

"You're probably wondering how I got my sex slaves. Actually, it was no problem. If you cruise down certain streets in Miami, it's easy to pick up prostitutes, hustling to make a dollar. Once I got them in the car, I took them to an apartment owned by the gang. The prostitutes were always glad to get liquor and drugs. I encouraged them to have whatever they wanted and as much as they wanted.

"When the prostitute was high enough or passed out, I took her into the bedroom, stripped off her clothes, tied her spread-eagle on the bed, and performed any kind of bizarre sex act I wanted to.

After I'd had as much of her as I wanted, I shared her with any gang member who happened to come in. I can remember one time when ten of the gang abused one prostitute. Usually, we made videos of our sex-capades and sold them for a very good price."

I shuddered again. *The woman may have been a prostitute, but no human being deserves that kind of violation.*

"By the time I was twenty-three, my outlook on life was pretty jaded. About that time something happened that changed my life.

"One day, one of the homosexual gang members picked up a male prostitute and brought him to the gang's apartment. He was drugged, stripped, and tied to the bed. The gang member, who was also very high on 'angel dust,' went berserk. When I arrived with my date, we heard ghastly noises coming from the bedroom before we even got in the house. I looked cautiously through the half-open bedroom door and saw to my absolute horror that the gang member was sawing at the neck of the male prostitute with a large butcher knife, trying to decapitate him. He had already severed the prostitute's private part, split his chest open, and cut out his heart."

This is too horrible to even hear! How can Carlos stand up there and talk about it? I don't know how much longer I can sit here and listen… it's too ghastly.

"I managed to overpower him and grab the knife. Apparently, someone had heard the screams and called the police because they arrived right after I did.

"They immediately took the gang member into custody and asked to search the property. I told them no. So they called for backup

"When the other officers arrived, they sent one to get a search warrant.

He returned shortly, and they scoured the

apartment. More than $250,000 worth of drugs was confiscated. The Feds were called in, and I was charged with 'possession to distribute (drugs). They charged the gang member with murder.

We both went to jail.

"Since I had plenty of money, I contacted one of my lawyer friends, and he got me out of jail in a few hours. But he warned me that, if convicted, I was looking at twenty-five years to life.

"The Sunday night before my trial date on Monday, I drove aimlessly around the streets of Miami. I felt so depressed. I was thinking seriously about suicide. Suddenly, something drew my attention to a small holiness church sandwiched between two taller buildings. I had no intention of going to any church that night, let alone, a holiness church. To this day, I don't really understand what made me stop and go inside, but I did. The minister started his sermon just as I sat down

"I didn't hear everything he said, but I heard hope. And I grabbed on to that hope with all my remaining strength. At the end of the sermon, I went down front and told the minister I wanted to accept Christ as my savior.

"Suddenly, there was someone to help me with the terrible load of guilt I'd been carrying. It felt like I was starting a new life, but I still had to face my trial. I didn't know what to do. If I pleaded guilty, I would automatically be sentenced. If I pleaded not guilty, it would be a lie. I wrestled with it most of the night.

"On Monday morning, I got up early, feeling like the world had been lifted off my shoulders. After a quick breakfast, I met my attorney at the federal building. I told him about my spiritual experience and that I wanted to plead guilty and ask for leniency. He thought I was crazy and told me the judge would throw the book at me. But my mind was made up, and I had him enter a guilty plea. The prosecutor agreed, and the judge gave me a ten-year sentence."

When Carlos stopped talking there was absolute silence. *If everyone feels like me, they don't know what to say. Even though Carlos' life has done a complete turn-around, the specter of what he described still hangs over us all.*

In December, we heard that Carlos had been transferred to a facility in Miami. The government normally permits inmates to serve time close to home, if they aren't politically involved in the community.

TEETH CLEANING TIME

(A Tooth Cleaned in Time Saves Nine)

During the first week of December, my name came up on the daily call-out sheet for a teeth-cleaning appointment. I had hoped Monica would forget about me, but experiences with my own dental hygienist in Talladega had always been good ones. So, in spite of occasional flashbacks to my root-canal ordeal, I approached this appointment with a little confidence. Walking the 100 yards across the compound to the dental office took no time at all, and I arrived 10 minutes early for my appointment.

All too soon Monica's smiling face appeared at the waiting room door, and her small, efficient hand beckoned me back to the rooms which held people captive for dental procedures. As I walked into the room, a flicker of anxiety rippled through my stomach. Even so, I tried to mount that black plastic chair with the confidence of John Wayne mounting his favorite horse.

Monica immediately slapped a lead apron over me like a pair of chaps. "Need to get some full-mouth x-rays to see if you have any cavities," she said, grunting slightly as she reached around to tie the top of the lead apron around my neck. "I'll also be checking to see if you've been brushing your teeth properly."

She picked up two large pürple tablets from the stainless steel tray next to the dental chair and handed them to me. "Chew these thoroughly, using all your teeth, but don't swallow. When you're done, rinse your mouth with water. The purple color will coat your teeth and show me any areas you aren't reaching with your toothbrush."

After rinsing, I laid back in the chair while she carefully examined the purple stains on my teeth and finally said, "Your teeth are in excellent shape, but you do have one area that needs a little more attention. You can do a lot for it by using the kind of toothbrush I'm going to give you. And you really do need to floss every day."

So far, so good. This is going to be a breeze. Wait! What is she doing?

"Open wide," Monica said, holding a thing that looked like a sand blaster near my quivering lips.

I know about sand blasters. You use them to get old paint off of houses or grime off of stone and brick buildings. But teeth?

Then she started. She blasted her way from tooth to tooth, exploding tiny pieces of plaque and grime away from my gum line. I never even knew the gunk existed, let alone that it had to be blown away like the side of a mountain. Endless flying fragments later, she stopped at last.

"What were you doing?" I asked. "Do I have any fillings left?"

Monica laughed. "All there. The sand blaster, as you call it, is actually the latest thing in dental cleaning equipment. It uses a combination of air and water forced through a small opening kind of like those do-it-yourself car washes that use high pressure water to get grime off your car."

"Oh," I said. I was impressed but nearly speechless. "Is

that it?" I asked with timid, but hopeful heart.

"No."

"Oh"

That's when the pain began. Real pain. Monica only weighed about 95 pounds but knew how to use every ounce with agonizing efficiency.

I wondered if I had made her mad. But how could I have? I don't even know her. She must have worked for a terrorist group before she became a dental hygienist.

"Open wide." she said again, and set up shop in my oral cavity. Soon, she had both hands and a small pick and shovel inside my mouth. Maybe the sandblasting hadn't loosened my fillings, but I was sure the pick-and-shovel method would do it. At one point, it felt like she had crawled inside my mouth and was standing on my bottom teeth, scraping my top ones.

The pick kept cutting my gums. I could taste the blood running freely, mixing with the miniscule amount of saliva I was able to produce in my anxiety. I wondered if I would need a transfusion. Just as drowning in my own blood seemed inevitable, Monica overcame her blood lust. She removed the pick and shovel and inserted the suction hose the same one that had nearly cost me my tongue and cheek linings during the root-canal procedure.

At least, the suction-hose action made it possible to breathe without fear of choking to death.

Then came the nylon cord. Back into my mouth she went with it, looping it like a lasso and forcing it between each tooth.

She neatly sliced my gums in several places, and the bleeding resumed.

She apparently wore down at last and removed all foreign objects from my beleaguered mouth.

"You can rinse now," Monica said calmly, as though nothing life-threatening had happened.

I did exactly what she told me to do but managed the courage to ask, "Did some of my enemies in Talladega ask you to rough me up? To be so little, you sure can inflict a lot of pain."

Monica and Dr. Leibetreau, who had stopped by to check the results of my torment, both chuckled.

"No pain, no gain," Monica said. "When I clean teeth I believe in doing a good job."

She was still talking as I edged out the door. "See you in about six months."

Not if I can help it. I hope I never need her services again! Get me back to Talladega, and put me in the gentle hands of my own dentist and hygienist. Lord willing and the creeks don't rise, they'll clean my teeth next time— if my mouth is healed by then.

CHRISTMAS IN PRISON

(The Happy Hours)

As the holidays drew near, we all felt a new excitement in the air. None of us could have anticipated the tragedy hovering in that same air. It was a happy time—visits from families, phone calls to relatives and friends, hundreds of cards and letters for inmates, and the bustle of preparation for the Christmas programs we were putting together.

We were issued only enough Christmas cards for our immediate families, so I took time in between all the activities to write a Christmas poem and used it instead of cards.

CHRISTMAS IN PRISON

It's Christmas time in prison

And yes, I'm doing fine

Just want to send a greeting

To thank you for being kind

Oh, yes, I do get lonely and

At times, the days drag by

But getting cards and letters

Makes the hours fly

As we celebrate Christ's birthday

I ask one gift from you

Pray that God will use me well

In all I say and do

MERRY CHRISTMAS

and

HAPPY NEW YEAR

Early in December, the Chaplain and our counselor, Mr. Farmer, asked us to contribute money to buy gifts for some local children whose parents had no extra money for Christmas presents. Some inmates resented being asked to give money toward gifts for unknown children when they had to be away from their own families. It was especially galling for those who made only eleven cents an hour. Somehow, in spite of their reluctance and ill will, the Christmas spirit prevailed, and over $5,000 was raised.

Inmates were allowed to attend a special party for the children. Mr. Farmer played Santa with a red suit, white beard, and fairly decent HO-HO-HO. He passed out gifts to 91 delighted children—dolls, bicycles, games, coloring books, baseball gloves and balls, and lots more.

After Santa's big moment, kids, and inmates dived into mounds of Christmas goodies spread out on long tables. Everyone kept their mouths stuffed so full, they could hardly sing Christmas carols led by the choir. When it was all over, even the disgruntled inmates admitted that the looks on the kids' faces had made it all worthwhile.

BILL—The Tragic Hours

On December 20th, while I was exchanging a pair of pants in the clothing room, an inmate called me over to him and said,

"Bill hung himself at Jessup."

Something ugly seemed to hit my heart and stomach at the same time. "Oh, no," I said softly through the sudden ache in my throat. Bill had worked in the clothing room and was one of first inmates I met after reporting to Eglin. He was a quiet man, neat about his person, and one of the nicest people I've ever met. He was given his clothing room job because of having been permanently disabled by a spinal injury caused in car accident several years before his imprisonment. As a result, he had to wear a back brace and use a cane to walk. While in the hospital recovering from his accident, he was diagnosed as a manic-depressive. He took medication for that and pain medicine for his back. Over the months, Bill and I became good friends. He always called me Mayor. We ate together, attended Sunday services together, and were visited by our families on the same weekends.

During lunch on December 5th, Bill was visibly upset.

"What's wrong, Bill?" I asked.

"They're transferring me to the Jessup, Georgia facility,

Mayor, because of my medical problems, but I don't want to leave Eglin. I'm doing okay with medicine, and I really like everyone at the base hospital. They take real good care of me. I have a job here I'm able to do and lots of friends.

"I don't think I can handle going to another camp. It's hard for someone like me to start all over—especially with only one year to go. I'm supposed to be out of here by this time next year. It just doesn't make sense."

Bill was starting his second year of a 24-month sentence on a tax charge. He had been permitted to self-surrender without being put in handcuffs and chains. Prison policy is to handcuff and chain the feet of everyone during transfers.

Surely they won't cuff and chain Bill.

The next day I was already eating breakfast when Bill came into the chow hall. I saw the dejected slump of his shoulders and the troubled expression on his face. I knew something was very wrong.

He limped over to the table, and I said, "What is it, Bill?"

His voice broke as he said, "Mayor, I've been informed that I'll be cuffed and have belly chains for the trip to Jessup."

"Oh no, Bill," I said, hiding the anger that exploded inside me.

How can they be so inflexible enforcing the policy? How do they justify cuffing and chaining a man barely able to walk, a man serving his time for a non-violent, white-collar crime in a facility where inmates can walk away any time they choose? How could anyone with an ounce of humanity treat him like a violent criminal or a dangerous dog?

"You'll be okay, Bill," I said, not really believing it but hoping it was true. "The trip won't take long. Once you get to Jessup, you'll make new friends and everything will be fine."

He picked at his food for a moment, then looked up at me with one of the saddest expressions I've ever seen and said, "I don't want to leave, Mayor. I just don't think I can handle it."

We finished breakfast, and as I carried our trays to the kitchen area, I kept trying to reassure Bill that the time would pass quickly, and he'd be all right. We said good-bye, and I watched him hobble away, not knowing that it would be the last time I saw him.

It took a long time to get over the shock and pain of Bill's suicide. That last conversation kept running over and over in my mind.

"I don't want to go, Mayor. I just don't think I can handle it" he had said

Was he trying to tell me something? Was he crying out for help? Was there something else I could have said? Was there anything I could have done to help prevent this tragedy? Did his family detect anything when they had visited the week before his transfer? Did he get a chance to call his 80-year-old mother before he killed himself?

I would probably never know the answer to these dismal questions.

But one thing I did know. Prison is bad, but death is forever.

PAT'S STORY

After several months of sharing a cube with my bunkee, Pat, we had become close friends. One day, just after we got back from mail call, I realized he was staring at me

"What is it, Pat?" I asked.

"Bunkee, you don't deserve to be in prison. I've been watching you, and I don't think you're guilty. I am guilty, but there's no way you are."

Pat had never discussed his crime with me, but today he wanted to talk

"I worked for the postal service for almost 20 years and had to retire because of a back injury. Before I retired, I was a claims adjuster for several ears. I didn't have to answer to anyone. In fact, I had the authority to write a check, regardless of the amount, to settle any claim against the postal service."

Pat was a very devout Catholic, a dedicated family man, and one of the nicest, most polite individuals I've ever met. But apparently, such carte blanche authority was more than he could resist.

"The case that was my downfall was one which involved a postal employee who collided with a private citizen while he was on duty. After the investigation was finished, I received the usual written request to settle the claim.

"I'm not sure to this day what made me do it, but a few months later I used that same accident report which described the original, legitimate claim, and wrote another check to the same person. But this time I cashed the check and kept the money. I had a friend in the check-cashing business and gave him a 4% fee for processing the checks. (The check-cashing business is no longer operational due to his friend's death.) Over a 12-year period, I was able to embezzle 5-1/2 million dollars from the postal service.

"When I was forced to go on disability, the employee who replaced me was familiarizing himself with the computer system and happened to call up the names of all the claimants. That's when he found out about all the checks made payable to the same person."

About three years after Pat's retirement, he was indicted for fraud and theft. He pled guilty and was sentenced to five and a half tears, and a fine of $1 million. He had to serve only thirty months fund continued to draw his monthly $2,000 disability check. He was responsible for paying the government $50 a month toward the one-million-dollar fine, and Pat was paid exactly that amount as an inmate operating a forklift.

In September 1995, Pat's mother passed away and he was denied a furlough to attend her funeral. From that day forward, Pat became very depressed and his demeanor and attitude completely changed.

On the 10th day of October, 1995, around 10:00 a.m. an officer came to our cube and asked me which locker was mine and which one belonged to Pat. Having showed him, I inquired if there was a problem with Pat.

"Pat won't be coming back.

He has been taken to the county jail for being drunk and in possession of alcoholic beverages," the officer said.

Pat's job on the Air Force Base afforded him plenty of freedom to move around without any or very little supervision. It was not uncommon for his wife to meet him at a motel on a frequent basis and spend several hours with her, according to Pat.

Apparently the death of his mother was more than he could endure, so he started drinking.

Pat was scheduled to go to a halfway house in February, 1996; instead, he was transferred to a higher security facility and lost his six months half-way house.

Pat's vacation will cost the taxpayers more than $65,000, plus being able to keep the 4-1/2 million.

ALFONZO, THE DRUGGIST

Dr. Alfonzo, could always be found sitting in front of Dorm 5, on one of the two seated benches placed outside each dorm.

Thursday morning February 2, 1995, I was walking back to the dorm, from the law library and Dr. Alfonzo greeted me, from where he was sitting, with "What's going on governor?" Ever since I had been at Eglin, Dr. Alfonzo had called me govemor. He knew that I had been the mayor of Talladega, but he remembered reading in the local paper about me running for Governor of Alabama several years back. *People never forget some things.*

"Just building time, Doc," I said. "How are you?"

Dr. Alfonzo knew that I had been interviewing different inmates, and obtaining material for my book. He had agreed to share with me his situation but kept putting me off.

"I'm doing fine Governor. If you've got a few minutes, I want to share with you about my case."

I stepped inside Dorm 5, to my cube, picked up my writing material and walked back outside the dorm to where Dr. Alfonzo was sitting. To be February, it was a beautiful, warm day. There was just enough breeze blowing to really make it a nice day for sitting outside.

Having met Dr. Alfonzo when I first came to Elgin, I had often wondered what a super nice, well-educated person like him had done to be sent to prison. Dr. Alfonzo, a very devout Catholic, was always helping out at Mass, and was always available for being a part of the religious activities.

As we talked, I learned that Dr. Alfonzo received his schooling in Havana, Cuba and New York. He had a degree in medicine.

Born in Cuba, he came to America (New York) in 1961 and received his citizenship. He lived in New York for 14 years before moving to the Miami, Florida, area, in 1974. With three grown children and six grandchildren, Dr. Alfonzo really loved

America. Prior to coming to prison, he was a very civic-minded, aw-abiding businessman. He was devoted to his family and church.

In 1962, Dr. Alfonzo and his wife decided to go in business or themselves.

They operated a pharmaceutical wholesale distributorship. They became what is known as diverters. They purchased all the merchandise from out of the U.S. and imported to the U.S. All his buyers were in N.Y., Detroit and Chicago. He and his wife were sole owners and operators. In 1983, Dr. Alfonzo entered into a contract with a very reputable pharmaceutical company located in Puerto Rica, and he was to be a distributor of birth control pills. Dr. Alfonzo was licensed through Health Rehabilitation Service (IIRS) to be a distributor of the birth control pill.

In 1962, according to Dr. Alfonzo, when the birth control sill was introduced to the public, approximately five companies controlled the market. Spain and France were excluded.

Dr. Alfonzo, through the pharmaceutical representative, purchased birth control pills for .50 cents per cycle (29 pills) and sold them for about $5 to his customers. At the same time, birth control pills from the other distributors were costing $9.50 wholesale and retailing for $15.

"How were you purchasing pills so cheap?" I asked. "I was buying in bulk from Guatemala, with invoice, having the merchandise shipped to Panama, a free zone, (no taxes) and then to Florida. I didn't have to pay all the tariffs by doing it this way," he explained. He went on to say that he had export license, wholesale pharmaceutical license and a contract with the company so he thought he was completely legal. He was paying all required income taxes on the profit. "I even had a letter of credit from a sank in Panama to guarantee payment and make the transaction above board," he continued. All the birth control pills came packaged with a national drug control (N.D.C.) number and expiration date and lot number printed on each package in English. He had approval from Food & Drug Administration (F.D.A.) to market the pill.

"With all these license and approval from the proper authorities, and an agent of the company selling me the pills, I thought I was doing everything proper," he said. "What happened to get you in court?" I asked.

"In 1984, FDA agents broke into our office, without any legal authority or warrants, and took all our records. This was shocking to us because we had their approval to distribute the pill "

Three years later, Feb 1987, Dr. Alfonzo and his wife were indicted on six counts. They were charged with wire and mail fraud and conspiracy to manufacture birth control pills.

Prior to going to court, Dr. Alfonzo and his wife were offered a sentence of 60 months if they would plead guilty. Both thinking they had not done anything illegal refused the offer. Some time later, Dr. Alfonzo's wife was allegedly made an offer. If she would testify against her husband, all charges against her would be dropped. She refused to testify.

They went to court, costing them, the government and the pharmaceutical company, more than S5 million dollars for legal fees and for attorneys.

During the trial, the Federal Government's main witness was the salesman who had entered the agreement to supply the birth control pills for all these years.

The salesman testified that he informed Dr. Alfonzo that the pill he was purchasing was to be sold in Latin America only, not in America.

The defense countered with evidence of all the license,

FDA approval, the contract with the company, writing on the package in English, and the invoices showing legal purchase receipts.

It didn't matter. The jury found Dr. and Mrs. Alfonzo guilty and was sentenced to 24 years in prison. They immediately appealed

They were not permitted to remain free on bond pending the appeal

Seven years later, they both are still in prison, waiting an answer from the courts. Since coming to prison, Dr. Alfonzo was injured in October, 8, 1987, while working for U.N.IC.O.R. (government agency). A box fell and hit him in the neck and back and caused permanent injury. Surgery cannot be performed, and he has to wear a neck and arm brace. He has been assigned as medically unable to do any work. This is why you can always find him in or around the dorm.

 Mrs. Alfonzo was injured in 1994 at the prison she is housed in. The dorm floor had been waxed, and no signs posted warning of the slickness. She slipped and fell, breaking her arm, injuring her head, and causing eye damage.

Laser surgery was done but burnt too much, causing loss of sight in one eye. A cast was placed on the arm wrong and caused nerve damage. To make matters worse, she was forced to go back to work in the kitchen or face being sent to the county jail.

In ending my interview, Dr. Alfonzo said he had learned that the competition had put so much pressure on the pharmaceutical company that they were forced to deny they knew Dr. Alfonzo was selling their pill in America. They were allegedly threatened with legal action and possibly looking at criminal charges if they did not cooperate with the Feds.

The cost to the taxpayers to keep Dr. and Mrs. Alfonzo in prison has already exceeded 1/2 million dollars. If they are required to serve their entire sentence, it will cost the taxpayers approximately 1-1/2 million dollars for the two.

I could not help but wonder how the streets were made safer by locking up a Dr. and his wife for selling a pill that the government had approved to be sold, but another government agency said that it could not be sold in America.

BARBERSHOP AND MEMORIES OF JR.

One morning, early in March, 1995, I went to the compound barbershop for a haircut. Ray, my regular barber, was grinning. Really grinning. Very unusual for him. Behind heavy, large-rim glasses, his eyes glittered with rare excitement.

"What's happening, Ray? You act like you just won the sweepstakes "

"Come on in, Mayor, and get a haircut from a short-timer.

I've been approved for halfway house. Is that great or what?"

"Great? It's fantastic, Ray. How in the world did it happen? I thought you had almost two more years to go."

"Would you believe a sentencing error in my favor? They reduced the sentence from 48 to 30 months. It's the best thing that's happened since my wife divorced me. Hey man, you know, maybe there really is a God who looks after people."

It was quite a speech for my reticent friend. The change in him was amazing. Normally, he had little to say and was less than cheerful. In fact, the other inmates disliked him because of his rather sour disposition. It might have been impossible to get to know him if we hadn't discovered a mutual love of barbering and politics. After several haircuts and conversations, he gradually opened up, and we became friends even though we were opposites in most respects. I discovered his hostility was largely due to the extreme bitterness he harbored because of having to spend time in prison a conspiracy charge. I don't know if the charge was valid, but I do know he was a model prisoner while at Eglin.

When inmates who have been model prisoners are awarded halfway house status, they're released and assigned to a facility, which is more like a home than an institution. They live in the halfway house for up to six months or 10% of their sentence, Halfway house status is not only a reward for having been a model prisoner but is also intended to help inmates re-acclimate to the outside world.

While in a half-way house, inmates are required to have regular urine testing for drugs, obtain and hold a job, and give a percentage of their earned income to the owner or manager of the half-way house for upkeep of the house— very much like a rental agreement with a landlord. They're allowed to visit relatives or friends as long as they're back by 9:00 p.m. However, if an inmate violates any of the rules or fails the drug tests, he loses his status and is sent back to prison.

"When are you due for release? And what will I do for a good haircut after you're gone?" I asked.

"I'm supposed to go in about four weeks. Don't worry about your hair. I trained those other guys real good," Ray said, referring to the four other inmate barbers. Suddenly, his scissors stopped snipping. He came around to the front of the chair and said, "Larry, why dont you apply for my job?"

Ray and I had talked about my adventures during the years

I'd been a barber, but his suggestion still took me by surprise. It hadn't occurred to me that I might be able to do something at Eglin 1 enjoyed as much as barbering.

"Why, Ray, I don't know. I like my job at V.T.S. (vocational Tech School), but I'll sure think about it."

I did think and pray about it and began to get excited. I knew I could handle the job because I had worked with some of the best barbers in Talladega and Birmingham, Alabama. Eddie Kemp.

Tom Pilkington, Bill Jones, and the late Alton Crawford, Junior Williams, and Z. D. Zenks were among the best. At one time, I had owned a three-chair barbershop myself. If I got the job, there would certainly be advantages. My pay would increase by about 25%, from 29 to 40 cents an hour. Also, I'd have more time for reading, Bible study, writing letters, and working on my book. There was also another advantage being able to talk and listen to most of the inmates at one time or another while cutting their hair. They shared many personal experiences which were invaluable in understanding how the judicial system works, or doesn't work, as the case may be.

I left the barbershop and walked back to the dorm, reminiscing about how good barbering had been to me through the years. It's a trade you can always fall back on, and can use to earn extra cash on weekends. A good barber is never out of work. The first time I ever cut anyone's hair was a fiasco. It was in 1957, right after Mary and I were married. I'd just been hired to work the graveyard shift at the Bauchmann-Uxbridge Textile plant in Talladega. Being a newly-wed who also had a hard time sleeping in the daytime, I wasn't exactly thrilled to be working 10 p.m. to 6 a.m.

Even before going to work at the plant, I had been thinking about trying my hand with a pair of scissors. My own barber, the late T. D. (Jr.) Williams, made a big impression on me. He was a good person and a very special man who was liked by everyone. Jr. couldn't work in a regular barbershop because he had a full-time job at the Bemis Bag Mill in Talladega. My father, the late B. W. Barton, and my mother, Ruby Barton, also worked there at the time. Since he couldn't work in a barbershop, Jr. had to give haircuts on his back porch, using an old wooden, straight-back chair for a barber chair.

Everyone knew Jr. liked his liquor, and there were all kinds of stories about his antics when he'd had a few. Like the time he was drinking and watching his brand new black and white TV. One of his favorite westerns was on, and the hero was pinned down by the bad guy who was easing around a building to take a shot at the hero. Jo, his wife, said she kept hearing Jr. yell, "Look out! Look out! He's sneakin' up on you!" The hollering kept up for a few seconds, and by the time Jo could walk from the kitchen to the den, Jr. had picked up his rifle and shot the bad guy, blowing the new TV to bits.

Jr.'s drinking didn't affect his barbering ability any.

One afternoon while sitting in Jr.'s rickety old chair getting a trim, I finally got my 17-year-old courage up enough to tell him I wanted to be a barber.

On that particular day, Jr. had already indulged in a drink or two … maybe three or four, and he was feeling good. Jr.'s wife, the late Josephine (Jo) Williams, fixed one of her wonderful cube steak suppers that evening with biscuits, green beans, potatoes and gravy, cold iced tea, and a sweet potato custard pie. The beans and sweet potatoes were especially good because Jr. was an avid gardener and raised them in his backyard. Jr.'s daughters, Sue and Sanky, finished eating just as Junior finished cutting my hair.

It so happened that Jerry Cooper, Jr.'s 12-year-old next door neighbor, was waiting to get a haircut. Clenched in his hand, like he hated to let it go, was 50 cents to pay for the haircut. When Jr. offered Jerry a free haircut if he'd let me practice on him, Jerry was quick to agree. He figured he'd be 50 cents richer and get a haircut to boot. His glee was short-lived. After he felt the way I cut off a few chunks of his hair, he began to have second thoughts about being used as a training device. He tried to talk his way out of the whole deal even though Jr. stood close by giving me instructions, assuring Jerry that everything was under control.

The back porch door opened into the kitchen where Jo and the girls had just finished eating. In the middle of Jerry's protests, Jr. ducked into the kitchen and quickly returned with a plate of gravy and biscuits. After that, every time Jerry opened his mouth to say something negative about my haircutting talents (or lack thereof), Jr. poked gravy and biscuits into it. In a blur of biscuits, gravy, and flying hair, Jerry got his haircut. Several weeks later most of his hair had grown back to a respectable length. In spite of the hair mutilation episode, Jerry and I have remained good friends through the years.

As happens so often with couples who have been married a long time, Jr. passed away a few months after Jo died. His daughters, Sue and Sanky, asked Jerry and me to conduct Junior's funeral service. It was sad for both of us, but we were honored to do it. Jr. was our friend, and I'll always be grateful to him for helping me become a barber.

Wrapped in warm memories, I couldn't resist stopping by to tell the job director that I wanted to apply for the barbering job. She gave me a "cop-out" form Eglin's term for the job change form— which must be submitted any time an inmate applies for a different job. When she told me several other inmates were also applying for the opening, I tried not to count on getting it but was really happy when told about a month later that if I still wanted the job, it was mine. I accepted gratefully and worked there until May, 1997.

DAVID

In April, 1995, when the bombing of the federal building in Oklahoma was headlines for months, the compound was a-buzz from different inmates who had experienced a run-in with various federal officials and especially the ATF agents. Most of the comments were sympathy for all the children who were killed but anger that more of the federal agents had not been blown away.

Having heard many stories from the different inmates as they attended vocational tech school and later as I worked as a barber, I was not really shocked at these type comments. To say that much bitterness exists is an understatement.

When any law enforcement agent has to make an arrest, regardless of whether the defendant is guilty or innocent, once that defendant is taken to court and stripped of home, car, bank accounts, everything he has worked all his life to accumulate, and then sentenced to a long time in prison, and then his family deserts him, when that person is released from prison, unless he is a Christian and possesses the ability to "not retaliate," in my opinion based on conversations by the inmates, the Oklahoma bombing could be one of many destined for the future. Also, I would not be surprised at some time in the future to hear or read of federal judges, prosecutors, law enforcement officials, and even some jurors being assassinated. I would never have believed this prior to being incarcerated and having been exposed to individuals from all walks of life and all nationalities.

While David is not a vindictive person, he has strong opinions about how some of the ATF agents are abusing their power.

David, about 5'10" tall and weighing about 160 pounds was one of the most knowledgeable persons I have every met when it comes to weapons. This was his business.

David was a family man who was a well-respected, law-abiding citizen and an employee of the federal government for over 10 years who held a security clearance. I found David to be an individual who would help you in any way he could, the type person who would give you the shirt off his back if it was needed.

Apparently, the willingness to help a friend, after his insistence, ruined his life, costing him everything he owned, including his family also a long prison term

One day while cutting David's hair, I asked him if he would be willing to share his story and permit it to be used in my book. He was more than willing. The following statement will make the average law-abiding citizen feel anger, as well as shock at the way some of the law enforcement agencies operate.

"Not having been informed of any charges against me, I was arrested by two agents of the BATF on January 25, 1992, at 8:20 p.m. in my home in Winter Park, Florida, along with my co-defendant who was visiting from Gainesville, Georgia, and taken to the Seminole County Jail.

"During a period of time beginning on October 6, 1991, wherein I initially met who was later to become the government informant, I reluctantly sold suppressed equipment with sound depressor (SD a silencer. The suppressor made the weapon illegal.). He had a Class III Federal Firearms License to deal in Class III weapons, and I had a Class I License, or what is commonly known as a Gun Dealers' License, and have had for 12 years. I had never been visited or inspected by any agent of the bureau or any other federal agency regarding any firearms transactions whatsoever. During the time of October 6 and terminating on January 25, 1992, I had received several phone calls from Brevard County, Florida, approximately 60 miles from my house. He was a fellow gun enthusiast and shooter as I was, and was learning or attempting to learn the ins and outs of handloading or reloading ammunition and or competitive shooting equipment/techniques, etc. I had met him at a gun show. He began calling me, telling me he wanted to acquire unregistered .22 Ruger Target pistols for his collection, and that he would "put them away" in his safe and not be sold under any conditions. I advised him of where in Brevard County he could legally purchase Title III handguns and register them with the BATF. After much conversation over three months, I finally told him I might know someone who had two that he might want to sell, but the price would be high $950 each. This high price was set to steer him away from me, and only a fool would pay such an inflated price for such a relatively inexpensive 22 rifle/pistol. He said money was no object, and he would pay cash upon delivery and would like to have them as soon as possible. I called a female friend in Gainesville, Georgia, from where I had just relocated, and asked her if she still wanted to sell her two guns. She was also a collector of weapons. She said yes, and we agreed on a price. In the next two weeks, she drove down from Gainesville, Georgia, and brought me the single 22 Ruger pistol and a 22 Ruger rifle. I contacted the supposed shooting buddy of mine via phone, and he arrived and paid for the weapons. He came two hours later than the agreed-upon time When asked why, he claimed car trouble. I had no reason to doubt him. During this delay and unbeknown to me then, he was meeting with the BATF to get 'wired up' for electronic monitoring of our conversations. After the initial sale, he then decided he wanted two more guns just like what he had just bought. I said they weren't available, and he would have to be satisfied with what he had just gotten. A few weeks later, he called me again and began to ask me to provide him with two more unregistered guns. He continued calling and made at least 12 phone calls to me during his initial inquiry and persuasion phase of this conspiracy. I contacted my friend in Gainesville, Georgia, and she said reluctantly that she might be able to get two more made. A friend of hers was equipped to manufacture weapons. Without going into a lot of details, two more transactions exactly like the first were made successfully, the last resulting in my arrest at my home five minutes after the third transaction. All the time he came to my home, he was wired, and 14 tape recordings of our conversations were used at trial.

"Three hours after arriving at the county jail, the agent in charge of this investigation took me to an interview room after reading me my rights, and said, 'You're looking at five years. Do you want to talk to us?' I said, 'I don't mind talking to you, but I think I should have my attorney present.' He said, 'Oh, so you want to play hardball, eh?' I said, 'No, I just think it best to have someone here to represent me. He then left the room with another fellow agent, and I haven't talked to him since.

"During my arrest at my residence, the following events occurred. My wife was knitting on the living room couch, and I was in the bedroom preparing some shooting equipment to take to the range the next day to test. The ATF employed the manpower of the Seminole County Sheriff's Department Special Weapons and Tactics team to assist them in executing their search warrant. The SWAT team used a battering ram on my front door, breaking it open. Simultaneously 3 concussion hand grenades were thrown in from the front living room windows, which they had broken for that purpose. An entry team used another ram to break all the glass in the sliding glass door on the patio area after cutting the screens out with military knives. The entry team from two different directions burst into our home carrying H&K MP-5 submachine guns equipped with silencers and laser sights, all wearing bulletproof vests and the typical tactical entry equipment such teams use. My wife screamed and ran in to the bedroom where I was and tried to hide next to my filing cabinet, while covering her head. She of course did not know what was going on. As soon as I heard the spoons from the grenades pop off, I knew what was happening. The people came into the living room area poised ready to shoot. Since I have been involved in SWAT team training organizations for 15 years, I knew what to do. I immediately hit the floor and put my hands over my head and told my co-defendant to do the same thing, which she did. I was immediately handcuffed as was she and brought to sit on the couch in the living room. The team broke out all the windows in the house, which was totally unnecessary. The smoke alarm was going off as a result from the smoke and heat from the grenades which added to the confusion. An agent said, 'Shoot the thing out.' They finally tore it down. The outside temperature was about 35 degrees, and we were freezing. They began searching the house and showed me the search warrant finally upon my request.

"I have a 750-pound gun safe to store all my weapons (legal) and the senior agent told me to open it. I'm now handcuffed. He said he would get a torch and burn it open. I spun the handle as it was unlocked and let him search it. Not finding anything illegal, they got mad and began going through our drawers in our bedroom and all other areas of the house. They took all my personal belongings out of my Buick Park Avenue and brought them into the house, making several trips and put everything on the kitchen table. Then they said they were seizing it—no reason given. Later, they came back in and said it had too many miles for them, so I could keep it. The only thing they took out of my house was a file folder in my file cabinet where I had ordered, bought, and paid for through the Treasury Department—ATF the necessary paperwork required to purchase and possess a legally suppressed Ruger .22 target pistol. There was my picture, fingerprint cards, and ATF application copies, along with the initial purchase receipt for the gun in question which was in transit from the manufacturer to the Class III dealer in Georgia. No other items or property was taken from my house after spending 7 hours going through it.

"I called my wife from the jail, and she told me they were still there, threatening to arrest her as they knew she was involved up to her eyeballs with me when she said she threw away all our phone receipts after paying them for our long-distance calls. That angered them, and when they didn't believe her, they started making threats of arresting her. My wife is a teacher of English to sixth and seventh graders. She knows very little about my guns/equipment or anything else. When she pleaded much ignorance, they responded with more threats and intimidation.

"I was standing outside my house with this informant five minutes before they broke into our house. They could have arrested me outside in the front yard since I was under visual surveillance at that very time, but they didn't

There were no threats, no weapons displayed, no reason to take me down like a fugitive who was a major criminal and had had trouble with the police or was a violent prospect. The informant informed them that I was a dangerous man because of my shooting abilities and my trophies. All my guns were legally registered to me, and there were no Class III weapons or destructive devices anywhere in my house or in my possessions.

The arrest was Saturday night. I was taken to Orlando for my preliminary hearing at 9:00 a.m. on the following Monday. By then, I had retained private counsel and was represented at the hearing. My wife and daughter also came. After several allegations made by the US attorney and the arresting agent to the judge, I felt compelled to dispute these charges and had my wife and daughter take the witness stand to refute allegations of my being a wife beater and possessing dynamite that I had allegedly stolen from a local Sheriff's Department in 1972. After all was said and done, I was denied a bond, but the judge granted another hearing for Wednesday morning. I had my wife remove all my gun collection and take it to a private storage area and place it under lock and key. She gave my attorney the key and surrendered (voluntarily) my passport to show I could not leave the country, did not have any of my guns in my possession any more, and was not a threat to anyone. This did not satisfy the agent or the US Attorney, and they said that I was a public safety factor, risk of flight, and would probably gun down the arresting agent, and then turn the gun on myself. Bail was denied. I went to trial in 67 days after the arrest. My attorney discredited the informant and my co-defendant and had the jury laughing at their credibility as they testified against me. The trial was four days long and resulted in the jury being hopelessly deadlocked three (3) times, according to the jury foreman. The judge, John Moore III, intimidated the jury foreman and told him that he would hate to have them come all the way back to Orlando the following Monday morning to continue deliberations and drive 75 mile each way until they completed their deliberations. The jury foreman reluctantly took the jury out at 4:15 Friday afternoon and came back in 15 minutes with a guilty verdict on three of four counts of conspiracy of possession of illegal weapons/manufacturing, etc. Sentencing was 89 days later 64 months, $2,500 fine, three years' probation, drug testing, etc. My co-defendant got one year, two years' probation, self-surrender, personal recognizance bond from the first day of arrest, and testified against me, saying that she was five times more guilty than me. She only had one count of conspiracy, but manufactured, transported across state lines, and purchased four additional guns for all these transactions.

"During the ensuing weeks waiting for incarceration in the Federal system, the insurance company canceled our house policy, the neighbors were harassed by the news media for a feature story on their dangerous neighbor, and continued to print my picture and a story about my former law enforcement anti-terrorist training background

"When I took the stand in my own defense, the US

Attorney objected to every question my attorney asked me, and the judge sustained the objection, saying he was 'leading the witness.' Every time we got to the point to show the jury the entrapment situation from the very beginning of this case, the government objected, and the judge sustained the objection. I could not have the opportunity to explain how I got into this situation with the informant to the jury, especially when we discredited him. The informant, even when on the stand, reluctantly cooperated. He refused to answer questions posed to him by my attorney and took the Fifth Amendment to not incriminate himself. The judge finally ordered him to answer and we eventually found out that he had 31 legally registered machine guns in his possession courtesy of the Treasury Department/BATF! I hired a private investigator to get other witnesses for me against him. A prominent gun shop owner in Brevard County told my attorney that the informant was in his shop on several occasions since my arrest and was bragging about setting me up for the illegal weapons charge in order to get a reduction in his Title II Firearms Permits from the BATF. This gun shop owner did not want to testify to this fact for me because of his fear of this same agent's harassing him at his place of business and possible closing him down for an inventory or inspection which could dampen his proceeds accordingly. I appealed this case, and on May 17, 1993, I was turned down by the 11 Circuit Court of Appeals even when there were 6 different precedent cases in the Circuit on this very issue of malicious objection by the government, and the malicious substantiation by the judge. That same day, I got my divorce papers in the mail!"

TRAGEDY

May, 1995, was filled with tragedy. Ken, an inmate who worked in the mess hall and still had three years left on his eight-year sentence, was a perfect specimen for one of the old Charles Atlas commercials. At fifty-one years of age, 6'1", and 250 pounds of pure muscle, he appeared to be in perfect health. Ken's wife, Beth, had recently moved from Miami, Florida to a community just outside the prison camp so she could visit as often as possible

Ken wasn't a religious man, but was one of the nicest, most polite people I've ever met. Like so many other inmates, he was serving time for conspiracy. He was very bitter about the justice system

One day, when the weather was a near-perfect 75 degrees, Ken had spent about an hour working out with weights. He finished the workout and started back to his dorm. He remarked to one of the inmates that he thought he might have strained himself because he was having some chest pain. By the time he reached the dorm, the chest pain had become more severe. He laid down on his bunk and asked the inmates to call the P.A. (physician's assistant) to come and check him. By this time the pain was so severe he couldn't walk 300 feet to the clinic. Before the P.A could get to the dorm, Ken cried out in an agonized voice, "I don't want to die in prison!" According to the inmates who had gathered around Ken's cube, those were the last words he ever said.

It was only two or three minutes before the P.A. arrived. The paramedic rescue team from Eglin A.F.B. had been notified and arrived with him. They did CPR on him and used the defibulator, but to no avail. Ken was dead

Ken died in prison with no chance to say goodbye to his wife who was only a few miles away. A few days later, due to very bad weather conditions during the night, inmates were not permitted to leave the dorm and go to their work assignments. By noon the weather had cleared, and inmates were told they could spend the rest of the day at their leisure.

Shaun, thirty-one, 5'10", 195 pounds, was like Ken--all muscle and apparently in perfect health. He decided to work out in the weight shack. By 7:00 p.m. he had been working out for several hours, and feeling some tightness in his chest, returned to his dorm. Shaun complained to his bunkee that he was having chest lain, but since his work schedule had kept him from working out or several days, he assumed he had overdone it. He took a shower and told his bunkee he was going to lie down for an hour or so to see if the pain would go away.

At 8:45 p.m. his bunkee tried for several moments to wake Shaun up, but got no response. He became alarmed and yelled for someone to help. One of the inmates activated the fire alarm which rings in the dorm and also at Eglin AFB Fire and Rescue station. Another called "Control" on the dorm's emergency phone which connects to the main officer's station. Within five minutes it looked like every inmate in the dorm was there, crowding around the numerous medical personnel working to revive Shaun. In the meantime, someone apparently notified the warden, captain (of the guards), and other ranking officials. They were also there and obviously concerned.

Shaun's cube was in my dorm. I stood outside looking in a window, watching as medical personnel administered CPR. I saw one of the doctors inject something into his heart in an effort to save him. But I had seen enough dead people when I worked in the embalming room at Talladega Funeral Home and Joe and Glenda Gassett's Funeral Home in Wetumpka, Alabama, to know that here was no hope for Shaun

As I watched the medics continue working on Shaun, my thoughts turned to yesterday's Sunday services. Like most Sundays, I was the pianist and had decided to stay seated at the piano during the sermon. From where I sat I could see the whole congregation. At the end of his sermon, Chaplain Becton gave everyone the invitation to accept Jesus or to re-dedicate his or her lives.

I happened to notice Shaun get up and walk out with another inmate during the invitation. At the time, I didn't think much about it.

But now, as I watched them put Shaun's body on a stretcher and roll him away, I wondered if he was a Christian or if he had unknowingly passed up his last chance to become one. Like Ken, he had no warning of death. No chance to say good-bye to friends and family.

It seemed so final when they put Shaun's body in the ambulance, and the thought crossed my mind,

"Is death like prison?" The words churned around in my brain, almost forcing me to go back to my cube and write the following poem:

Is Death like prison?

Is death like prison?

The dark thought came to me

Away from all our loved ones

What a sad time it will be.

Prison days are endless

And long the dark night sky,

But there's one consolation—

Pris'ners go home by and by.

Death can't be like prison;

It can hit us without warning,

And there's no second chance

Whether evening, night, or morning.

No more friends or family visits

In the Bible it does tell

We'll not spend eternity in prison

But in heaven or in hell.

If a person knows not Jesus

As their Savior and their Friend,

They should call on him today;

Tomorrow may be their end.

Two weeks after Shaun died, I was asked to sing a special song for the Sunday morning service. Although I have played the piano since age ten, it was usually to accompany other people's singing. That' probably why I had trouble thinking of something I'd feel comfortable singing. Finally, the lyrics of a song written in the 940's, "If We Never Meet Again This Side of Heaven," came to lind. I had played it many times for Ruby Barton (my mother), Idessa Gravette, and Dessie Morris who is the mother of my dear friend and national evangelist, Rev. Max Morris. They made up the church trio then, and sang it often--usually at funerals. Richard, a dentist serving time for conspiracy who also played a mean piano, greed to accompany me, and we were able to rehearse several mes before the service.

Sunday morning the chapel was packed with inmates and visitors (visitors are permitted to attend services with an inmate relative or friend). Ken and Shaun were heavy on my mind, so I decided to say a few words to the congregation before I sang.

"You know," I said, "Ken and Shaun left this life without raring. They had no chance to say good-bye to anyone. If they weren't already Christians, they had no last minute chance to be saved. Maybe today is a good time for each of you to consider there you'll spend eternity.

"The only way any of us will ever be reunited with family or friends after death is either in Heaven or Hell, and no one wants it a be in Hell. You'll have a chance-maybe your last chance-to accept Jesus or re-dedicate your lives at the end of the service. Don't put it off. We never know when or who death will strike ext."

Richard had been playing softly while I was talking. I began to sing

"Soon we'll come to the end of our journey

And perhaps we'll never meet any more

Till we gather in heaven's bright city

Where we'll live there for evermore.

"If we never meet again this side of heaven,

As we struggle through this world and its strife,

There's another meeting place somewhere in heaven,

By the side of the river of life

Where the charming roses bloom for ever

And where separation comes no more

If we never meet again this side of heaven

We will meet on that beautiful shore."

THE SECONDS YEARS BEGINS

As the days, weeks, and months turned into my second year in prison, I had perfected a routine for staying busy. Evenings and weekends were filled by answering letters, practicing songs for Sunday services with various groups, studying the bible, and working on my book. My regular barbershop job took up the daytime hours during the week.

I still had faith that the 11 Court of Appeals, Atlanta, Georgia, would review my case, realize that I'd been wrongfully charged, and reverse my conviction. Like a personal litany, I repeated John 14:13,14 over and over to myself.. *"Whatsoever ye shall ask in my name, that I will do... "* And I knew that thousands of Max Morris' World-wide Prayer Partners, along with hundreds of others from throughout the United States, were praying that my case would be reviewed and the conviction overturned. I felt great.

In June of 1995, my attorney, Bill Dawson notified me that my appeal had been denied. What a blow! Thinking there just have been some mistake, I immediately called Bill to ask him to file for a re-hearing. Two weeks later, I received notice that the court had refused to rehear my case.

Disheartened I called Bill again and asked if he thought we should appeal to the U.S. Supreme Court. He wasn't too enthused about it simply because the Supreme Court receives thousands of cases each year, and only about one out of a thousand actually gets reviewed

"But I'll be glad to file it, if you want me to," he said.

I labored over the decision for several days, praying for guidance to do the right thing. How, I wondered, could reasonable men who were supposed to be well versed in the law not decide in my Javor and reverse the conviction? Finally, I decided to take my chances. I called and told him to go ahead and file.

Next, I called Max Morris and told him what I'd decided to do.

"I'll notify the Prayer Partners around the world." he said.

While doing my own praying, I arrogantly reminded God of His promise in John 15:16—… *"Whatsoever ye shall ask of my Father in my name, he may give it to you.*

On January 22, 1996, I got an apologetic letter from Bill, telling me the Supreme Court had refused to review my case. There was no place left to go.

For the first time since coming to prison, I was really angry. When the judicial system failed me the first time, I was upset, and it had hurt to leave my family and lose my job. But somehow, I always had faith that the appeals courts, at least, would give me a fair hearing. I was wrong.

It was the pits. My faith in the judicial system was wiped out. For 20 months I'd seen inmates come and go. Most of them convicted of far more serious crimes than my alleged money laundering. Yet, it seemed they were the ones getting breaks-not me.

To me, the bitter irony was that many of the inmates getting reduced or over-turned sentences were atheists with little respect for the judicial system or anything else. And here I was, trusting in God and believing that ultimately, justice would prevail, and I would be released. Yet, I continued running into judicial walls time after time after time.

That night, after calling my wife and Max to tell them the bad news, I dragged myself back to my cube, head bowed and shoulders slumped in defeat. I crawled into my bunk and let go with great heaving sobs. I berated God for having failed me.

"How could You let this happen?" I asked between sobs. "You say to ask anything in your name, and you will do it. Maybe 1 can understand it if you don't listen to me, but how can you ignore my mother who has served You faithfully for 65 years and my wife, Mary who has served You without question for more than 40 years? Dear Mary, who struggles so hard, keeping everything together, while I live in this country club of a prison. And how can You ignore the prayers of people like Max Morris and all the thousands throughout the world who are praying for me?"

You bet I was angry. Angry at the system that had failed me. Angry at God for not answering prayers. As the sobbing and anger slowly wound down, I was feeling more than a little sorry for myself and couldn't even see the self-righteousness in vowing that even though God had let me down, and even if Mary and I lost everything we owned, we would still serve God. The next morning I called Mother and told her the sad news about the Supreme Court's refusal. I needed and wanted to be comforted. I should have known what Mother would say.

"Just keep looking up and trusting God," she said.

That wasn't exactly what I wanted to hear just then, and forgetting what I had vowed the night before, I said angrily, "I did trust in God, and He let me down."

"Don't let the Devil deceive you, Larry. God's word is true, and He will answer your prayers," she said gently.

I knew if I wanted her to say anything else, I was wasting my time. If it's in the Bible, Mother believes it, and that's that. In spite of knowing this, I said, "Mother, the

Supreme Court has already ruled. There's no use praying for them to change the verdict. They've refused to even consider my case."

As she hung up, Mother said, "Larry, don't ever give up on God. We may not understand the reasons for everything, but His word is true."

By then, it was almost noon, and I needed a shower before my afternoon shift at the barbershop. The shower is a great place to argue with yourself, trying to reason out any situation. In prison, it's about the only "prayer closet" around. The steam from the shower mixed with the steam still coming from my anger. Try as I would, I just couldn't understand the way God was doing things. I found myself wondering if He was truly in charge of everything.

Then, suddenly, softly a voice spoke inside my mind.

"Just settle down, and know that I am God. Understand that my reasons for the way things happen are not always clear. You're upset, but remember, I always keep My word."

Tears of relief mixed with the water streaming down over me, and I finally realized that the forces of evil had blinded me to the faith I should have kept, no matter how unreasonable or unfair the situation seemed. In my heart, I knew that blaming God certainly wasn't the answer and that whatever small satisfaction I might gain from venting my hurt and anger was a bad bargain against the loss of my faith in God's purpose.

I began to feel better. I remembered that since I'd come to Eglin, attendance at Sunday morning services had gone from about 50 to a standing-room only crowd, and the choir had grown from four to more than 15. I felt even better. Not that I was personally responsible for all of it, but I'd taken an active part in helping make it happen. Maybe, I thought, it was part of God's purpose that I should be here. In my mind's eye, I saw the many inmates who had become Christians—men who might never have given serious thought to God or his wonderful promises to mankind if they hadn't been at this particular place in time. Humbled, I wondered who I thought I was to question God's reasons and purposes.

That afternoon at mail call I received an inspiring letter from a lovely lady, Sharon Morgan, a World-Wide Prayer Partner, who had been stricken with M.S. (multiple sclerosis) several years ago. As I read her letter, I began to realize what being strong is really all about. Here are some excerpts from that letter and my reply to it

January 18, 1996

Dear Larry,

Thank you so much for your letter. I really appreciate your prayers and the time you took to write. I have never given up during my battle with this disease... that I didn't have bad days. There have been times when Satan has worked EXTRA hard on me...as I am sure he has on you too... but when it seems that I've just 'bout reached the bottom and believe no one cares, God reminds me that He still loves me and that there are people who care...God's people... people like you who are praying for me and who will take the time to write. That is so very encouraging.

My illness has made it difficult for me to get out much. I am now on permanent disability from my job. I can get around my story house pretty well as long as I'm near furniture. When I go out. I walk with Canadian Crutches... the ones that hook on your arms. They're BRIGHT RED. For trips of any distance, like the mall, large stores, airports, just about anywhere besides home, I have to take my wheelchair. It's PURPLE. If you're going to be disabled, you should at least make a fashion statement!

My husband works very hard at the new BMW plant; then comes home to do most of the housework, cooking. grocery shopping. etc.

Please remember him in your prayers also. He is a wonderful Christian, and I am blessed to have him. We met at Lee College when we were both in the Lee Singers. He sang in the bass section, and I was the pianist. We are going toward our 24th anniversary. When I became ill, fortunately we had been married 20 years and had established a good marriage. My doctor kept telling me that if we needed counseling, his office provided those services. He told me that 85% of his 100 female MS patients (MS strikes mostly women) were divorced— the husbands couldn't adjust to the changes in their lives.

When I was first diagnosed with Multiple Sclerosis, October of 1983, my first reaction was "Why me?" I reminded God that I had been a good Christian— since I was 7. Daughter of a Church of God Minister—my husband was the Music Minister at a large church of God in Tampa—I went to Lee College—played the piano for the Lee Singers—we were doing God's work—I had just finished my Master's Degree in Piano Performance, etc., etc. I kept rationalizing with God why I didn't deserve this illness, and then I realized Why not me?" — was I better than all the millions of people who suffer in this world? No. And I have what many people in the world do not have—I have a wonderful Savior who has been with me throughout the days of blindness, hospitalizations, paralysis, unending pain and fatigue. I am never alone. He is always there for me. He did not promise me a life free from illness, death, hardships, tragedy—but He did promise me that He would be with me in everything I faced, and that through Him I would be triumphant.

The day I came home from the doctor following the diagnosis, I was of course devastated I could hardly find the strength to pray. I was hurt and confused. How was I going to be able to face what was ahead of me? I knew God was there for me, but I knew I faced an illness full of surprises. A Russian-roulette illness. An illness you rarely die from but many times wish you could. An illness that keeps eating away at all of your bodily functions. I desperately needed a word from the Lord. I had never been one to say. "I'll just open my Bible, and whatever I put my finger on is just for me." But that day was different. I needed something from his Word that would give me some perspective on my situation—help me make sense of it all. I prayed for that special message and opened my Bible. Right before me, underlined in ink from a previous reading, was Romans 8:18: "For I reckon that the sufferings of this present time are not worthy to be compared with the glory which shall be revealed in us. " When I get to feeling sorry for myself. I read this scripture over and over.

My experience with MS has taught me to truly trust in the Lord. My faith in His ability to heal me never wavered—I guess because I was brought up in the Church of God, had been healed many times as a child, had seen healing in my father's ministry. But I have discovered that the test of real faith comes by completely trusting that God is in control of your life and as you said in your letter, "While we don't always understand why God permits us to experience financial, physical, and emotional storms in our life. He is able to keep us safe and sustain us." I don't understand the purpose for my disease just as I'm sure you don't understand the purpose for your imprisonment. But I do trust God and I trust His timetable for me and for you. And while we wait. we can pray for each other. It will help me just knowing I'm on your prayer list.

Well, I didn't mean to ramble on and on. I hope that this new year will be a better one for you and bring you closer to an overturned verdict. I can tell by your letter that God has been very real in your life. It is very encouraging to know that God's grace is always sufficient and always there just when we need it.

God bless you and keep you.

Sharon

As 1 finished reading Sharon's letter, with tears streaming down my face, I said, "God, help me to never, ever complain about anything. Upon my release from prison, whenever it is, I pledge to do whatever you want me to do."

That night after returning from work, all the other inmates had gone to bed, and I was sitting at the desk area in my cube. I read Sharon's letter again and then wrote her the following letter.

January 24, 1996

Wed. Night

Dear Sharon,

You may never really know what your letter meant to me and its arrival had to be the work of God.

I had just received a letter from my attorney, with the notice from the U.S. Supreme Court, advising me they refused to review my appeal. I had such high hopes they would reverse the injustice. There are hundreds of people throughout the world praying that this would be done. John 14:14 says.

"If ye shall ask anything in my name, I will do

it." I have been raised in the church and always believed the scriptures.

Receiving this adverse news presented the devil a golden opportunity to attack my faith.

As I read your letter, tears flowed freely, and I knew God saw what was headed my way and used you to strengthen me.

Sharon, I am writing a manuscript and hope to publish it upon release, and if you don't mind. I may want to use part or all of your letter, with your permission.

Thank you for letting God work through you to help me. Take care until next time and keep me in your prayers. You are in my prayers. I also thank God for your husband. My wife and I have been married for 39 years (since I was 16). December 14. 1995, and she is a jewel.

Love,
Larry Barton

February 1, 1996

Dear Larry,

Thank you for your letter. I'm so glad my previous letter ministered to you in some way. And you are welcome to use the letter if you wish. I told Reid I wasn't sure what I said that was of benefit, but I'm glad it meant something to you. I was so sorry to read about the Supreme Court decision. I know that was terrible news to hear, and to understand, especially, as you say, since so many people are praying for you.

While my situation is not as difficult as yours, I do know how it feels to wonder why God is not "responding to all the prayers from so many people. People constantly tell me—throughout the Church and across this country—that they have been praying for me. And I've even said, "God, I have such faith in you I know it really only takes ME praying to receive from you. But since so many people-good Christian people are also praying for my healing, why haven't I received that miracle?" I haven't really come up with any good answers except the one from Paul in I Corinthians 12:8-10, where Paul asked the Lord three times to remove his thorn in the flesh. And if anyone ever had the ear of God it had to be Paul.

"For this thing I besought the Lord thrice, that it might depart from me. And he said unto me, 'My grace is sufficient for thee, for my strength is made perfect in weakness.' Most gladly therefore will I rather in glory in my infirmities, that the power of Christ may rest upon me. Therefore I take pleasure in infirmities, in reproaches, in necessities, in persecutions, in distresses for Christ's sake: for when I am weak, then am I strong."

I sometimes feel like people think I have "given up," or I just don't have enough faith—since I haven't been healed in these past 13 years—and everybody is praying "so hard." I can only keep trusting in Him. I have told God that I have absolute faith that I can be healed—but I also have absolute acceptance of His will in my life. Just because I do not see healing right now does not mean he cannot or will not heal me at some time. I am often concerned by Christians who believe there should be no suffering in this Christian life you know, "pie-in-the-sky" believers. If you're a "Good Christian, you should be healthy, wealthy, and have no problems. That isn't very scriptural. The Lord himself said, "And he that taketh not his cross and followeth after me is not worthy of me. "

People often misquote that and say we're to take up "his" cross, referring to Christ's cross—that's not what it says. Christ is the speaker in this scripture and the "his" is US. We're to take up OUR cross—our—burden and yet still follow Him. How can we partake in Christ's suffering if we don't suffer ourselves? Well, I hope you don't mind me going on and on. This is good therapy for me. It helps to write if -to see it on paper—to reinforce my faith; and maybe it will help you in some way. At least it's something to read.

The tape I was going to send you was a tape of my piano playing. When I became ill in '83. 1 had no idea how long I would be able to play. so Reid, my *husband, helped me tape it in the church sanctuary. The quality is not very good since it was not done in a studio. But my father had nice covers put on it, and it has become a "keepsake" of sorts for family and friends. My ability to play has come and gone over the years—I am now having difficulty with my left arm and have been unable to play since before Christmas. Reid is supposed to sing Sunday night—I'm hoping I can play enough to get through his song.*

That has been my greatest heartache and perhaps the most difficult thing for me to understand. That was always my way to express my love and worship of God—through my music. And we had been doing church work for 10 years when I became ill. I wasn't sure why God chose to affect the talent He gave me and one I had always used for Him. So 1 have had to work through this more than anything else.

I went from playing 6 hours a day, playing for all the church services, choirs, teaching piano—to not playing at all. Then I got little better about a year ago and could play for the Sanctuary Choir. But I can no longer practice for any length—the arms just aren't strong enough. I practice in my head—since I can't practice for any length at the keyboard. I played a solo recently at Lee College for Homecoming— and God was so good to me. He helped me get through 2 nights. That was a miracle in itself. They had a "nostalgia" section on the program, where they featured several alumni. I told someone I didn't realize I was getting old until it dawned on me, I was part of a "nostalgic" section! Then I had another attack and have not been able to play since before Christmas. It's a frustrating disease.

I will send the tape to Mary. I'm going to warn her not to compare it to anything of Max's. Everything he produces is so professional. This tape is rather rough around the edges. But maybe she'll hear something in it that will speak to her heart. I was definitely playing from mine.

I pray daily for you and your family. I pray that God's presence will be so real to you—surround you with His wonderful peace! That He will give you a sense of purpose when you wonder what will come from this difficult time in your life. I pray that you will stay encouraged when you feel so alone. And that you will remember there are people who care although I am not family or one of your close friends. I care.

And when I say I'm praying for you, I really am praying for you. Not just once, but every day. I hear "God bless you; we're praying for you"—all the time. Not that I doubt people's sincerity, but I do often wonder how many people are REALLY PRAYING FOR ME. They walk away, and I'm soon forgotten. Not that they mean to be uncaring; I think people do care and would like to see me better. But people are busy—they have their own lives and things to do. "Out of sight— out of mind. "

But you and I are imprisoned—you behind bars, me behind an illness. We live with our chains every day. Other people's lives go on, but we can never get away from our shackles. I don't think many people really know what that means. Please believe that when I say "I am praying for you." I really am praying for you—I remind the lord about you many times during the day. When I ask Him to please relieve the terrible pain I'm in, I ask Him to remember the pain you're experiencing away from your family and friends, and what you have to live through every day. The pain of "absence" must be so great in your life. I wish I could help. If we never meet. I want you to know you have a friend who cares about you and your situation.

With love and prayers for a better, brighter tomorrow.

Sharon

JESSICA

There was one bright spot in May Jessica. She's my beautiful granddaughter who is twelve, going on twenty. Her birthday is May 30th, and having been imprisoned May 27, 1994, I missed her eleventh birthday. Jessica wasn't about to let me miss her twelfth one.

Jessica had come with my wife, Mary, to visit many times luring my first year at Eglin, but they had never made the five Hundred mile round-trip by themselves. Usually, they rode with Our son, Delane, or my brother, Charles, when they and their wives tame to visit.

Not this weekend. Jessica informed Mary that just the two of them were going to spend her birthday with me, and it was a wonderful visit.

Jessica, like myself, never meets a stranger. During previous visits, she had gotten acquainted with many families and their children. And she charmed the prison officers. It was always more like a family reunion when Jessica came to Eglin.

Jessica is an Auburn University "Tiger" fan and has been almost from the time she was able to say the word, football. This is rather strange because I'm an alumnus of the University of Alabama, and Mary, Delane and daughter-in-law Becky are all Alabama football fans. We've sometimes wondered if the hospital switched Delane and Becky's baby for some other child. More likely, Jessica simply fell in love with Auburn's mascot, the tiger. I can't remember exactly when I nicknamed Jessica "Tiger Lou," but it stuck, and I still affectionately refer to her as my little Tiger Lou.

It was amazing how much Jessica had grown during the past year. As I watched her chatting with the guards, pictures of the past flicked through my mind, and I remembered a time when she was only 6 1/2 months—a baby (she's still MY baby). It was December, and Delane and Becky were in the process of moving to a new house. Because they didn't want to drag the baby back and forth in the cold weather, they asked Mary and me if we'd mind keeping Jessica for three or four days while they moved and got the new house in order. It wasn't the first time we'd kept her, but it was the longest period of time. Of course, we didn't mind

We were always looking for reasons to take care of her.

At the time, the new parents were trying to train Jessica to sleep alone in her baby bed, but when she stayed with Mary and me, we let her sleep between us in our king-size bed. Naturally, when she went home Delane and Becky would have a tough time getting her to sleep in her own bed. They claimed we were spoiling her, but we certainly wouldn't spoil the most beautiful grandchild in the world! *What does a young couple know about a six-month-old baby, anyway?*

The night Delane brought Jessica over, the December temperature was in the low twenties, and we were glad they had decided to leave her with us. After telling his mother what all she should to do to properly take care of Jessica, Delane added one final remark as he was leaving.

"Don't let Jessica sleep in the bed with you and Dad. I don't want to go through all that crying when she comes home and has to sleep in her own bed."

But Delane," said Mary, "we don't have a baby bed and I'm afraid to leave her alone on a regular bed—she might roll off and fall to the floor."

"Well, make a pallet on the floor with lots of quilts for her, but promise you won't let her sleep in your bed."

Reluctantly, Mary agreed. I stayed out of the conversation, but at this time, I'd been married to Mary for more than twenty-five years and couldn't help wondering what was going through her mind. I was sure it included some alternate plan. I also thought about the pallet Delane had suggested. Sure, I knew about sleeping on pallets. I'd done it many times and even liked doing it—especially when I was a kid. But who ever heard of a baby grandchild being made to sleep on the floor? It seemed like child abuse to me!

About 9:30 p.m., Mary and I were sitting in the den, watching TV and enjoying a big fire in the fireplace. Occasionally, one of us looked at Jessica who was cooing and gurgling contentedly while she played with her toys on the floor. Mary had been rather quiet for some time. I glanced at her, and noticed she had the alternate plan look in her eye. A little while later, Jessica began to get cranky, and I suggested that we put her to bed, still aware of Mary's promise not to let her sleep in our bed.

I was bursting with curiosity about what she would do because I knew when Mary gave her word to someone, it was like money in the bank.

Without saying a word, Mary got up from the couch and left the room. In a few moments she returned, dressed for bed and carrying a huge armload of quilts, blankets sheets and pillows. She carefully built a very well padded, king-size pallet. When it was done to her satisfaction, she put on Jessica's pajamas, placed her in the middle of the pallet and laid down beside her.

She looked at me, grinned like a Cheshire cat and said, "I promised Delane we wouldn't let Jessica sleep in our bed. I never said we wouldn't sleep with her on the pallet!"

Sometimes, grandparents have to do what they have to do.

Yes, they do. The day was quickly coming to an end, but I had learned that Jessica made the A-honor roll for the year, and had received several awards at the end of the school year for outstanding work. She was also presented with the Presidential Award for a science project. Mrs. Sadie Curry, one of her favorite teachers and the mother of Fran Curry, TV personality, made the presentation. To top off her well-rounded academic year, she was doing great in band and making fine progress studying piano. *Was I a proud grandpa or what?*

Yet, for all this, Jessica was still a rough and tumble girl. Sometimes, I believe she could demolish an anvil. A few weeks before her twelfth birthday she demolished her go-kart by running into a culvert on the edge of the road. Thank God, she wasn't injured. However, a few days later, she was visiting one of her friends, and they were taking turns riding her friend's mo-ped At least, they took the precaution of riding in an open field, away from traffic. Jessica had ridden to their turn-around spot and was going to come back to let her friend take a turn. She wheeled the moped around, going only about five miles an hour. The mo-ped apparently hit a rock, throwing Jessica off. She landed on her left arm, and it was broken between the shoulder and elbow. Fortunately, she had on her helmet. That probably prevented a serious head injury, which could have crippled or killed her. At first, the doctor thought that due to the location of the break, he might have to put her in a half body cast, but he decided to try a different kind of contraption, and it was successful. In a few weeks, the x-rays showed the bone had knit, and she was as good as new.

Meanwhile, Jessica had talked her Ma-Bart (which is what she calls Mary—I'm Papa-Bart) into buying her a pair of skates for her birthday. When I found out, I suggested they both might be in need of psychiatric help. I had no chance to buy a present for my Tiger Lou", so I wrote the following poem and presented it to her.

Jessica (Tiger Lou) Barton

My granddaughter's name is Jessica.

There's no one quite as smart.

She's mighty cute and musically inclined

But dangerous on mo-peds or go-karts.

Tiger Lou is what I call her.

She's lovely as a pearl.

On May 30th this year, she'll be

My special birthday girl.

It's true I can't be with her

Because I'm far away,

But Tiger knows I love her

On this and every day.

HAPPY BIRTHDAY— I LOVE YOU!

Papa Bart

All too soon, visiting time came to a close. I thought of all the tragedies during May and couldn't help wondering if I'd ever get to see them again. As Mary and Jessica got up to leave, they hugged and kissed me and told me how much they loved me. I felt as if my heart would burst.

I had always tried to hold my emotions in and not break down in front any of my relatives, but it's almost impossible at the end of visits. To me that's the worst part of being in prison--not knowing when or if you will ever see your loved ones again.

I watched them walk away. Then, the ache in my throat spilled over. Tears streamed down my face as I walked back to my dorm with the words of the old gospel song rolling through my mind... *"If we never meet again this side of heaven, we will meet on that beautiful shore."*

CHILI PEPPER

Chili Pepper from Chili without a doubt is one of the most outstanding drummers in the country. When I found out he could play, I convinced him to join our church group. Chili is married and is the father of three beautiful children. Even though Chili Pepper is not an American citizen, he holds the proper papers, which entitle him to live in America. His wife is an American Citizen

One night after choir practice, Chili Pepper and I were sitting around talking, and the subject came up about why we both were in prison. Chili Pepper had been an investor dealing in stocks and bonds. A very successful businessman who had become one of Chili's clients allegedly was in the drug business, unknown to Chili Pepper. Over a period of several months, he had invested over one million dollars for the client. The client was arrested and worked out a deal with the feds to testify against Chili Pepper. A plan was concocted to insure a conviction of Chili Pepper.

Arrangements were made for the client to take Chili Pepper and his wife and daughter out for supper. Chili Pepper had no knowledge that his client had already been arrested

According to Chili Pepper, there was no business discussed at this supper, just a friendly get-together. A few days later, Chili Pepper was indicted on money laundering charges of over a million dollars. He refused to plead guilty.

The day his trial was to begin. Chili Pepper was approached by the prosecutor and told that if he did not plead guilty, the grand jury was meeting in another part of the building, and his wife and daughter would be indicted for conspiracy. Chili Pepper told the prosecutor that his family had no knowledge of his business and was not involved in any transactions. The prosecutor informed Chili Pepper they had evidence of the alleged business meeting at the restaurant. The prosecutor informed

Chili Pepper that he could get the grand jury to believe him Chili Pepper pleaded guilty to protect his family. He was sentenced to 60 months. If he had gone to court and been found guilty, he could have received more than 25 years, and his wife and daughter could have been sentenced to 10-20 years.

Chili Pepper's vacation at Club Fed will cost the taxpayers more than $125,000.00, and the drug dealer is on probation for cooperating.

A REQUEST FOR INVESTIGATOR SURRETT

On or about December 8, 1995, I was made aware of an incident that took place in Atlanta, Georgia involving a Jerry Jackson. According to the news release, two police officers by the name of Wayne L. Pinckney and W.T. Sauls had been suspended following an investigation into a shootout at a motorcycle repair shop that killed Mr. Jackson. Witnesses said the officers deliberately shot the man.

The witness interviews and forensic evidence "raises some very troubling concerns about the actions" of the officers, said Mayor Bill Campbell.

Police have said Jerry Jackson was killed December 7, 1995 by ricocheting bullets in the shootout between plainclothes officers who thought a robbery was in progress and a mechanic who thought the police were armed robbers.

The coroner agreed that the bullets had ricocheted and a ballistics test showed the fatal bullet was fired from Officer Pinckney's gun.

But witnesses have said that Pinckney intentionally shot

Jackson as he lay on the sidewalk outside the motorcycle shop, pleading for his life.

"Particularly troublesome is the statement of an eye witness given police on December 7, who describes officer Pinckney as shooting in the direction of Mr. Jackson," Mayor Campbell stated.

The Georgia Bureau of Investigation crime lab also turned up significant evidence to conclude bullet fragments recovered from Jackson's body were from Pinckney's gun, said Gib Heuett, Chief Assistant Deputy Director.

The officers will be suspended with pay for five days. After that, they will receive no pay and will have a chance to appeal. The police department will turn over its findings to the district attorney and U.S. Attorney's office for a possible grand jury investigation, Police Chief Beverly Harvard said. A civilian review board also will look at the evidence according to the newspaper story.

As I read the article, my heart begin to beat faster as I wondered if this was the same Jerry Jackson that had worked for Jamie and the city of Talladega. *If I could prove this is the same person, I could file a brief with the courts asking them to give me a new trial based on this evidence,* I reasoned.

Being Christmas season and staying busy with my job as well as involved with the various chapel services, I kept delaying following up on the news article.

On Wednesday, January 10, 1996, I wrote the following letter to Talladega County District Attorney Investigator Dennis Surrett, and included a copy of the newspaper article.

Dear Dennis,

Please find enclosed a copy of a news article that was in the local paper.

After reading the article, I recalled where you were instrumental in helping a man get out of prison that had been incarcerated wrongfully. I recall you worked as hard to get him freed, as the effort was made to convict him.

While I am the first to admit that I was very negligent in the way I handled transactions with Jerry Jackson, he does or did exist and received every dime that he worked for. I have no way of knowing if this Jerry Jackson in Atlanta, Georgia, is the same one that worked with Jamie and the city, but as I told you in the interview, Jerry allegedly lived in or around Douglasville and Atlanta.

Other than being away from the family, I am doing fine. I have met a lot of professional people to include professional football players. congressmen, lawyers, doctors. dentist, preachers, policemen, prosecutors, judges, and several sheriff's, as well as numerous other professions. My full-time job is working in the barbershop, as well as serving as pianist for the various services.

Thank you in advance for looking into this for me, and I will know if this is the same one if I can see a picture of him.

Sincerely,

Larry Barton

cc: Bill Dawson, Attorney

Rod Giddens

On January 12, 1996, I received a letter from a long-time friend and a strong supporter. Her husband of more than 50 years had recently passed away and I had written her a letter of condolence. If had been home, I would have been there with the family. I had always done these type things. The following is the letter.

1/8/96

Dear Larry,

It was so nice to hear from you. It's such a shock about my husband. He had been feeling good for the last 3 months, out cutting grass and raking leaves. Then he fell. Took a step back and fell over a little bush and broke his hip in 3 places. He often spoke of you. He loved you too. He said he couldn't understand why that guy didn't tell the truth about cutting those trees because he talked to him and he told Albert you was paying him to cut them, and the name on the truck was Jackson. Everybody says that if you run for mayor again you will get ir. This mayor up there now won't do nothing. These two families in our neighborhood sell dope and boy do they have some awful carrying on out there. Sex acts and cussing like you never know. This bunch up here won't do nothing about if. We got a little snow Sat. night which didn't help my feelings a bit. You know I broke my hip last March 15. and I had to go to Birmingham with it and they had to open it again. Now the pin is working out and one day I will have to have it took out But right now I can't stand the thought of it. But when it hurts bad enough I will. Oh yes, my husband was taking a sack of trash out the door in June and broke his arm and could you believe I picked him up. Well, Larry, you will just have to guess at my writing.

Always your friend,

Bertha

As I read the letter, I thought if only this information had been available before or during my trial. I couldn't help but wonder how many other people are out there that maybe met Jerry but did not realize how important to me it was for them to come forward. People are hesitant about getting involved, I reasoned.

A few days later after receiving the letter from Bertha, I was talking to my sister, Edith, on the phone, and I asked her to contact her and get her permission for me to send a copy of this letter to Dennis Surrett. Edith wrote me a few days later and informed me that Bertha had approved my request to share her letter with Dennis.

On February 5, 1996, I sent the following letter to Dennis and included the letter of my friend, as well as the one from Suzanne Scott.

Dear Dennis.

While going through some of my legal papers last week, I found the enclosed letter. I do not know this person, but I recall a lady from Munford called me during the last days of my trial and shared with me that she and this Ms. Scott had been at a nightclub in Anniston with Jerry.

The letter from Ms. Suzanne Scott came to me after the trial, and after I called her in New Orleans and asked her to share with me in writing what she knew about Jerry.

I may never find Jerry, but I will keep on trying. Jerry Jackson does exist, if he isn't dead, and all the tree work was done that he was paid for plus everything else he did for Jamie.

On February 8, 1996, the following news article caught my attention

A grand jury Thursday decided not to indict two undercover officers in the death of an unarmed man who witnesses said was executed as he crawled on the sidewalk outside a motorcycle shop.

The grand jury had weighed murder charges against Officers Wayne L. Pinckney and W.T. Sauls in the December 7 death of Jerry Jackson. He was slain after a shootout that resulted from a series of misunderstandings.

Both officers had been suspended without pay. After Thursday's decision, Mayor Bill Campbell reinstated Sauls. He said Pinckney will remain suspended but will receive pay.

The police department is still investigating Pinckney's role in the shootout, and questions remain about how he used his gun, Campbell said.

Pinckney and Sauls were working in plain clothes when they went into the MotoCycles shop with their guns drawn. The officers said they mistakenly thought the business was being robbed.

A shop employee who thought he was being held up opened fire on the officers, and they returned fire. Jackson, a customer at the shop, was killed.

Witnesses said they saw Pinckney aim at Jackson as he lay on the sidewalk, but Pinckney denied he deliberately shot anyone. Ballistics tests showed Jackson was killed by ricocheting bullets from Pinckney's gun, according to the news release.

As I finished reading the article, I still wondered if this was the same Jerry Jackson that had worked with Jamie and the city and if he had been deliberately killed. Had someone from Talladega learned his whereabouts and was successful in hiring one of the Atlanta policemen to murder him? From all accounts, it was apparent that Jerry was lying on the ground when he was killed. Sure was strange. At least the mayor was concerned about the shooting and didn't believe it was justified

I never received any type response from D.A. Rumsey's investigator Dennis Surrett in regard to my letter.

THE DRUG SCENE

As 1995 ended, my naiveté about what went on prisons pretty much ended with it. During the long months, I'd heard lots of discussions--in the barbershop, the dining room, the dorms, and on the compound. It no longer shocked me to know that drugs, booze, sex, or anything else an inmate desired was available. For a price.

P.J. is a drug addict who did cocaine, speed, heroin or whatever he could get his hands on. He told me drugs were as easy to get as gum or candy bars. He was sentenced to prison because of the burglaries he committed to feed his drug habit.

"Hey, man," he said, "when I found out I could get the same drugs in prison I'd been using on the streets, I thought maybe prison wouldn't be so bad after all."

At the time, I couldn't believe what he told me. I thought that prisons, of all places, would be drug-free. A place to rehabilitate drug addicts and alcoholics. - What a laugh! I'm still laughing.

P.J.'s revelation reminded me of what Jack Cowley, former warden at Oklahoma State Reformatory had said about the drug situation in America and its prisons.

"The war on drugs is a failure and a success. It's a miserable failure because it hasn't stopped drug use in this country, but it's a success because it's the best economic boom we've ever seen

"Prisons are big business. It's the growth industry of the 90's, and profits are over-riding the expenses. The public isn't willing to change because the upper class hasn't felt the pain, yet. Poor folks are the clients of the system. Until the more affluent feel the effects, nothing's going to change."

It is estimated that 75 to 90 percent of federal and state inmates are serving time for drug-related charges an overwhelmingly large factor in the problem of overcrowded prisons.

According to Justice Department figures, the number of adults in state and federal prisons for drug-related charges more than tripled between 1986 and 1991.

Alleged offenders receive sentences ranging from six months to in excess of 400 years. In this way, the justice system attempts to remove them from society and separate them from drugs.

Obviously, this approach is a dismal failure, and perpetuates not only overcrowded conditions, but also the drug problem... with taxpayers picking up the tab S. T., a crack dealer serving 20 years, will quickly tell you he's been selling drugs ever since he came to prison in 1992. S. T. claims he averages between $1,500 and $2,000 a month selling drugs. He's never been caught.

"Anything they sell on the street costs triple here," he said. "A bag of dope worth $10 on the street goes for as much as $40 in prison. And everybody wants a piece of the pie."

How does S. T. smuggle the drugs past the guards and into the prison compound? Girlfriends. He has lots of "girlfriends." They smuggle the drugs in rubber gloves, condoms or balloons inserted in their vaginas. Once they're past the guard checkpoint, S. T. is notified that he has a visitor. Shortly after his arrival in the visiting area, the "girlfriend" goes to the restroom, quickly removes the drug-filled container from her vagina and passes it to S. T. He then goes to the men's restroom and inserts it in his anus for transport back to the dorm.

But less than 20% of his drugs come through the visiting room. Most of the drugs he smuggles in come from someone at Eglin Air Force Base where S. T. works during the day. Prisoners are allowed to roam around the base with little or no supervision, as long as they report for work and return to the prison compound when they're supposed to. When S. T. plans to smuggle drugs, he always picks a day when certain guards are working who don't search inmates going through the prison checkpoint.

Allegedly, S. T. also has a connection with a commissary employee who picks up various items at the warehouse commissary on base and delivers them each week to the prison commissary where they're sold to inmates The employee makes drug pick-up while at the commissary warehouse and puts the rugs in plastic bags. He buries the plastic bags in three or four irs of peanut butter.

Later, when S. T. makes his weekly purchase at the prison commissary, he simply orders the prearranged number of jars with the stash inside. He takes them back to the dorm, removes the plastic bags and re-bags the drugs after mixing them with baking soda or crushed aspirin to make them go further. Then, he's ready for business

Another inmate doing 15 years for drug smuggling said, just like on the streets where you have drug cartels supported by corrupt government officials, the major drug operations in prison rely on cooperation with the guards who abuse their power for profit.

"Before I was transferred here from Atlanta, I had two wards who picked up drugs for me at a post office box. They got raid on the street by my dealers association," he said.

This inmate's left leg was amputated below the knee in a car wreck several years ago, and he has an artificial leg. Because of his handicap, he was assigned to work as a truck driver on the air force base. The job allows him to go everywhere on the base, making it imperatively simple to pick up his supply of drugs

His prosthesis is approximately 20 inches long, but what the guards don't know is that he went to the hobby shop and hollowed just a hidden compartment in it large enough to hold up to two rounds of heroin or cocaine

"Heroin is the most popular prison drug because it puts you in an I-don't-care kind of mood. You nod out and chill. Pot is dangerous because it stays in your system too long. Cocaine's not much in demand because it's too expensive. It gives you a great sigh but only lasts for a little while. A $30 bag of heroin can produce a nine-hour high where as $30 worth of cocaine only lasts an hour"

His ingenuity doesn't end with the prosthesis and peanut butter scams. He sports a hairstyle similar to that of boxing promoter, Don King, a style six to nine inches tall. The barber who styles this towering mass of hair says that the inmate comes in the evening before he's due to make a drug pick-up. He has the barber cut out a large pocket in the center of his hair, then styles an outer layer of hair back in place to hide the hole. Apparently, there's plenty of room for a good-sized packet of drugs.

Inmates who are really strung out, and won't trade sex for drugs, will trade or sell things bought for them by their families—sneakers, shirts, shoes, underwear, etc. Eventually, they run out of things to sell and have no money left in their commissary accounts to pay their drug bills. Often, their only option is running to the warden and asking for protective custody. Usually such inmates are transferred to another facility, and the inmate to whom he owes money is transferred to a different facility.

Even if inmates aren't addicted to drugs, alcohol or gay sex when they enter prison, they're prone to pick up the habits, especially if they have long sentences. Although I have no firsthand knowledge of these things, so many inmates have shared with me that I have no doubt they exist as described.

Further evidence of the validity of these inmates' stories is as follows.

October 27. 1995—four correction officers at the Atlanta Federal Prison were indicted on charges of trying to smuggle marijuana, cocaine and heroin into the prison

Since 1989—thirteen staff members at a Pennsylvania prison have been arrested on charges of trying to smuggle drugs. Eleven prisoners have died at this facility from drug overdoses and urine tests show that at least 20% of the inmates are using drugs.

March, 1995—three prisoners were found in their cells with assorted needles and syringes, unconscious from drug overdoses. Before serving time at Eglin, I wouldn't have believed what an expensive joke on American taxpayers the prison system has become. Now, there's no doubt in my mind, and it's obvious to me the American government isn't serious about winning the war on drugs.

Elected officials, as well as those hoping to be elected, talk rough on crime. New laws are passed, resulting in the conviction & more alleged drug offenders. Those convicted are crammed into ready overcrowded prisons where it's probably easier to obtain rugs than it was on the streets

Officials resist legalizing drugs, ostensibly on moral and ethical grounds. But alcohol is considered an insidiously dangerous rug by professional personnel associated with drug abuse treatment and rehabilitation programs. Half a century ago alcohol as made illegal, creating a large and lucrative black market for any ne willing to risk making or selling it. Officials finally threw in the dwel and repealed the Prohibition law when they realized they couldn't gain control of the monster they had created

No, I am not advocating legalizing marijuana, cocaine, etc., but think about what would happen if drugs were legalized and sold nder even stricter guidelines than alcoholic beverages. Gigantic profits would be taken away from the current drug trade, thus rippling and eventually destroying trafficking networks. Arrests and convictions for drug-related offenses would dwindle drastically, egating the need for the large numbers of police officers, drug Agents, lawyers, and support personnel currently involved with various aspects of the drug dinosaur. Prison overcrowding would e reduced, and the need for extra prison employees to handle the overload would be eliminated.

Over a period of time, the government could save trillions f dollars. But this ain't gonna happen in my lifetime. *Drugs and prisons are BIG business.*

Prisons have become taxpayer-supported crime colleges here inmates can get excellent on-the-job training in such subjects s drug procurement, obtaining sexual gratification of any kind or description, robbing banks, embezzling, making crack, counterfeiting, telemarketing scams, and an almost endless list of other crime skills. Inmates may not be given diplomas when they're released, but they'll be among the best-educated criminals anywhere.

DEAN AND GENE

Dean and Gene, twins, only 5 feet tall, were probably as popular with the inmates as anyone in camp. They were always in the company of "Big John," a 6-foot, 7-inch tall, black man, a former pro-football player. Dean and Gene told everyone they were his "bodyguards."

According to the twins, Dean owned a fifty-foot trawler used for commercial fishing. One day, Gene asked Dean to loan him the boat for the day to be used for some friends. Dean was going to be out of town for a few days, so he obliged.

During the course of the day, Gene and his friends sailed into federal waters, unbeknown to them. After about an hour of fishing, the coast guard approached them and came on board. Gene and his friends had in their possession $6,000 worth of legal fish and 66 groupers that were less than 20 inches long. According to Gene, federal regulations prohibit the possession of a grouper less than 20 inches.

The government seized the trawler, valued at $100,000, the $6,000 worth of fish, and three years later, indicted Dean and Gene for conspiracy to commit fraud.

Even though Dean had been out of town, he was the owner of the trawler and was given an option to plead guilty and be sentenced to four (4) months in prison or go to court and take a chance on being sentenced to five to seven years. Dean and Gene plead guilty, forfeited the boat, and the $6,000 that the fish brought and went to Eglin for four months. Justice served, our waterways made safer, and it only cost the taxpayers $25,000.

MAIL CALL AND LAWRENCE

Like everyone else away from home, inmates look forward to mail call. About three-thirty every afternoon, a prison officer hands out the mail. If you get a letter, it's the high point of the day. But a lot of inmates don't. Many go for days without getting mail. A few never do.

I was lucky. On some days, I received as many as seventeen letters— some from people I didn't know but who had heard of my case and had written a letter of encouragement and support. If there was a return address, I answered them.

One afternoon, Lawrence, an inmate with whom I had become friends, sat next to me at mail call. We had met each other's families on visiting days and both attended the same university, Louisiana State in Baton Rouge. Lawrence had been a C.P.A. for over 20 years when he was indicted for conspiracy. At the time, he was an elder in the Presbyterian Church, president of a civic group, a little league coach, and owner of an accounting firm, a prominent and well-respected member of his community.

According to Lawrence, a long-time client asked him to prepare a financial statement in order to secure a $500,000 loan at a local bank. Lawrence's firm prepared the statement, using figures supplied by the client. The loan was approved, based on the financial statement his firm prepared. Shortly after the loan was approved, the bank went into receivership and was taken over by the FDIC (Federal Deposit Insurance Corporation).

The loan made to Lawrence's client was among those audited after the takeover. Auditors discovered that the client had neglected to list some of his large liabilities on the financial statement. Whether the omission was intentional or not, Lawrence and his client were both charged with conspiracy to defraud a bank.

Lawrence's client happened to be the personal friend of a high-ranking official in New Orleans, and this official just happened to be a friend of the right person in the court system. The client was offered probation if he would plead guilty and testify that Lawrence knew the information on the financial statement was false. He did, and got his probation.

By contrast, Lawrence was told he would be wise to plead guilty and take a 24-month sentence; otherwise, they told him, if the case went to trial, he could get ten years or more. Fearful at the prospect of getting such a long prison term, he pled guilty. He lost his reputation, his business, and two years out of his life away from his wife and children.

Taxpayers will end up spending over $50,000 for those two years out of Lawrence's life. Do you wonder, like I do, how this serves justice?

THE DAY MARY SANG

Sunday, February 18, 1996 was one of the most memorable days I ever spent at Eglin. It was the day Mary sang.

For whatever reason, when I arrived at Eglin in May 1994, there was a policy prohibiting family members from taking part in the singing programs at prison religious services. At that time, there was only one inmate who played piano for the services, four or five regular choir members, and a couple of special singers who made up the rest of the musical group. The average attendance at Sunday services was about fifty.

The pianist read music but couldn't play "by ear" (accompany a singer without written music). For me, it was just the opposite. I read very little music, but could accompany most singers without it. Usually, I was able to play any song after hearing it only once or twice. This makes it easier for both singer and player.

Word traveled fast about the new inmate who could play gospel music, southern (quartet) style, and before I could turn around, I was the new assistant piano player. At first, I played mostly for the special singers. Interest in the services grew as the beat and spirit of the good old gospel songs rang through the air. More and more inmates volunteered to sing solos and asked to join the choir. They liked working with someone who helped make the singing easier, more relaxed and even fun.

A few months later, when the regular pianist was transferred to another prison camp, I took his place. About the same time, the civilian choir director took a leave of absence, and left me holding the bag. Fortunately as a member of the Chaplain's Protestant Council, I had a little clout, allowing me to do things different from the norm.

Charles, a chiropractor who had been charged with fraud, was sentenced to Eglin. It happened he had also been a professional blues singer with a broad musical background. He eagerly agreed to fill in as temporary choir director, and the two of us were able to turn the music program around.

I doubt there are many church choirs which have a convicted blues singer directing, a convicted politician serving as pianist and an odd assortment of other people convicted of a multitude of crimes singing and playing at every service. But it worked for us.

Within two months our choir membership was running about 15-20 singers, and there were several new soloists backed up by a couple of newly formed quartets. We also recruited several drummers, a bass player, a guy who played a mean lead guitar and a harmonica player. The icing on the cake was Richard, a dentist who came to Eglin during all the recruiting. He turned out to be at least as talented on the piano as he probably had been with a dental drill, leaving me free to play the electric (piano) keyboard

There's a very special feeling you get from gospel music. Once you start singing and clapping your hands in time to the music, it's almost impossible to be depressed because it just plain makes you feel good. I think that feeling kept inmates coming back to services time after time, and the news spread around the compound. Charles and I weren't bashful about helping things along. Every Sunday morning we opened the back doors of the chapel and used the public address system to send music out all over the compound.

Within six months Sunday morning attendance had increased to more than 125.

Over a year after I became involved in the music program, the Chaplain was transferred to another prison facility and replaced by Reverend Minster, an Assembly of God preacher. Chaplain Minster gave excellent sermons and really loved music. Inmates were delighted when, a few weeks after his arrival, he changed the policy prohibiting family member participation. I was especially glad because my wife, Mary, and I love to sing and have sung in a gospel group called "The Pioneers" for more than 25 years. We've also done a lot of singing and playing in our church, Cherry Street Church of God, in Talladega.

On February 18, 1996, I was scheduled to sing a special. It just so happened that Mary was scheduled to visit that weekend. I realized it was a golden opportunity to substitute her in my place on the program. The Sunday bulletin was printed as usual, listing me to sing the special song. When the time came for me to sing, I told the congregation I wanted Mary to sing instead, and that I would join the other musicians to accompany her on the keyboard.

I handed the mike to Mary, walked over to the keyboard, and glanced around the chapel. The ushers had set up 200 chairs for the service, but so many inmates came that they had to set up 25 more. Every seat was filled and inmates standing against the walls. When they opened the back doors of the chapel there were over 50 more standing outside.

Then Mary started to sing. Her clear, sweet voice filled the air with the wonderful words of an old gospel.

Trials dark on every hand, and we cannot understand.

All the way that God will lead us, to that blessed promised land,

But He'll guide us with His eye, and we'll follow until we die,

We will understand it, better by and by."

A surge of feeling ran through the inmates like the swell of an ocean wave. They couldn't sit still as the power of the music seemed to lift their very bones. Soon everyone was clapping in time to the music, and when the choir joined Mary on the chorus, every single inmate came to his feet. She immediately went into the chorus of another song

"Jesus on the main line, tell Him what you want,

Call him up and tell Him what you want.

The tempo increased, the music swelled. The inmates were singing, clapping their hands and some were even shouting. The music made them feel so good they weren't about to let Mary stop.

She had to do two encores before they let her hand over the mike to Chaplain Minster. The response was so great, I wondered if they would lock her up for conspiracy. Not only did they not lock Mary up, but Chaplain Minster asked her to sing again in the following month. As he closed out the service, he said it was the largest attendance ever recorded at a prison service.

I looked out over the audience while Mary was singing, and didn't see drug dealers, bank robbers, convicted lawyers, doctors, politicians, or bank presidents. I saw human beings, people written off by society but not written off by God. I couldn't help wondering if the devil was in a phone booth somewhere, dialing 911 and begging for relief (mercy).

JOSE'

The "BOCCI Court" is utilized more by the older inmates than some of the other games. BOCCI is a very enjoyable game and requires very little physical ability.

Jose', an 80-year-old inmate was seen daily with his rake, shovel, and bucket getting the court ready for the inmates. This was the job he had been assigned upon arrival at Eglin. He was extremely efficient and took a lot of pride in seeing that the court was just right. Unless the temperature was extremely cold, Jose was always without a shirt, his overweight, suntanned body exposed. The BOCCI court consisted of a dirt strip, approximately 50 feet long and four feet wide. There was a one-inch by four-inch wood board imbedded in the ground that ran the length of the dirt strip. The object of the game was to roll a small rubber ball to the end of the court and then take round wooden balls that looked like miniature bowling balls and roll them down to where the rubber ball lay. If a player hit the rubber ball with the wooden ball, he received four points. The wooden ball stopping closest to the rubber ball received one point. The player who received twenty-five points first won. The BOCCI court is within ten feet of the area where the stationary bicycles are located.

As I was finishing up my daily, early morning bicycle ride, I observed Jose' working on the court. "How are you this morning?" I asked. "Fine," he responded. I had heard through the grapevine" that Jose' would be leaving soon. "Heard you were a short timer."

"Yep, leaving in four months." I stopped peddling, and as the wheels of the bike stopped turning, I slid off and walked over to where Jose' was working. He had his rake and was leveling the dirt.

"How long you been at Eglin?" I asked. "Three years," he responded. Walking beside him as he moved the length of the court, Jose told me he had been in the "system" six years. He was 73 years of age when arrested.

Jose' had been a supplier for heroin for over twenty years. His dealings were overseas. He had not sold any heroin in the U.S.

"How did you get caught?" I asked.

"Seven pair of pants," he responded. Jose laughed and repeated, "Seven pair of pants got me seven years and cost me $490,000."

According to Jose', he owned four garment factories two in China and two in Japan. He had buyers from all over the world that purchases pants. He would sew their label inside the pants and ship them.

For twenty years, he had been taking packets of heroin, sewing them into one of the pockets of the pants, and shipping to his drug customers. Each pocket contained $70,000 worth of heroin. Jose' had several customers in the United States that purchased from him but were not into the drug scene.

Jose' concluded this wild story by saying that seven pair of pants with the heroin sewed into the pocket got mixed up in an order going to an American customer. When the customer discovered the heroin, the authorities were called, and Jose' was arrested. Jose' said the prosecutor told him, that due to his age, if he would plead guilty, he would ask the judge to only sentence him to seven years. Jose pled guilty.

As I started to leave, Jose said, "When I get out, I'm going to write a book about 'Seven Pair of Pants'"

BEN

On September 2, 1996, the day of our annual Labor Day barbecue cookout, when we finished stuffing ourselves, several inmates had a tennis play-off. Ben Cain, a 62-year-old black man, about 5' 8", 135 pounds, was an ex-semi-pro tennis player. The games began and lasted until late that night. Ben ended up playing fifteen consecutive sets. He was incredible he was unbeatable.

About 8:30 the next morning, I walked by Ben's dorm on the way to the law library. My mind was on the research I needed to do for my upcoming appeal, but a crowd of staff members and inmates gathered around someone lying on the ground caught my attention.

"What happened?" I asked one of the inmates.

"Ben's dead," he said sadly. "He was sitting on a bench outside Dorm 3, and he just fell over."

I moved in closer and saw that the paramedics from Eglin Air Force Base and our camp medical personnel were working together, trying to get Ben breathing again. Minutes after I arrived, Chaplain Minster pushed his way through the crowd, barely acknowledging inmates who were trying to tell him about Ben. He made his way to where Ben lay so still and unmoving. I wasn't close enough to hear what he said, but I saw him reach down and touch Ben's foot as he bowed his head and prayed.

I guess my time sense was distorted; everyone appeared to be moving in slow motion, but it seemed only seconds before medical personnel loaded Ben on a stretcher and shoved him through the rear door of the ambulance. According to inmates who were on the scene from the time Ben was found, the combined medical team had worked on him for approximately thirty minutes.

With heavy heart, I watched the ambulance move away toward Eglin Air Force Base Hospital where Ben would be officially pronounced dead. Inmates rarely died in camp. They always died "in route to the hospital" or in the hospital. Prison officials probably thought it was easier on the families not to say that their loved ones had died in prison.

Word travels fast in a prison camp, so it wasn't long before the members of various prayer groups were praying for Ben. I heard one of the inmates say, "It's a little late to be praying for 'ole Ben now...he's already dead "

Later that morning, I met Chaplain Minister walking on the compound. "Hi, Larry. I've got some good news for you," he said. When Ben arrived in the emergency room, the medics were doing their final check of his vital signs before they pronounced him dead and detected a faint pulse and immediately put him on life support equipment. Now they're just waiting to see what happens."

Two days later, I stopped by the Chaplain's office. "What's the latest on Ben?"

The Chaplain looked up from some papers he was studying and said, "I saw him yesterday morning, and they had taken him off all the life support equipment. I could hardly believe it when I saw him sitting up in bed!"

"Does he remember what happened to him?"

"Partly. He says he remembers being in church Sunday, and he remembers playing tennis. But everything else is a blank. I told him God had spared his life for some reason and as soon as he felt up to it, I wanted him to share his experience with the other inmates during Sunday morning services," the Chaplain said

A few days later, Ben was flown to a medical center in another state for further observation and testing. All the tests were negative. Medical personnel were baffled. They found nothing wrong with Ben...no trace of damage to his heart...no damage to his brain. By rights, after thirty minutes of attempted resuscitation, even if it was successful, Ben should have been a vegetable. But he wasn't.

The miracle of Ben's resurrection brought the story of Lazarus to mind. Lazarus had been dead for four days, and Jesus "resuscitated" him. When Dr. Jesus heals, there is no damage to the to the heart, brain, or anything else!

FOSSI

"Precious Metals" are the words used to describe a building where several of the inmates work. According to Fossi, an employee at "Precious Metals," this is where all surplus equipment from various government agencies is shipped and stored until disposition.

There are several ways of disposing of these items: sell at public auction, private auction, sealed bids, contract with private business, or mark items as "destroyed" and give them to friends. "Precious Metals" is comprised of desks, chairs, computers, heavy equipment, and much more.

According to another inmate who works at "Precious

Metals," he has seen secretaries sabotage their computers in order to get a new modern one. These computers cost around $5,000 each and are sold for as little as $150.

Fossi shared with me that a trailer to haul chemicals in that cost the government $250,000 to purchase in 1979 was put on the market for $35,000. When it did not sell, the government spent $20,000 completely renovating the trailer and sold it for $7,000 to a friend of an elected official. There was a lot of speculation that the official was a silent partner in the business of the purchaser.

Fossi went on to tell about desks and chairs that cost the government $500 to - $700 a piece being sold for as little as $25 for the desks and $3 for the chairs.

According to Fossi, it is not unusual to carry truckloads of typewriters, adding machines, computers, and other office equipment out into the woods, dig holes with the bulldozer, and bury the equipment. Millions of dollars of equipment buried. All inmate employees are threatened with retaliation if they are caught telling about this operation.

THE THIRD YEAR BEGINS

I glanced at the calendar. How could it already be May 27, 1996--the beginning of my third year in prison? Although I always counted the days, time slipped by almost without my noticing. So much was happening, and I wondered if it would be possible to finish all the projects I had started in one more year. Of course, I hated being away from my wife, family, and friends. Loss of income was no fun either. But other than that, I wasn't doing too badly.

Thanks to my friend, Max Morris, I received cards and letters from all over the world Just answering all the correspondence from the W.W.P.P. (WorldWide Prayer Partners) could have kept me busy. But I also got mail from old and new friends in the Talladega area, and if there was a return address, I always answered. I appreciated each one having taken the time to write, and it helped make me feel more a part of what was going on at home.

The captain I worked for managed to get funds for a new air-conditioned barbershop, complete with state of the art equipment. I initiated the policy of making appointments for haircuts, and it worked out well. Inmates no longer had to wait in long lines for a turn with the barbers, leaving them free to do other things until time for their appointments.

The chapel's music program was going great. When former choir director, Carol Nations, returned from her leave, she continued the variety of music programs we had created. Prayer groups of every denomination were in full swing, and I ever decided to learn to play the trumpet. As a former politician, I figured I had enough hot air to make some kind of sound on the horn!

My third manuscript was nearly finished, and I put out feelers to a few publishers to see if they were interested. I even wrote a song. Thanks to Max Morris and Charles Towler, it was published in King's Praise songbook in March, 1996.

GOD ANSWER PRAYERS

Some people don't consider themselves to be religious, and may attribute the small miracles in their lives to coincidence or fate. But I believe that God answers prayers, and the small miracles which follow were a result of prayers.

On a Sunday in mid-June, 1996, 1 called Mary to check on things at home. After talking to her for a couple of minutes, I could tell something was bothering her--nearly forty years of marriage had given me a kind of marital ESP.

"What's wrong, Mary?" I asked. She hesitated, then said, "I hate to tell you, but the air conditioner quit working. I don't know what's wrong with it. I called George Ambrester Electric and left a message, but they haven't called back yet."

The central heating and cooling unit is over eleven years old—plenty old enough to have worn parts needing to be replaced or repaired. With only one income, Mary was already stretched to her limit with house payments, car maintenance, utilities and food. I was frustrated, knowing Mary had to face day-to-day problems alone, and I prayed it wasn't the compressor or motor, either of which can cost hundreds or even thousands of dollars to replace.

After talking to Mary, I went back to the dorm. I was glad my cube was empty because it was time to talk to God. Even though I believe God knows our problems, I needed to pray about Mary's difficult situation—she couldn't afford minor repairs, let alone a compressor or new motor. As I said, "Amen." I felt at peace, knowing that Mary was in more powerful hands than mine.

Monday morning I called Mary before she left for work.

"George Armbrester called," she said. "He's coming over to check the unit. He said he'd let me know what was wrong and how much it will cost … wait, hold on a minute."

Shortly, she came back, on the line. "What's the matter, Mary?" I asked. "I was trying to get my panty hose on while we were talking. The house is so hot, they keep sticking to my legs."

Monday night I called again to find out what George had said "After you hung up this morning, I decided to pray for that old air conditioner before I went to work. God must have been listening, because when I came home this evening the house was cool, and there was a note from George. It was only a minor problem after all" Three days later, Mary received a bill in the mail for only $85, and the payment wasn't due until the first of July.

When it rains, it pours, and a couple of days later the starter in the car went out. This cost Mary another $150. Billy Bartlett, owner and operator of the Talladega service station where Mary trades, said she could take all the time she needed to pay. Billy's that kind of person. Maybe that's why hundreds of people know they can depend on him for good car maintenance.

Two weeks later, just before the bills were due, a retired minister from Delaware, was inspired to send a $100 check to our friend, Max Morris. The minister requested that the check be sent to Mary. Mary and I have never met this man. We've never even been to Delaware. He found out about my imprisonment through Max and the W.W.P.P. (World Wide Prayer Partners).

A few days after that, a senior citizen I've known for thirty years, but with whom I have nothing in common—church, civic or socially—came to Mary's office at the Alabama Power Company and handed her $100.00. This lady had no way of knowing our financial need except through God. Yet, in spite of these generous gifts, Mary was still $35 short.

During the time all this was taking place, the car insurance premium was due. Mary had saved a little each week to pay the semi-annual premium. When Doug Camp's State Farm Insurance premium notice came, it had been reduced $50. Mary had just enough to pay the bills

Another week or so went by, and Mary discovered that holes had burned in the muffler of her car, and the tail pipe had rusted badly. Not only was it noisy, but also a potential danger from fumes coming into the car. She talked to me about it, and I suggested she contact my life-long friend, Reuben Sizemore, who owned a muffler shop in Talladega. He told her it would cost about $60 to replace the muffler and tail pipe. Mary gave him the go-ahead, hoping he wouldn't bill her for a few days.

The day Reuben did the work, a check came from Max Morris. The check was dated two days prior to Mary finding out she would have to have the muffler and tail pipe replaced. Her prayers were answered even before she uttered them. I found out about the straw that almost broke the proverbial camel's back on Labor Day.

When I called Mary that day she said, "Oh, Larry, there must be a black cloud hanging over my head--one of the caps on my teeth broke off. It was so old, it just crumbled." By now, she was almost in tears. "I talked to Dr. McKinney. He said it would be about $300.00 to fix it, and that doesn't even include the cost of the x-rays. Maybe I can get him to let me pay him monthly."

I suspected that she could. Dr. Tony McKinney has been our family dentist for years. Not only is he an excellent dentist, but he is also known for working with his patients. The dental work was scheduled to begin September 10th. On September 5th, while I was taking my daily two-mile walk and jog, something kept telling me to call

Mary. Normally, I don't call her until late evening, but the message in my head was so strong by 10:00 a.m. I could no longer resist and called her at work. When she realized it was me she became very excited and said, "Do you know what? Charles just came by the office and handed me an envelope. After he left, I opened it, and there was $500 in it!"

Mary and I both started crying. Charles is my brother. Mary had told no one about her dental problems except God, Dr. McKinney and me. God is the only one who could have talked to Charles and his wife, Gail, about Mary's need. Dr. McKinney and I sure didn't. Normally, our phone calls last only three or four minutes, at 23 cents a minute, it gets expensive fast. But Ma Bell picked up a little extra that day for crying time. So many miracles Some not so small. And there was one more little miracle yet to come.

Standing in line is a way of life at Eglin-to eat, brush your teeth, use the toilet, the shower, to go on sick call, do your laundry, etc. After talking to Mary, I went to the commissary and stood in line, waiting my turn. Ralph, an inmate and one of my barbershop customers, was right behind me.

"I don't really need anything today," he said, "but I wanted to get me a Blue Bell ice cream.

"Maybe I'll get one too," I said. Blue Bell ice cream is a favorite of all the inmates, and Blue Bell makes it all … vanilla, strawberry, chocolate, banana split, cookies and cream, to name a few. I've been a chocoholic as far back as I can remember, and my mouth watered just thinking about that luscious ice cream. While mayor at Talladega, I averaged going to the Dairy Queen or Fincher's Delite several times a week. The Finchers—Pansy, Wayne and their daughter, Renea owned a shop similar to a Dairy Queen and made chocolate malts so thick, I had to eat them with a spoon.

On top of that, my mother usually called two or three times a week to tell me she had made a chocolate cake (with batter and chocolate fudge icing made from scratch). It was good enough to wallow in. "I'm saving the pan to sop for you," she always told me. I think it's largely her fault that I became a "sop-oholic as well as a chocoholic. I can sop a pan clean better than anyone in the world. My chocolate-wallow daydream was interrupted by my turn to buy commissary items. After buying a few essentials like soap and stamps, there wasn't enough left in my account for the dreamed-of ice cream. I told myself I didn't really need the fattening ice cream anyway. Ralph must have noticed because when I got back to the dorm, he came in right behind me, holding two Blue Bells—my favorite— cookies and cream.

Seeing the expression on my face, he said, "I bought one for you for always keeping my hair looking so good." If I could have gotten inside that pint of ice cream, I would probably have one old-fashioned wallowing and sopping. I thanked Ralph and in my heart I thanked God for the ice cream and all He had done for Mary and me. Don't tell me God doesn't answer prayers

ANN WHITE WALLACE SURRETT

The second week in September 1996, the headlines of the *Daily Home read "SURRETT INDICTED FOR THEFT."* I had always been taught that vengeance belonged to the Lord, and as individuals, we were not supposed to get even... but to forgive someone for any wrong they had done to you. When you are serving time in prison for charges you are not guilty of, and this has been brought about by unscrupulous law enforcement officials, sometimes it is tough to forgive and not want to get even.

As I read the article that told how the former DA's Investigator, Ann White Wallace Surrett, a woman who once helped build criminal cases against others in Talladega County now faces criminal charges herself for stealing more than $100,000 from the District Attorney's office and the 29th Judicial Drug Task Force, I was elated and I also felt compassion. Even though Ann Surrett, along with her husband, Dennis, had been less than honest in helping get me convicted, I knew what she was facing if convicted and sent to prison.

As I read the *Daily Home* news article about how Ann allegedly had used the stolen funds to pay off her VISA, American Express, and Spiegel accounts, as well as purchase household items, clothing, and other items, my thoughts returned to what Policewoman Jamie Grace, Director of UNO, shared with me about a week prior to her being found dead. *"Mayor, there is some money and drugs missing from the DA.'s office and Dennis and Ann are blaming me for it. They are vicious, especially Ann. She has threatened me."*

As I continued to read the article how Assistant Attorney General Bruce Liberman was successful in obtaining three indictments against Ann to include four counts of first-degree theft of property, two counts of fraudulent use of credit cards, and nine counts of possession of a forged instrument, in my mind I reasoned that maybe this was the beginning of pay back time for the way Jamie Grace, myself, and hundreds of others had been mistreated through the years by Ann White Wallace Surrett.

According to Assistant A.G. Liberman, even though Dennis Surrett, the husband of Ann and also an investigator for the D.A., had not been implicated or indicted, I wondered how he could work side by side with his wife, sleep, eat, and live with her and not be aware of her new-found wealth. *If Dennis is that naive, then why don't the D.A. fire him, or does Dennis and Ann know too much about the D.A., I thought.*

In view of the indictment and ongoing investigation, I decided to write a letter to Attorney General Sessions and request he re-open an investigation into the death of Jamie Grace. Mr.

Sessions had only been in office for a short while but was making an impact on the state of Alabama in his effort to help clean up the state from corrupt elected officials. Mr. Sessions also was a candidate for the U. S. Senate seat that was being vacated by retiring Senator Howell Heflin due to his retirement.

The following is the letter:

September 16, 1996

Honorable Jeff Sessions

Attorney General

Montgomery, Alabama

Dear Mr. Sessions,

On August 3, 1992, an African American lady by the name of Jamie Grace was found dead at her apartment from what Talladega County D.A. Robert Rumsey stated was suicide. Ms. Grace served as head of United Narcotics Operation (UNO) under the direction of Mr. Rumsey.

At the time of the death of Ms. Grace, I was in my third term (9th) year as mayor of Talladega. Based on what Ms. Grace had shared with me a few days prior to her death, and information provided me after her death, by an informant by the name of Jerry Jackson, I had reason to doubt that Ms. Grace committed suicide. I made a verbal complaint to then Attorney General Jimmy Evans and was assured he would check into my complaint. I learned later that Mr. Evans and D.A. Rumsey were best of buddies, and I never heard any thing from Mr. Evans.

A few months after my complaint was registered with Mr. Evans, 1 became the target of an investigation and was eventually charged with one count of fraud and 26 counts of money laundering of $5,925 which was paid to Jerry Jackson. I was convicted by a federal judge and sentenced to fifty-one months. I am presently in my twenty-eighth month at Eglin A.F.B. prison camp, and scheduled to be released in 97, so this is not an attempt to have my sentence reduced

I am enclosing a document for your consideration and I have additional information that deserves consideration that I feel will prove Ms. Grace did not commit suicide.

I respectively request an investigator from your office contact me and let me share with them what I know. Once this is done, I trust you will conduct your own investigation and learn that Ms. Grace was murdered and made to look like suicide. I strongly believe that one or more persons connected with Mr. Robert Rumsey was involved in this cover-up.

Thank you in advance for your assistance to my request and concern.

Sincerely yours,

Larry Barton 19228-001
P.0 600-Dorm 5-F.P.C.
Eglin A.F.B., Fla., 32542

On or about September 28,1996, I received the following letter:

October 21, 1996

Dear Mr. McFadden,

I learned today that the autopsy report on Jamie Grace reveals there was no powder burn test performed. Wonder why?

As a former mortuary science student and a partner in a local funeral home, I know that the standard procedure in an autopsy on the person who died from a gunshot wound would be:

1. Determine the trajectory of the bullet by entry and exit wound(s),

2. Test for powder burns around wound(s).

Testing for powder burns would be common and necessary for determining the possibility of suicide.

I also recall a conversation with a police officer who indicated the gun allegedly used in the death of Jamie is not the same weapon she normally carried

I don't want to bother you, but I am convinced that Jamie Grace was murdered, and I want the person(s) responsible brought to justice.

Once again, thanks for everything you are doing.

Larry Barton 19228-001
P.0 600-Dorm 5-F.P.C.
Eglin A.F.B., Fla., 32542-7606

In the fall of 1996, Attorney General Jeff Sessions was elected to the U.S. Senate. Having received no further correspondence from anyone about my request, I wrote the following letter to the new Attorney General.

February 4, 1997

Dear Mr. Pryor:

First of all, congratulations on being appointed to serve as Attorney General. I know you will do an outstanding job. Secondly, on September 16, 1996, I wrote a letter to then Attorney General Sessions requesting an investigation in the death of former Chief of U.N.O.

(United Narcotic Organization) Jamie Grace

On September 26, 1996, Mr. Sessions acknowledged receipt of my letter through correspondence from Mr. Edward F. McFadden, Chief Investigator.

Since the letter of September 26, 1996, even though I have forwarded three letters containing information that I felt would benefit him in his investigation, I have not received any further correspondence.

Mr. Pryor, I am confident that Ms. Jamie Grace did not commit suicide, and I hope all effort will be made to bring her murderer to justice.

Please don't permit this outrageous act to be swept under the rug. like it has so far.

Thank you in advance for your assistance and I would appreciate it if you could bring me up-to-date on the investigation.

Sincerely,

Larry Barton 19228-001
P.O. Box 600-Dorm 5-FPC
Eglin AFB, Fla., 32542-7606

MOTHER

My mother celebrated her 85th birthday December 15, 1996. She has been blessed with good health all her life, but lately, I had noticed a problem with her writing in the letters she wrote to me, and her voice sounded weak when we talked on the phone.

Near the end of the Christmas holidays, I called Mother, and my sister, Edith, answered the phone. At first, I thought I had dialed Edith's number by mistake.

"You have the right number. I'm at Mother's house," Edith said

"What are you doing there at this time of day?" I asked.

Edith began to cry and said, "I think Mother has a problem. You know her back is still weak from that slipped disc surgery she had a few years ago. " Edith stopped a moment, took a deep breath, and continued.

"She got into the bathtub and couldn't get back out."

"What?" I asked, shocked by what Edith said.

"Well, I called her several times. When she didn't answer, I got worried. I told Elvin (Edith's husband) about it and asked him to go with me to check on her.

"The front door was locked, so I used my key to get in.

We ran through the house calling to her, and when we got near the bathroom, I heard her faintly calling out to us. We rushed to the door, but it was locked, too.

"Mother!" I yelled through the door, "What in the world happened?"

"You know the habit I got into of folding my legs under me in the tub after I had my surgery?" Her voice was so weak I had to put my ear against the door to hear her.

"I remember."

"Well, they went to sleep, and I couldn't get them back out from under me. That's why I wasn't able to get out of the tub. I'm sorry about the door. I always lock it when I'm taking a bath.

"Don't worry, Mother. Well call Glenn, our handyman's son. He can bring over some tools to use on the door. You just hang on."

"I'm okay.

I drained the water out of the tub, but I'm getting awfully cold."

After Glenn got the door open, Edith wrapped Mother in a blanket. Glenn and Elvin lifted her out of the tub an easy task since Mother only weighs about 100 pounds. She was so chilled that she was on the verge of shock, and we were somewhat concerned that her legs might be partially paralyzed, but after a few days, she bounced right back.

Mother has lived alone ever since my Dad passed away in 1991. They had been married more than fifty years when he died. She did amazingly well by herself until the bathtub incident. After that, Edith urged her to take extra precautions like not sitting down on a low couch or chair for fear she couldn't get up. Everything went smoothly for a while, but several days later when I made my daily call to Mother, Edith answered again.

"Are you off for lunch?" I asked.

"No, it's Mother again. She's been getting weaker, and it seems like her memory has gotten worse. Elvin and I were worried about her, so he went over to check on her, but couldn't get in because the front door was locked. He said he knocked real loud several times and heard Mother's voice, but couldn't tell where it was coming from. He walked around the side of the house to the bedroom window and hollered again. This time he heard her voice coming from the bedroom. She said she was on the floor and couldn't get up

"That's when Elvin called me, and I brought the house key over. We went in and found Mother on her knees by her bed. She told us that in spite of the trouble she's been having with her knees, about nine last night she decided to kneel down and say her prayers. Just like I've done all my life and then couldn't get up. Oh, Larry, we didn't get into the house until around nine this morning. Poor Mother was trapped on her knees for twelve hours! Thank God, the thermostat was set high enough or she might have frozen to death."

During all this time, my efforts to get Mother to go for a check-up had been useless. Although she had a doctor, she hardly ever went to see him.. All her life she had trusted in God to heal her, and her faith never wavered. I love and respect Mother and believe God can do anything, but I also know that God helps those who help themselves. Her health was failing, and she needed some medical attention-a physical exam and blood tests, at the very least.

Not long after I talked to Edith, I got a poorly written, fatalistic letter from Mother. At the end of the letter she wrote, "Son, I hope God will let me live until you come home." That broke my heart. I called her the next day. "How are you feeling, Mother?" I asked.

"Who is this?" Her voice sounded weak and distant.

"It's me. Larry. Are you OK?"

"Where are you?" she asked, evidently confused.

Being in prison away from family is bad enough when everyone is well, but when your own Mother is so ill she can't remember who or where you are, it's too much. I called Edith immediately after talking to Mother and insisted she make a doctor's appointment for Mother so we could find out what was going on.

Later that week, Mother was examined and blood tests were done. The tests and exam showed that she had a severe bladder infection—so bad that the bacteria had spread throughout her body, affecting her entire system. The doctor gave her some strong antibiotics, told her to drink lots of fluids and to rest as much as possible. No one knew if the infection would have a permanent effect on Mother. *Even if the medicine cleared it up, would she survive? If so, would her memory return? Would she regain her strength and better use of her legs?*

All these questions ran through my mind as I lay in my cubicle that night, and I began to hear the nagging, but persistent voice of the Devil telling me that Mother was finished ... that God had let her down. "She won't live until you get home," the devilish voice told me. "You'll never see her again." I tossed and turned and finally got up, turned on the small reading light, and opened my Bible. And there it was... the story I needed to read… in II. Kings, 20: 1-11, the story about King Hezekiah being sick. He was apparently very ill because the prophet, Isaiah, came to him and said, "Put your house in order for you will not recover. You are going to die." Hezekiah turned his face to the wall and prayed, ". O Lord, remember how I have walked before thee in truth and with a perfect heart..." Hezekiah wept bitterly.

Then, just before Isaiah left the king's house, God spoke to Then, just before Isaiah lef the king's house, God spoke to him and told him to go back and say to Hezekiah,...I have heard thy prayer and .. will heal thee." God not only added fifteen years to Hezekiah's life, but also delivered him and his city from the hand of his enemy, the king of Assyria.

Thoughtfully, I closed my Bible and began to pray. Weaving Hezekiah's story through my prayer, I compared Mother's situation to his sixty years of faithful Christian service, tithing, supporting her church, teaching Sunday school, singing in the choir, and trusting in God for everything. I felt in my heart that she was just as deserving of being healed and enjoying a few more years of life as Hezekiah had been, and I made my feelings part of my prayer.

When I finished praying I called Max Morris and described Mother's condition to him. I asked him to alert the WorldWide Prayer Partners to pray for her. For the first time, I felt at peace about the situation.

After our last scare with Mother, I was concerned that the infection might have caused some kind of residual damage and asked Edith to arrange a complete x-ray exam with a doctor recommended by my brother Charles' son, Dennis. On the day the scan was scheduled I called Mother and she informed me, "This is a waste of time. The doctor is going to find that I'm okay."

Obviously, her memory was better, and she certainly hadn't lost her faith in God's healing power! Edith, Charles, and my son, Delane, all went with Mother for the scan. It took quite a while, and afterward the doctor spent some more time going over the results. When he finally called everyone into his office he said, "For an 85year-old woman, Mrs. Barton is in excellent health. Other than a little brain shrinkage which is normal as we age, I can't find a thing wrong with her."

When Mother told me the results of the scan, I thanked God for what He had done. She had been forced to go to the doctor, but her faith in God never wavered

On Saturday, April 19th, Edith and Mary brought Mother for a visit. I hadn't seen Edith and Mother since October or Mary since Christmas. I was so glad they had come on Saturday because I was allowed to visit with them for six hours both days of the weekend. Other than being a little weaker than normal, Mother seemed to be her old self again.

My newfound ability to play the trumpet had progressed so well that in the Sunday morning service I was able to play

"How Great Thou Art," accompanied by Dr. Richard. Afterward, the inmates wanted Mary to sing all their favorite songs: *"Bye and Bye," "When the Morning Comes,"* and *"Jesus on the Main Line, Tell Him What You Want."*

Just before Mary sang I told the audience that this would probably be the last time my family would visit. I had a certain release date of September 9th, but since I was going back to court for re-sentencing, I might be leaving even sooner. I turned to Mother and asked her to say a few words. She shared some experiences she's had over the years, which she felt clearly illustrated how good God had been to her. And she told them how she had come to love all the friends she had made on her visits to see me. While she spoke my thoughts flashed back to that dark night when I could hear the Devil in my mind, mocking me with the words, "She will not live until you get home. You will not see her again." But I did see her again, thanks to her unwavering faith and the prayers of people around the world

Mother sat down and Mary began to sing the old hymns. As usual, everyone stood up and sang along with her. My heart filled with joy, uplifted by the music, and I silently gave thanks for my Mother's life and the hope I had been given for a reduced sentence.

It was a wonderful visit, but like all of them, over all too quickly. Mary, Edith and Mother were saying their good-byes, but Mother broke down when she hugged me and said, "Oh, Larry, I love you so. I wish you could leave now and go back with us."

My throat ached with unshed tears. "It won't be long now, Mother. I'll be home soon, and I'm going to be there to help when you celebrate your 100th birthday." Nothing is impossible with God, and I believe He will give her the fifteen years that will bring her to that birthday.

COWBOY BANDIT

One evening, a new inmate sauntered into the poolroom where several of us were gathered. We stared because he looked like a teenager—too young to be at Club Fed. He glanced around and sat down next to an inmate named Bill.

Bill turned to me, grinned and said, "Larry, meet Larry. This young fella' is living proof that if you had robbed a few banks, you'd have gotten a lighter sentence."

"Are you really a bank robber, or is Bill pulling my leg?" I asked young Larry.

"No, Bill's right. It's true. If you're really interested, I'll tell you how it happened."

I was interested and I told him so.

"Okay. Well, I used to be in the construction business and made over $100,000 a year. There was an accident, and I broke my back. I had lots of pain and a long hospital stay. While I recuperated, I got hooked on morphine. When I got out, my back wasn't good enough for me to keep on managing a construction business, and I had a drug addiction to boot. To make matters worse, my wife got hooked, too.

"How did that happen?" I asked.

"Oh, she said the drugs helped her cope with the stress of all the financial problems we were having. It was a bad scene.

Things had gotten to the point that we needed about $1,200 a week just for drugs. With no income and two drug habits to support, I lost my business and eventually my house as well. We had to move in with my mother.

"My mother loves me, but she wasn't all that thrilled to have me, my wife, and the kids coming down on her. We were completely out of money. I racked my brain for ways to get some, and finally, in desperation, decided to rob a bank. I talked it over with my wife, and after the initial shock of the idea, she was willing to go along with it-she pretty much did whatever I wanted to do.

"We were very nervous the day we robbed our first bank, but we'd gone over the plan so many times, we were sure it would work "

"How did you do it?" I asked.

"Simple. First, we drove around until we found a bank staffed with mostly female employees. We figured they wouldn't be as likely to chase me after the robbery and would probably scare easier. We also checked for banks with lots of trees and shrubbery around them. We figured that way, I could take cover if I needed to, and the bank employees couldn't see which way I went when I left the bank.

"The other important thing to our plan was that the bank had to be within walking distance of a Wal-mart or some other big shopping center parking lot. That way, we figured the Bronco wouldn't be noticed parked with all the other cars. Plus, it was an easy walk to the bank."

"Before a bank job I always let my beard grow out for four or five days and then used some dark spray stuff I mail-ordered to make it look even heavier. I guess the idea of robbing banks made me feel like Jesse James because I decided to wear cowboy clothes.

You know, faded jeans, a checkered shirt, and a big brimmed hat pulled low over my eyes. That's why they started calling me the 'Cowboy Bandit."

"Do you have any pictures of yourself in disguise?" I asked.

"Sure. I'll show you one tomorrow," he said.

"Did your wife go with you into the bank?"

"No. After we spotted the right bank, we'd drive around town until we found a Bronco the same model and color as ours, steal the license tags, and put them on our Bronco. Then, we parked the Bronco in the parking lot we'd located near the bank.

"While I walked to the bank, my wife stayed near the Bronco and used the nearest phone booth to call in a phony emergency to the police or sheriff's office. She always made it sound so bad, they'd think lots of officers needed to respond.

"Meanwhile, I was entering the target bank, acting like any ordinary customer. I'd get in line and make friendly conversation with the other customers. The only difference was, when my turn came at the teller window, I gave them a handwritten note instead of making a deposit or withdrawal."

"What kind of note?"

"Well, I usually wrote the note on the back of one of their bank forms. It said something like, Put all your money in a bag.

Leave out all the dye packs. (Packets of money covered with a dye invisible to the naked eye but apparent when a black light is shined on the hands of anyone who's handled it.) Hand me the bag. Don't try any funny stuff because my partners are across the street watching you. Then I'd give them a crooked cowboy grin and saunter out the door.

"I never stayed in a bank more than a couple of minutes. That gave me a small safety margin in case I didn't notice someone hitting a silent alarm. It takes police three to five minutes to respond—even to an emergency call."

Cowboy Bandit Larry told me that he never actually had partners other than his wife and no weapons of any kind. But the bank personnel didn't know that.

"What did you do after you left the bank?" I asked.

"That's when the cover of trees and shrubs around the bank came in handy. I was able to slip away behind them and go directly back to the Bronco. My wife and I would drive around for a while to make sure no one followed us. Then we'd pull into another parking lot or service station, replace the stolen tags with our own, and go home "

"How many bank jobs were you able to pull off before you got caught?"

"Well, we pulled eleven jobs without a hitch, using the same old plan every time. But our luck ran out on number twelve."

"What happened?"

"I think we got too cocky. On that last job, we didn't take time to call in the usual phony report to the police. Just as I left the bank, one of the tellers hit a silent alarm. I guess we were meant to be caught that day because a city detective just happened to be driving by, saw me leaving the bank, and followed at a distance.

I got into the Bronco, and we drove away, never knowing we'd been made. By the time we got half a mile down the road, cops were coming at us from every direction. We were surrounded."

Cowboy Bandit Larry's story was already bizarre, but there was a final twist. The F.B.I. had no real evidence proving that he and his wife were involved in the other eleven robberies, so they offered the couple a deal. If they would plead guilty to all twelve bank jobs, he and his wife would only get three years and would only have to serve part of the sentence. Of course, they accepted the offer.

Bill turned to me and said, "Don't you wish you had robbed some banks? Cowboy Bandit will be home before you are."

I couldn't answer. A wave of bitterness came over, me. How could our justice system force someone like me to serve more time for a $5,900 crime I didn't commit than a guy who robbed twelve banks and walked away with over $250,000?

BEN IS BACK

On Friday, January 17, 1997, Ben Cain, the inmate who had been pronounced dead in September 1996, and then having been revived had returned from Rochester, Minn.

On Sunday Morning January 19, Ben was in chapel service and Chaplain Minster requested he give his testimony.

Prior to Ben speaking, Chaplain Minster stated that when he first heard about Ben's situation in September, he had walked over to where Ben was lying on the cot. "I knew it looked bad. The thought kept running through my mind that it would be my responsibility to notify Ben's wife and family that he had died in prison," he said.

Chaplain Minster continued. "As the medics was preparing to place Ben in the ambulance, I was able to touch his foot and I asked God to restore life back to Ben. Upon returning to my office, even though I had prayed asking God to restore life, I had doubts. I knew God could and I knew prayer groups over the compound were praying. All I could think of was having to notify Ben's family."

As the Chaplain continued, he shared with the congregation how he had visited the Talladega prison facility and at that time was having trouble with diabetes. There were a group of inmates who had a prayer group and they learned about me being sick while at Talladega and wanted to pray for me. "God healed me and I have not had any more problems with diabetes," he said.

Chaplain Minster went on to tell that later in the day, he received a phone call sharing with him that Ben was alive. The medical personnel were baffled and had no other details other than Ben was alive. "For the next few days, I visited Ben and talked with him. I shared with him that God had spared his life for some reason and when he returned to camp, I wanted him to give his testimony." Ben was transferred to Minn. a few days later.

As Ben Cain walked to the pulpit, the inmates and their family that packed the chapel came to their feet giving Ben and God a standing ovation. Tears were streaming down Ben's face as he began to address the audience. Ben had prepared the following typewritten comments.

Good morning, everyone, and a Happy New Year to those I have not spoken with since my return to Eglin. I have written a short thank you note for all that were instrumental in saving my life last September '96'. My mind is not as functional as it was, so I feel setter reading to you what I wrote, so I won't forget.

First of all, I'd like to express my appreciation to those mates and staff members who greeted me when I returned to the compound on Friday night. I am very grateful to know that all of You exemplified a great deal of sympathy and sorrow for me while I was unconscious and also during my stay in the hospital. The concern all of you showed toward my family, my wife, and my children were more than remarkable and I very much appreciate jour concern and I am extremely grateful.

I'd like to give special thanks to those inmates who were in he area of the incident and contributed all they could in assisting toward my revival. Their concern and help will never be forgotten. Very, very special thanks go out to counselor Stickler for everything he did, from getting the physician assistant, to mouth to mouth resuscitation. Inmate Gregg Thomas, I understand went as far as he could trying to revive me until the officials arrived and ordered him to stop. I'll always be indebted to Gregg.

Many of the inmates began to pray for me at this time and I am very grateful. A very special thanks goes out from my heart to Chaplain Minister who so happened to be on the compound when he attack occurred. He was able to send a direct message to my Lord and savior to request for Him to let His will be done.

I am almost sure Chaplain Minster said something like this… "Lord, if it is your will so shall it be, but dear God if Cain can be of any further service here on this earth, please save him for another minute. Amen.

Last but not least. The angel that never thought about giving up was the Physician Assistant Ms. Lawrence. After everything tried did not work, she continued every effort she could think of, and all she had been taught. I am almost sure she asked the good Lord above to enter the arena and give her a helping hand. From the compound to the hospital I do believe Ms. Lawrence and our Savior, Jesus Christ played a tag team, and she tagged Him in after she had done everything in her power. Again thanks to everyone and remember 'God is Alive." God Bless.

As Ben returned to where he had been sitting, there was another standing ovation and no dry eyes. At the end of the sermon, Chaplain Minster did something that had not been done in a Sunday morning service. He emphasized again that he believes in miracles and provided an opportunity for anyone that had a need to come forward. Several inmates responded. At the end of the prayer, Chaplain Minster asked if I would lead the congregation in a chorus of *"It Is No Secret, What God Can Do."*

That night in a special Sunday night service, eight more inmates were saved. God is alive and in control at Eglin.

NED

The International Toastmasters, is one of several organizations that meet on a regular basis, in camp. Each Saturday, an educational program is sponsored by the Toastmasters for any inmate who would like to attend. With the number of professional people serving time, it is no problem to secure speakers.

On this particular Saturday, I had been invited to give a talk about banking and politics. I was to share the hour with "Ned," a former new car dealer. Having spent over 20 years of my life in banking and finance, I accepted the invitation.

Upon completion of my presentation and having afforded an opportunity for questions, I introduced Ned.

Ned, from Atlanta, Georgia, shared with the inmates about arranging financing for the customer on a new car purchase. During each presentation by the inmates, they are asked to share why they are in prison. An inmate is allowed to be as brief or in depth as they want.

According to Ned, he was serving, 30 months, for mail fraud. He allegedly was submitting an application, for customers purchasing a new car, to the different financing companies, in search for the best possible financing arrangement. In many cases, if a customer did not have a down payment, but their credit was good, Ned would list on the loan application that the customer was making a good size down payment. Since Ned owned the dealership, he did not see a problem with this.

However, when Ned supplied the financing bank with a false financial application, is where he became entangled with the government. When the bank approved the loan by phone, Ned would finish up the paperwork and forward it to the bank by mail At some point, a customer lost his job and had to give up his car. For whatever reason, it was learned that the customer had not madethe down payment that had been indicated on the loan application.

Ned was indicted for mail fraud and afforded an opportunity to plead guilty or go to court and maybe be sentenced to twice the amount of time. It will cost the taxpayers a minimum of $62,000 for his vacation at "Club Fed."

Having worked for three different auto dealers, Jim Preuitt, Roebuck Chrysler-Plymouth and Regal Pontiac, I couldn't help but reflect back to some of the deals that had been pulled by the sales manager and owners to obtain financing. If the "Feds" ever decide to investigate automobile dealers, they could have a long vacation at "Club Fed," too!

PAUL AND LINDA WESSON

Around the first of February 1997, in a telephone conversation with Max Morris, he shared with me that our good friend Dr. Paul Wesson's left eye began to bleed internally. This was his best eye, and now he is blind again in the eye and has very little sight in his right eye.

Max shared that he had been on the telephone prayer line with Paul, and his spirit is excellent in spite of this set-back. Paul has been confined to his home, getting total rest.

As Max shared with me about Paul, my thoughts turned to how he and his lovely wife, Linda, have stuck by me while at Eglin.

Shortly after arriving at Eglin, I was in need of a pair of tennis shoes, but would not let Mary know due to the financial hardship she was facing with the loss of my income. I turned the matter over to God, and a short time later, I received a check in the mail from Paul and Linda that was more than enough to purchase a pair of tennis shoes. Even though they are almost worn out I still wear them and have asked God to let them last until I am released. I reminded God that the children of Israel wandered in the wilderness for forty-years and their clothes lasted .... why can't a pair of tennis shoes last three years?

Paul, the son of a minister, is a successful businessman, who owns his own pharmacy in Sylacauga, Alabama, without a doubt has suffered more pain and heartache than most anyone I have ever been associated with. Paul suffers from diabetes. This afliction took both of his kidneys and now he lives on a transplanted kidney.

In addition, Paul lost his eyesight. After seven major operations on his eyes, he could see until this recent setback. If this was not enough physical suffering, the enemy made sure there would be more. Paul lost both of his legs due to diabetes. He presently walks on two artificial legs—so much pain!

On November 3, 1993, the devil sent more suffering and pain Paul and Linda's way. Their only daughter ... two days before her planned wedding day ... with her wedding dress in the back seat of her automobile was killed in an accident in Montgomery, Alabama.

Paul and Max had visited me on several occasions, driving the 500 mile round trip to Eglin. Max shared with me that not one time had Paul ever complained about making the trip. Paul also had to hire a druggist at $23 an hour to run the business while he was away. For a man to endure the pain that his body must have felt and to pay $230 for help in order to visit me, that is a true friend who cares.

On March 21, 1997, Max and Paul came to visit me again—their fifth visit. Long time Friends, Jimmy Jordan, a graduate of the Alabama School for the Blind and a retiree of the Industries for the Blind, and Reverend Harvey Bowlin, pastor of Trinity Lighthouse Church of God, also came to visit on this date. This was not their first trip.

As we visited, Paul shared with me about his recent setback but was quick to share with me that God had healed him Paul said, "When I returned to the doctor for a check-up, I was informed that I had 20/20 vision."

THE GENERAL

The last Sunday in September, Mary came to visit accompanied by relatives, Chester and Gaynell Smith who are also members of Max Morris' World Wide Prayer Partners (W.W.P.P.). They arrived in time to attend the chapel service. Mary and I were scheduled to sing.

The morning before, a former two-star general who had become a good friend of mine, came into the barber shop for a haircut. He is one of the most dedicated Christians I have ever known. The General reads his bible regularly and is what I call a real "prayer warrior". We had talked a lot during all his haircuts, and among other things, he shared with me about a veritable miracle concerning his wife. I asked him if he would share this news with everyone in the Sunday service. He said he would be honored to share. The following is his testimony.

"A year ago, my wife's doctor told her he had discovered a tumor, but that the tumor was inoperable because of its inaccessible location in her abdomen. Over the next few months, the tumor grew to the size of a cantaloupe, and my wife felt a little sicker every day. The doctors finally decided to try a biopsy, and were able to get one. Test results showed the tumor to be malignant.

Because it was growing so fast, they believed that in a short time she would die. They gave her chemotherapy, but it wasn't really effective; it only made her sicker every time she had a treatment.

"I started praying ... not asking, but thanking God for healing my wife, in spite of doctors who kept telling my wife and me, 'It's just a matter of time'

"I told several friends about my wife's condition, and asked them to pray for her. Not long after, I found out they had involved people all over the world--people we had met during the past forty years of our travels with the Army, and many we didn't know, were praying for her. I also asked the prayer groups here in camp to pray for her. I truly believed that if enough people prayed for her, God would heal her.

"During the next month and a half the tumor began shrinking, and my wife had fewer episodes of nausea. Then, two weeks ago, her x-rays were negative. The doctors were astounded. They couldn't even find evidence of where the tumor had ever been.

"It was a wonderful miracle. You can't know how humbly thankful I am for that miracle, and to know God is keeping watch while I can't be there for her. I praise Him, and give Him all the credit for healing her."

As the general finished his testimony, I thought of this old hymn:

It Is No Secret (What God Can Do)

There is no night for in his sight

You'll never walk alone,

Always feel at home,

Wherever You may roam.

There is no power can conquer you,

While God is on your side.

Take him at His promise,

Don't run away and hide.

It is no secret what God can do.

What He's done for others, He'll do for you.

With arms wide open, he'll welcome you.

It is no secret what God can do.

PHIL

Phil, the nephew of a very popular Grand Ole Opry country singer, and a professional country singer himself, shared with me his story.

He and a friend purchased a plot of land containing several acres. They owned the land for several years, prior to the sudden death of his partner. Shortly thereafter, Phil was indicted for conspiracy.

According to Phil, who had a hit record overseas and was 36th on the chart in America, had permitted his partner to look after the land primarily because Phil was traveling with his band all over the world. When Phil was indicted, the authorities informed him that his partner had leased this piece of land to some drug dealers to be used for a landing strip. Phil was unaware of this transaction and even though he was offered probation to plead guilty, he chose to defend himself in court. Phil a law abiding family man had confidence in the judicial system.

During the trial, the drug dealer testified that he did not know Phil nor had any dealings with him. The prosecutor convinced the jurors that this was not important. The main thing was Phil was a partner and he was as guilty as his partner who had allegedly leased the land to the drug dealer for $40,000. The court found Phil guilty and was sentenced to nine years in prison.

Having been afforded an opportunity to play piano for Phil to sing in chapel service and live in the dorm with him for 3 years, become acquainted with his family and share meals together, I am convinced Phil is no more guilty of his crime than I am of mine. At the end of Phil's sentence, it will have cost the taxpayers more than $200,000, for his vacation.

MIKE

By March, 1997, 1 had been at Eglin for thirty-four months. Hundreds of inmates had swapped stories with me, telling about why they were serving time. Mike was one of the large percentage of them who were former drug dealers.

Mike was 36 years old, 6'2", and 215 pounds. He had once been very muscular and physically fit, and was working on becoming that way again. Before being imprisoned, he was a resident of south Florida. He served in the Navy for five years as a gunner's mate and held the rank of petty officer, Ist class. While serving he trained as a Navy Seal--Navy Seals are an elite first-strike group, which usually carry out secret operations. His assignments took him all over the world bringing him into contact with lots of different people, some of whom had drug connections. After his discharge, Mike became involved in drug trafficking, and in a short time, worked his way into the big-time operations.

One day I had a chance to talk to Mike, and I asked him, "How did you actually get involved in the drug scene?"

"Well, I didn't go into the business green," he said. "While I was in the Seals, I became good friends with this guy and got to know his family.

Some time later, my friend died. His family moved to Jamaica, but we stayed in touch. A few months later, I found out my friend's Dad was running marijuana from Jamaica to the U.S. One day his boat captain was sick, and he needed someone to operate the boat. I was experienced and he trusted me, so I agreed to help with the delivery. The next thing I knew I was knee deep in drugs."

"Your friend must live like a king in Jamaica," I said.

Mike laughed. "He lives in a colorfully painted clapboard shack up in the mountains. His swimming pool is carved out in the mountain rock and fed by a mountain stream. He keeps his new Mercedes in a garage built better than the house he lives in. That's the way he enjoys living. He knows every palm that needs greasing to keep heads turned the other way so he can make sure all his buyers have safe passage."

"How did you manage to get yourself set up as an dependent buyer?" I asked.

"After I worked for my friend a few times and learned the pes, I decided to start my own business. My usual routine was to to Jamaica where the marijuana was grown and select what I wanted to buy. Naturally, the better the grade of marijuana, the ore money it would bring at the other end. I always brought the plastic wrappers to package it in because they weren't available in maica. After making the deal on the grade of marijuana I wanted, would sail to Cuncay, Catcay, Bemini, or one of the other islands the Bahamian chain, wait until my contact let me know my stuff is packaged and ready for delivery. That's when my contact let e know which island was going to be the staging island (island here the marijuana was delivered to the buyer).

"My friend was in thick with the proper authorities, but if ru wanted to be left alone by authorities in other areas, you had to ty them off, too. For instance, paying off the Bahamas Defense irce guaranteed an escort to U.S. waters ... even as far as the Gulf ream. Sometimes the cost of doing business was a percentage of e total pounds of marijuana being transported. Other times, it as money--in one case $10,000. And don't think the Americans e any different.

"Sounds like you were doing pretty well, Mike. I've never been involved with drugs, but it seems like a terrible risk to me. you must have been making a whole lot of money to keep taking .such chances."

"Larry, I was buying 2,000 pounds of marijuana every trip a cost of $50.00 a pound, wrapped. If I wanted it delivered, it as $150.00 a pound. In the states, it brought $850 to $1,000 a pound, so it was well worth paying off officials for safe passage and asking going to jail. I made so much money, I was able to buy two very fast, specially built, thirty-six foot boats. They could run 80 ph loaded and 100 mph unloaded. I also bought a twin engine, avaho Chieftain plane for half a million dollars cash. Not to mention my house right on the water which is worth about 140.000 "

I interrupted. "Wait a minute, Mike. If my math is right, a person could make $200,000 profit on 2,000 pounds. No wonder people are willing to take such big risks!"

"You got that right, Larry, and even though I'd never risk getting involved with cocaine or any other hard drugs, that's where the real money is."

"You mean there's even more profit in hard drugs?"

"You bet there is. A person can purchase cocaine in Columbia for $500 to $750 per kilo (one kilo equals 2.2 pounds).

After it's sold to the dealer, he cuts it by mixing it with baking soda, crushed aspirin or whatever's popular and easily available.

After it's cut, that same kilo purchased for $500 or so and sold to the dealer for $15 to $20 thousand has the potential of bringing $40 to $50 thousand on the streets.

"So, if someone buys 220 kilos of coke in Columbia and pays $500.00 per kilo, the cost will be $10,000, but it will him bring $3 million, give or take a little. After the street dealer cuts and mixes it, the weight increases to 5,000 pounds, and it brings about $6 million when he distributes it."

"Pretty lucrative business," I said.

"It sure is. That's what makes drug smuggling and making fast cash look so good to the average person making minimum wage or even to those making $20 to $30 thousand a year. But they don't realize how dangerous it is. People get killed.

"A personal friend of mine decided he wanted to get into the business and went to Columbia to put a deal together. He hasn't been heard from since. I suspect that only about four out of ten people who go to Jamaica or the Bahamas ever complete a deal. The other six wind up getting killed, robbed or arrested."

"Why does that happen?"

"First of all, you have to show money to the person you're trying to deal with--just to prove you've got enough to buy the drugs. Someone going in green doesn't know if the dealers are truly reliable. They're forced into a blind trust situation. If the dealer turns out to be bogus, more than likely the greenhorn buyer will be robbed, beaten or even killed. It's a very dangerous business ... especially if you don't know whom you're dealing with.

"Several times, when I was heading home with a load, boats came up along side my boat and fired shots. Some of the Bahamians and Jamaicans are regular pirates and will take your load if they can. If they succeed, it's clear profit for them."

"How did you keep them from taking your load, Mike? And how did they know what you were carrying?"

"They know you're running dope when you're not displaying lights on board at night. I survived by always being prepared for them. I kept plenty of firepower on board. If they fired, I returned fire, and they would take off. Most new drug dealers don't know these pirates exist and aren't prepared for an attack "

"Sounds like you had everything figured out. How did you get caught?"

"It's not an unusual story, Larry. It was because of a man that I considered my friend. I'd known him a long time and would have trusted him with my life But I didn't know he'd been caught by the DEA (Drug Enforcement Agency]. They threatened him with a life sentence and a tremendous fine. Then, true to form, they promised him a lesser sentence if he would cooperate in helping to set up the people he knew in the drug business.

"He contacted me and asked if I'd pick up a load of marijuana for him, He said he would pay me 60% of the profit to deliver it in the states. It sounded good to me, so I agreed to do it. The day I was arrested, my boat was loaded with 2,000 pounds of marijuana. Just as I sailed into the island staging area, my boat was suddenly surrounded by helicopters flying overhead. I tried to make a run for it, but with a load that big I couldn't outrun the helicopters. Unfortunately, it was too late when I figured out there were DEA agents on board the helicopters. If I had only known, I could have dumped the load overboard, and they wouldn't have caught my boat--I'd been able to out-run them before when the boat was empty. I still tried to get away, but when they started firing at my boat with a 30-caliber machine gun, it encouraged me to stop." Mike laughed and seemed lost in his own thoughts for a few moments.

I interrupted his musing and said, "What happened then, Mike?"

"I'll never forget September 8, 1994. It was about ten that morning when the DEA agents arrested me and the person who was helping with the load and took us back to Bahama." His eyes got that faraway look again. "To think I could have gone free and rich."

"What do you mean, Mike?"

"Well, when we got to Bahama, they put me in a room alone with one of the DEA agents."

"I can make you rich and you can go home,' he said.

I looked at the agent. "What do you mean? Are you offering me a deal?"

'You could say that. If you cooperate and give us the names of all the people you do business with in the states so we can catch them, you'll get 25-35% of what we confiscate.'

"Larry, I spit in his face. I may be a lot of things, but I'm not a snitch.

"What did the agent do when you spit on him?"

"I was handcuffed, beaten and left alone. The agent came back every once in a while to see if I'd changed my mind. He really got upset when he realized I wasn't going to turn in my customers."

"Mike, I don't know anything about the drug scene, so I'm curious. Were your contacts low income blacks and whites or what?

"Larry, my man, I was selling to construction company owners, judges, lawyers, and a lot of other so-called professional people who were purchasing marijuana for resale. There's profit from the top to the final buyer. It's not like dealing in cocaine you don't have to carry a gun when you're delivering marijuana to those people."

"I didn't mean to side-track you, Mike. What happened after the DEA agent realized you wouldn't give up your contacts?"

"It was a nightmare, Larry. They held my partner and me on Catcay Island for about two hours, then they turned us over to the Bahamian Drug Enforcement Unit (DU) for incarceration and interrogation. The DU interrogated us continuously for thirteen hours, asking a lot of questions we couldn't answer because we simply didn't know the answers. Finally, around midnight they put us in a small cell. It had a cold, damp, concrete floor and was infested with roaches, rats and other vermin. Our requests for blankets and everything else were denied.

The next day, after spending a sleepless night in barbaric conditions, they took us back to the DEU interrogation room. We repeatedly requested one telephone call so we could contact the American Embassy, but they refused. We were told that when they were through with us we'd be turned over to Bahamian customs, and maybe when customs finished with us, the Embassy would be contacted. All during this part of our ordeal, we begged for food and water, but they said, 'You Americans have no rights here.'

"After another round of questioning we were taken back to that same cold, filthy cell. Around noon a Bahamian customs officer came and questioned us for about fifteen minutes. He only asked for standard information … name, address, what we were doing in the Bahamas, etc., and then left. By that time, our hunger and thirst was severe. In desperation, we made enough racket to get the guards' attention and pleaded with them to give us some food or, at least, a little water. We also asked what we were supposed to do about relieving ourselves of normal body waste and personal hygiene. The guards raked their nightsticks back and forth across the cell bars, drowning out our question about whether or not the embassy had been contacted. It didn't take any more to convince us they were serious when they laughed and yelled at us,

'Both of you better shut up or you'll get another beating!' They left us alone for the rest of that night.

"About 10:00 a.m. the next morning, the guard told us we had a visitor from the embassy. He led us to a small room where a representative of the American Embassy was waiting. We quickly explained our sorry situation— no food, no water, and no sanitation.

He said he was just there to confirm that there were, in fact, two American citizens being detained at central holding, but that he would try to get the Bahamian authorities to allow us to make a phone call. Finally, at eleven that night we were allowed to make a call. I called my wife and asked her to retain counsel and come to Nassau as soon as possible. They took us back to our cell immediately after the call. We still had gotten no food or water, but they did give us a cup of tea.

"The morning of September 11th dawned and at 7:00 a.m. they gave us another cup of tea and a piece of hardtack bread. We asked the guard if there was any way we could get more food, and he said, 'If you have someone to buy it and deliver it, you can have it. When we asked about relieving ourselves he said, 'Pee in your tea cup… you can either keep it to drink or throw it out.'"

"At two that afternoon our wives arrived with an attorney from Miami. The attorney told us she couldn't practice in the Bahamas, but would find out about a good local attorney who could represent us. They left and came back with food, water, blankets, candy bars, etc. which the guard delivered to us about five that evening. We felt a little better even though we were still in the same cell.

The morning of September 12th they gave us tea and hardtack again. It was nearly noon before our wives and the attomey arrived. They brought more food and water, and the good news that they had been able to retain local council. He got there around 4:30 p.m. and said the charges were unclear, but that a court date had been set for the 14th or 15th in Magistrate Court #6. On September 15th we were taken to appear before the magistrate and pled not guilty on all charges. He set the trial date for October 26th, but our attorney was able to get it moved up to October 12th

"On September 17th they moved us to Foxhill Prison where we were segregated from all the other prisoners. The guard who accompanied us was told to take us to the West Wing better known as the Hellhole because it had the worst possible conditions at Foxhill. They separated us and put us each in a different 6'x 9', four-man cell. Only a bucket was provided for bodily functions, but hygiene was non-existent. It was two more days before we were permitted to shower.

We were kept in these tiny cells for weeks with only twenty minutes each week to bathe and brush our teeth. There was no such thing as being allowed outside to exercise or get a breath of fresh air. Even worse, no phone calls were allowed...not even to our attorney. Finally, on September 21st our attorney managed to get in to see us and brought fruit, water, candy bars, and other things we desperately needed or wanted.

The prison guards promptly stole everything for themselves. We kept asking for water, so they brought us some laced with kerosene I still have skin rashes and other problems from drinking that contaminated water.

"Prison days pass with agonizing slowness and the boredom and discomforts nearly drive you crazy. But at long last, on October 12th, we were taken to court and appeared before the Magistrate. We pled guilty to possession of marijuana. The magistrate gave us four years and sent us back to Foxhill. Five days later, they handcuffed, waist-chained and shackled me, then pushed me into a room where I was interrogated and severely beaten—especially my face and body. Apparently, the interrogation only lasted about ten minutes, but it felt like hours. I remember the captain of the guard saying, 'Give him about ten days and another beating ... maybe hell regain his memory. They did the same thing to the person who was arrested with me."

I shuddered and said, "It must have been awful for you,

Mike. I can't even imagine what it must have done to you."

"Well, Larry, let's just say I hope I'm never again forced to go through that or the things they did afterwards. I just couldn't take it."

"What happened after the beating, Mike?"

"About a week later our attorney showed up. We asked if he'd brought us any food and water, and he said the guards at the front gate had it. He said he tried to prevent them from taking it by appealing to the authorities, but was told we were now inmates and no one except the warden had a right to give us anything. To make matters worse, we found out that although we were getting letters, the guards threw them away. Luckily, when our attorney visited we were able to give him letters for our wives, and he got them out and mailed them for us.

"On October 29th we were again chained and shackled and taken to the "beating room". I was severely beaten in the kidney area, and after that session, had large amounts of blood in my stools and urine. The bleeding persisted for a month, but medical attention was denied. Two days later, our food was intentionally contaminated with glass and wire. We were subjected to constant racial harassment by inmates and guards.

Food was often withheld as a means of racial harassment. When we did get food, it had usually been tampered with in some way, making it virtually inedible. Around November 9th an embassy official appeared and made arrangements for us to get two gallons of water daily, but we only got one gallon of it. Guards and inmates stole the rest along with our magazines which had been delivered by the embassy and approved by prison officials

"Things went on like that until November 24th when our wives and mothers were finally allowed to visit. A priest came with them and told us he had also tried to arrange for us to get food and water, but had been unsuccessful. During their visit we found out we were supposed to have been transferred to another facility, but the paperwork was tied up due to red tape. It was also during this visit that my wife saw the ugly bruises and multiple abrasions I had from the beatings.

"The Bahamian prisoners were allowed visits of up to one hour, but ours were always limited to fifteen minutes. When we asked the guards why ours were so short they said, 'Because Americans are rich. Your families can afford to stay in the Bahamas, spend money and come back for more visits.'

"Our attorney came November 30th and told us our transfer papers were finally complete, and we would be leaving some time in December to go to a stateside federal prison. He couldn't give us a firm date for 'security reasons.' "It should be before Christmas,' he said."

"Just about this same time we were informed that officials from the U.S. Board would be coming to take a look at American prisoners. The next day we were taken out of our cells, stripped naked in front of fifteen or twenty guards, slapped around and given another beating. The guards said they were giving us a 'good farewell'. Even the Bahamian inmates were upset this time and protested our cruel treatment. So, the guards beat them, too.

"The day after our good farewell we were taken out to see the U.S. Board members. When the chief of the prison saw the bruises, abrasions and other effects of our beatings, he sent us all back to our cells, refusing to let U.S. officials see us in such poor condition. On December 13th, with our attorney present, U.S. Board members were permitted to meet with us. The spokesperson explained that we were being returned to U.S. soil and would serve the rest of our time in a federal prison. On the 20th of December, after more than three months of hell, the guards woke us up around 3:30 a.m. and ordered us to pick up what little was left of our belongings. We were taken to the airport and turned over to the U.S. Marshal Service.

"What a horrible ordeal for you, Mike," I said.

"That's putting it mildly, Larry. I've never been so thankful to leave a place in my entire life. The results of physical abuse were easy to see, but the effects of the mental abuse we were subjected to from the day of our arrest were just as damaging. A lot of it I described to you, but some things are beyond description. There were plenty of times when we were afraid we'd never make it home alive.

When we arrived in the U.S., a prison doctor examined us. I weighed 170 pounds. My normal weight is 265. My partner's weight had dropped from 180 to 130 pounds. The doctor said it was a good thing we'd been in good physical condition when they arrested us or it would have been a lot worse. Still, when we got to the Miami Corrections Center (MCC), we were so weak from malnutrition and related fatigue that we had to stop and rest between 'F° Unit (where we were staying) and the chow hall which is only about 500 yards away. And now, although we've put on some weight, we haven't regained our health and probably won't get back to the kind of condition as we were in before all this happened. The mental and emotional scars -they haven't really even begun to heal. We'll probably be lucky just to stop having nightmares.

"Mike, I know you've suffered terribly, but you're a family man with five children, and it's hard for me to understand how you could have ever become involved with drugs. I've always been adamantly anti-drugs. A lot of that feeling comes from my belief that drugs destroy our kids and anyone else who becomes addicted."

"Larry, if I had it to do over, I'd do a lot of things different. Believe me, I've learned from my mistakes. As for being destroyed by drugs, I know lots of bankers, lawyers, judges, and a long list of others considered pillars of their community who smoke marijuana regularly and are still doing their jobs well. I've smoked it since I was sixteen and have served in the military, and raised a family. I owned my own successful construction company before I started running drugs. I've never had any desire to do hard drugs. What you've heard about marijuana leading to hard drug use is, for the most part, scare tactics used by members of law enforcement to help insure their job security.

"You don't hear of people overdosing on marijuana or robbing stores and banks for money to buy marijuana. It's cocaine and other hard drugs that hook people and cause them to commit crimes like that. I do agree that we need strong laws to help prevent hard drug abuse, but alcohol and tobacco kill more people, and alcohol causes more violence than marijuana ever has or ever will. A policeman who's a friend of mine told me he'd much rather go into a place where people are smoking marijuana to make an arrest than to enter a nightclub where they're serving liquor. He says it's less dangerous because marijuana smokers are seldom violent, but a bunch of drunks often want to fight or kill someone.

"In answer to your original question I would never encourage anyone to become involved with drugs. My involvement as a dealer has cost me my health and nearly my sanity. I've paid thousands in lawyer fees, I'm doing time in prison, and my wife has filed for a divorce. The potential fortunes that can be made just aren't worth the risk of losing your family or your life. You're better off making less money legally without always having to look over your shoulder.

"Running drugs sure ain't what it used to be. The new generation of drug dealers are cowards. They'll sell you out in a heartbeat to keep from going to prison themselves. They don't want to lose their houses, cars, boats and airplanes. So, when they're caught they snitch you out, and you wind up doing their time. They stay out on the streets, still dealing drugs paid for by the DEA, while someone like me who refuses to sell out his friends sits in prison. They called me a crook, and now I'm a convicted felon, but some of the law enforcement officers are no better. They arrest you for dealing drugs, take everything of value you own, put it all up for auction, and bid on it for low dollars. Indirectly, they're also getting rich off drugs. Look around any town and see what the law enforcement officials are driving and the houses they live in. Then ask yourself how they can afford all that on $25-35,000 or less a year. The government doesn't want drugs legalized because it would cost them too much. Until the American people use their voting power to turn things around, my getting out of the drug business isn't going to make much difference … except to my own life."

2255

On January 22, 1996) I filed another motion called a "2255" requesting the court vacate my sentence due to ineffective assistance by attorney Bill Dawson. Even though my case had been to the Supreme Court with no relief, I knew I was not guilty of the charges. There had to be someone in authority who would review my case and realize that a mistake had been made.

At my sentencing hearing in April 94, obstruction of justice charges had been added. When asked by Judge Nelson what the obstruction charges were for, Prosecutor Barnett alleged that I had given one of the government witnesses, James "Peanut" Thrower money to testify an asked him not to talk to the police. I knew this accusation was an outright lie. "Peanut" didn't know anything about my case, good or bad, to testify.

When Mr. Barnett reminded the judge that "Peanut" had testified that I gave him money, all of a sudden Judge Nelson asked my attorney Bill Dawson, "Response, Mr. Dawson? I believe Mr. Thrower did testify ... generally along those lines; did he not, Mr. Dawson?"

Bill responded, "Yes, sir, of course, we deny that that's accurate or truthful. Judge Nelson responded with, "As I recall, Mr. Thrower testified, and I think you told me a moment ago, that there was some contact and some inquiry about what Mr. Thrower was going to testify about or what he was providing to police officers. That sure sounds like. ...if you read those obstruction statutes, they are pretty broad. It doesn't take much to find yourself in violation of one or more of those statutes. Those statutes are, next to making a threat on the life of a president, probably the broadest criminal statutes in the code. I find by preponderance that it did happen, and that constitutes obstruction." Before the judge imposed the sentence, he asked if anyone had anything to say. My attorney refused to comment. The judge then asked if there was anything I would like to say before he imposed the sentence.

"Yes, your Honor, a couple of things. First of all, I have much respect for the judicial system, have always supported it. But there's no doubt in my mind that the jury erred in finding me guilty of something I'm not guilty of.

"Second of all, Mr. Thrower is a life-long friend. About twenty-five years ago, I owned a service station. I hired him. When I became mayor several years ago, I hired him as a city employee.

He's worked for me off and on for several years. When his son got his eye shot out, I gave him donations to help him with his hospital expense. When he had his foot injured and in the hospital, I gave him expense money. He came to me, said his lights had been turned out, his family hungry, and wanted to know if he could have some money. If that's obstructing justice by helping a person that's down and out, then I guess I'm guilty of it, your Honor. But the only time we met and talked about this case, Mr. Giddens, my other attorney, was present. And my comment to Mr. Thrower was, 'You tell the truth, exactly like you know it If that's obstructing justice, then I'm guilty of it."

On February 8, 1996, less than a month after filing my, motion to vacate my sentence, Judge Edwin Nelson denied my request stating that, at trial, James "Peanut" Thrower testified that though Mr. Barton had refused to loan him money before the indictment in this case, Mr. Barton later initiated contact with him on two different occasions and loaned him $20 and $100. Mr.

Thrower testified that Mr. Barton had instructed him not to talk to the police about the matter. The matter was raised at sentencing and the court made a specific finding that the above recited facts were correct and added two (2) points."

Second, had the issue been raised on appeal, the court of appeals would have reviewed the trial court's action on a clearly erroneous basis. The trial court's decision was supported by evidence which the trial court believed. Any such claim made on appeal almost certainly would have been rejected. Appellate counsel is not ineffective when he fails to raise a meritless ground.

Third, with the two points added for obstruction of justice, Mr. Barton had an offense level of twenty-four (24) and a criminal history category of Roman Numeral I. Those levels yielded a guideline range of fifty-one (51) to sixty-three (63) months. He was sentenced to fifty-one months. Had Mr. Barton not been given two points for obstruction, his offense level would have been twenty-two (22), which in conjunction with a criminal history category of Roman Numeral I, would have yielded a guideline imprisonment range of forty-one (41) to fifty-one (51) months. Fifty-one months was and is an appropriate sentence in this case and the court certifies that were it required to resentence Mr. Barton without the two points added for obstruction of justice, all other things being the same, it would sentence Mr. Barton to fifty-one months.

For these reasons, the motion to vacate should be and the same hereby is DENIED." Done this 8th day of February, 1996.

I could not believe what I was reading. Judge Nelson was still stating that he remembers remarks that were never made.

On the 20th day of February, I filed another motion back to Judge Nelson, along with the transcript of "Peanut" Thrower's testimony in an effort to get him to reconsider.

On Feb. 26, six days later, Judge Nelson denied my motion. On August 15, 1996, I filed a motion with the Eleventh Circuit of Appeals in Atlanta, Georgia, asking them to review my case. I requested that the obstruction of justice be overturned. March 27, 1997, more than seven months from the date of filing with them, and having already served thirty-four (34) months in prison for charges I knew I was not guilty of, the Eleventh Court issued the following order.

Before TJOFLAT and COX, Circuit Judges, and RONEY, Senior Circuit Judge. PER CURIAM: Larry Barton, a federal inmate, appeals the district court's denial of his pro se motion (this meaning serving as my own attorney) to vacate, set aside, or correct his sentence, 28 U.S.C. $2255. Inasmuch as the district court was of the mistaken opinion that Barton had engaged in the obstruction of justice and his counsel had mistakenly supported that opinion, we vacate and remand for re-sentence.

The opinion was a seven-page document filled with numerous cases citing their authority to issue their ruling. As I read and re-read the order, I was thrilled to know that there are still some judges that are honest and will try to see that justice is served. I thanked God for I knew He was still in control.

In the last paragraph of the order, the three judges stated, "Although this court has complete confidence in the ability of this trial judge to fairly sentence the defendant, in the interest of the appearance of fairness, since he has indicated what he would do on remand, we suggest to the Chief Judge (Judge Pointer) of the Northern District of Alabama that the sentencing should be scheduled before a different judge. That judge can then re-sentence the defendant with complete disregard of any claim of obstruction of justice, all other factors remaining the same. VACATED AND REMANDED.

As of March 27., 1997, I was serving time in prison but did not have a sentence. I now had to wait for Chief Judge Pointer to either preside over my re-sentence or appoint another judge. I immediately notified my family of this good news. Even though I had already been approved to leave Eglin September 9th for halfway house, if the judge would be fair and hold the hearing soon, I could be finished with my sentence and not have to serve any halfway house time.

I shared the court ruling with Chaplain Minster, and he wrote the following letter to the court on my behalf.

U.S. Department of Justice

Federal Prison System

Federal Prison Camp

Eglin Air Force Base, FL 32542-7606

April 11, 1997

To Whom It May Concern:

I am the Chaplain at Eglin Federal Prison Camp, Florida. I has come to my attention that one of my key chapel participants, inmate Larry Barton, will be returning to court for a re-sentencing in the near future.

While I am in no position to judge the guilt or innocence of Mr. Barton, I would like to share with you some current, positive and helpful information regarding his contributions while incarcerated.

Since his arrival at Eglin, Larry has been an active participant in various chapel programs. He has served as a member of our Protestant Chaplain's Council, having been elected to that position by his fellow inmates. As a member of that committee, his duties included selecting the weekly Sunday Bible readers from among the Christian inmate population, selecting a Christian inmate to welcome the outside visitors and lead us in prayer and to schedule the special music for each Sunday service.

An accomplished piano player, Larry has served faithfully as our chapel pianist, playing for two evening choir practices each week, special music practices as arranged throughout the week and then plays for the Sunday morning Protestant Christian Worship Service. In addition, Mr. Barton provides the music for the Saturday night Full Gospel Businessmen's Fellowship, an international organization with a chapter here at Eglin.

Twice a year we present plays; one for Easter and one for Christmas. Mr. Barton has participated in an important way to bring the message of Christ to the audience. He has provided musical support and played vital roles in these dramas.

Mary Barton, Larry's wife, visits often and the two of them provide special music for the Protestant Worship Service. Mr. Barton's mother, who is in her 80's, used to sing with them but now is unable to travel. Larry is a devoted family man and, unlike many men sent to prison, his family has been very supportive throughout their long separation.

Larry Barton is widely known on the compound and is looked up to by staff and inmates alike. While it would be a loss to the chapel services, I would be remiss if I did not recommend that every consideration be given to granting Mr. Barton time served when he returns for his hearing.

Thank you for allowing me to share my thoughts on Larry Barton

Sincerely.

Rev. R.A Minister, Chaplain

SURRETT PLEADS GUILTY

In an earlier chapter, I shared with you that one of the D.A's investigator who had been instrumental in helping get me indicted, had been indicted herself.

According to the September 24, 1996 edition of The *Daily Home*, Ann Wallace White Surrett, a former investigator for District Attorney Robert Rumsey has been indicted for allegedly stealing more than $100,000.00 from the District Attorney's office and the 29th Judicial Drug Task Force. Mrs. Surrett was also charged with multiple counts of possession of a forged instrument.

Having posted bonds totaling more than $105,000.00, Mrs. Surrett was released. was released. According to The *Daily Home*, Assistant Attorney General Bruce Liberman, who was responsible for obtaining an indictment, indicated, if convicted of the charges, Mrs. Surrett could be sentenced to a maximum prison sentence of 150 years in prison.

On October 2, 1996, Ann Surrett opted not to appear in court, and her attorney filed a written waiver to plead not guilty to theft and forgery charges against her.

In the October 30 edition of the *Daily Home*, the mayor and city council members of Lincoln, Alabama, agreed to hire D.A. investigator Dennis Surrett, the husband of Ann Wallace White Surrett, as chief of police. However according to D.A. Robert Rumsey, Dennis had not turned in a resignation but assumed since he had been named police chief, he felt the resignation would be forthcoming

In choosing Dennis Surrett as chief of police for the city of Lincoln, the city officials claimed they had checked him out and were convinced that Dennis had no involvement or knowledge of his wife's criminal activity.

Council member Kurt Kuykendall is quoted in the October 30th edition of the *Daily Home* as saying,"I have conducted my own investigation of Surrett, and I am convinced that he had nothing to do with the alleged crimes of his wife. As the request of Mayor Lew Watson, I went to every law enforcement official in the county, including District Attorney Robert Rumsey and Circuit Judges Jerry Fielding and Julian King and was assured that there was nothing in his background that was illegal."

"Judge King said he (Surrett) would make us (Lincoln) a good police officer, and if (King) were us, he'd have no trouble 'hiring him in a heartbeat.' Mr. Rumsey said Mr. Surrett is one of the best investigators he's ever had, and his resume shows almost two pages of schooling he's had in law enforcement," Kuykendall added.

Deputy Attorney General Bruce Liberman, the prosecutor assigned to Mrs. Surrett's cases, said there was no evidence at this time to warrant Dennis Surrett's being charged under the state's complicity statute.

"I think that in order to charge someone under the complicity law, you have to have some evidence that the person encouraged or assisted in the commission of the crime. There is no evidence at this time to substantiate that charge," Liberman said.

As I read *Daily Home* articles about how D. A. Rumsey was quoted as saying Mr. Surrett is one of the best investigators he's ever had and Deputy Attorney General Liberman stating there was no evidence to warrant Dennis being charged, I was amused.

How in the name of common sense can such an outstanding investigator, the best the D.A. ever had, not have known about his wife's newfound wealth. He worked side by side with her daily, shared meals together, lived in the same house together, etc., and now she has been charged with stealing more than $100,000 from the DA.'s office, and he has no knowledge about this?

WHEN HE AND ANN WERE INVESTIGATING ME AND I ASKED ABOUT HIRING A PRIVATE INVESTIGATOR TO HELP

FIND JERRY, DENNIS INFORMED ME THAT I HAD THE BEST (referring to himself and Ann) LOOKING FOR JERRY. NO WONDER I WAS RAILROADED.

In the November 26 edition of the *Daily Home*, the headlines read, 'FORMER D.A. INVESTIGATOR PLEADS GUILTY."

According to the story, Ann Wallace Surrett, a former investigator with the Talladega County District Attorney's office, pleaded guilty to theft and forgery charges in Circuit Court before presiding Judge Jerry L. Fielding.

Through a plea bargain she entered into with the Attorney General's office, Mrs. Surrett will be sentenced to a total of 110 years for two counts of theft and nine forgery counts. The agreement states that she will receive a 10-year split sentence for each count and will serve three years. The sentences will run concurrently, which means she will only have to serve time on one of the sentences. Ann Surrett will also have to make restitution in the amount of $104,361.92.

As I read the article, I could not believe what I was reading. Dennis and Ann, along with Ken Sisk and Pee Wee Hurst charged me with a $5,925 charge, and I was sentenced to si months in prison.. and then along comes the D.A.'s right-hand woman who pleads guilty to stealing more than $100,000 and is only going to have to serve three years. If that had been some poor white or black person, that person would never get out of jail.

In the December 10t edition of the *Daily Home*, the headlines read "WOMAN FILES COMPLAINTS AGAINST ANN SURRETT."

According to the story, three warrants were issued for Mrs. Surrett's arrest on December 9th on complaints filed by Billie Cavender of Childersburg. Mrs. Surrett turned herself in at the Childersburg Police Department that same night, was processed in and out on three bonds totaling $1,500, according to Police Chief Ken Flowers. Ann had been charged with harassing communications, criminal trespassing and third-degree harassment, Chief Flowers said.

According to Mrs. Cavender, in a telephone interview with *Daily Home* reporter Cheryl Marsh, Ann Surrett and her mother came to her home in Childersburg around 9:00 a.m. on the previous Friday. Mrs. Cavender explained to the reporter how it all started.

"I called her mother last Friday morning to ask her what lawyer they used when her daughter Wendy (White) got in trouble with Craddock Clinic. The mother said she didn't know what I was talking about, and I told her maybe I had the wrong Wendy, and I told her I was sorry and hung up. Well, 3 minutes later, Ann called me back an used every foul word there is," Mrs. Cavender said.

"I hung up on her. Then, as I was getting dressed to go to Birmingham, the doorbell rang. I went straight to the door and opened it, and Ann and her mother came in. She cursed me and called me all kinds of nasty, vulgar names, words you've never heard before. She told me I just called her mother to hurt her, but I didn't. I had no idea her mother didn't know about Wendy because everybody down here did." she said.

Mrs. Cavender said she was inquiring because she has a family member who needs legal representation.

"I had no idea Ann's mother didn't know about Wendy's situation. I would never hurt anybody," Mrs. Cavender said.

A source who has knowledge of the situation said District Attorney Robert Rumsey's office was contacted by Craddock Clinic about two and half years ago concerning funds missing from the clinic. Rumsey turned the case over to the Alabama Bureau of Investigation because at that time Mrs. Surrett worked for his office. There was about $13,000 missing, and Ms. White was suspected of taking the money. Five to six thousand dollars of the money was in cash, and the remainder was in checks that were never cashed, the source said,

After the money was paid back by Ms. White, officials at the clinic asked that no charges be brought against her, the source said

Rumsey recused himself form the matter but asked that a state official from Montgomery present the theft case involving the missing funds to a Talladega county grand jury in August. That case was no-billed, the source explained.

Mrs. Cavender said Mrs. Surrett told her Friday that she hadn't heard the last of her.

"I kept asking her (Ann) to leave, and I don't even believe she heard me because of the rage she was in. She never interrupted her line of using those ugly words. She got in my face one time. I thought she was gonna hit me, that's why I sat down. She headed for the door, then she stopped and told me, "I'll get you for this if it's the last thing I ever do in my lifetime," Mrs. Cavender said Mrs. Surrett told her.

"She also told me that if her daddy ever found out about my talking to her mother than I would wish for the rest of my life that he had not. She continued to use curse words all the while," she added.

As I read about the alleged threats made by Ann, my thoughts immediately turned to what Jamie had shared with me a few nights before her death.

THE D.A., DENNIS, AND ANN ARE THREATENING ME! YOU DON'T KNOW THEM…I WORK WITH THEM, AND THEY ARE VICIOUS…ESPECIALLY ANN. I KNOW WHAT THEY HAVE GOING ON IN THE D.A. 'S OFFICE. I HAVE IT IN A FILE, AND WHEN I COMPLETE MY INVESTIGATION, I WILL SHARE WITH YOU, AND THEN WE CAN GO TO THE F.B.I OR THE JUSTICE DEPARTMENT.

As I reread the article, my thoughts reflected back to what Jerry had shared with me on Friday prior to Jamie's being found dead on Monday.

"MAYOR, HAVE YOU HEARD THAT ANN JUMPED ON JAMIE, BEAT HER UP, AND THREATENED HER WITH A GUN?" Then I thought about Dennis Surrett's ex-wife, Sandra, sharing with me about Ann allegedly jumping on Jamie.

IS IT POSSIBLE THAT ANN KILLED JAMIE?

In the January 10th, 1997, edition of the *Daily Home*, the headlines stated, "ANN SURRETT BEGINS SERVING PRISON TIME."

According to the story, the former D.A. investigator, Ann Wallace Surrett was sentenced to two 10-year split sentences Thursday, January 9th and was immediately taken to Julia Tutwiler Prison in Wetumpka, Alabama. Talladega County Circuit Judge Jerry F. Fielding imposed the sentence.

Although Ms. Surrett's cases appeared at the end of the docket, Judge Fielding called her up to the bench to be sentenced first. Mrs. Surrett stood before the judge with one of her attorneys, Jim Sizemore. Fielding explained that she was to serve three years of the sentence, and after that, she'll be paroled and put on probation for five years. She will also be expected to pay restitution

On February 14th, 1997, Ann White Surrett was found guilty of harassment but innocent of trespassing and harassing communication stemming from a phone call In his closing statement, Childersburg city attorney Greg Wood said testimony and evidence show that Mrs. Surrett was angry when she arrived at Mrs. Cavender's home, and she drove quickly to get there.

Mrs. Surrett testified that she only cursed Mrs. Cavender once but did not threaten her and was not asked to leave. Mrs. Surrett was sentenced to 10 days in jail and ordered to pay a $500 fine. The jail sentence will be suspended on payment of the fine and court costs. Presiding Judge Hewitt Conwill of Columbiana said that, due to Ann's present prison term, she would be obligated to his judgment after she is released from prison. Another part of her sentence is a one-year probation period with the condition she will have no contact with that the defendant, Mrs. Cavender.

According to the March 26th edition of the *Daily Home*, after being in prison just two months and 15 days, Ann Wallace Surrett, a woman who stole thousand's of dollars from the Talladega County District Attorney's Office has been granted the privilege of transferring to work release in the state penal system.

Mr. Tom Gilkeson, a spokesman for the Alabama Department of Corrections confirmed that Ann Wallace Surrett, 42, is currently housed at the Birmingham Work Release Center for Women

Mr. Gilkeson was unable to answer or provide proof as to how long she had been at the Birmingham facility and was not sure if any other prisoner had been allowed this privilege after serving such a short amount of time

In a further attempt to justify their action, Mr. Gilkerson said that around February 8", Ann's husband, Dennis Surrett, Chief of Police at Lincoln and former D.A. investigator, came to visit her at prison, and some of the inmates recognized him and started to threaten Ann.

In learning of the alleged special treatment of Ann Surrett, Assistant Attorney General Bruce Liberman stated, "This is news to me. If our office was notified, I didn't receive it. This is the first notification I've received. I am very shocked. I've been prosecuting criminal cases across the state for 10 years, and I am amazed that a former public employee can violate public trust and steal more than $100,900 from a law enforcement office and serve less than two months in prison out of a three-year sentence."

Liberman went on to say that he had learned of this situation from a Talladega County resident who was upset that this sort of thing was happening. Mr. Liberman said, "The citizen stated that Mrs. Surrett had been seen at her home in Sylacauga sweeping her porch."

In the May 14th issue of the *Daily Home*, Alabama state auditors released their findings in relation to the Ann Surrett theft Five days into the audit, financial records for the Child Support Enforcement Fund (a.k.a. the D.A.'s Expense Fund) were discovered missing. After auditors determined that records were missing. D.A. Rumsey told Mrs. Surrett to contact credit card companies the office dealt with to obtain supporting documents for the disbursements of the $384,235.20 that was in the account. After that request was made of her, Mrs. Surrett resigned from her job April 30, 1996. The audit was commenced on October 18, 1995.

According to the audit, Ann Surrett began stealing from the 29th Judicial Drug Task Force shortly after she became administrator of the entity's financial records during the summer of 1994. Mrs. Surrett pleaded guilty of stealing more than $105,000 from the fund, and part of her sentence was restitution.

RETALIATION OR PROTECTION

Shortly after the Eleventh Court overturned my sentence, I was contacted by Rose Livingston, reporter for the *Birmingham News*, which is one of the largest newspapers in Alabama. Rose, a long-time friend, wanted to visit me at Eglin and interview me concerning my victory and my view of prison life. Having agreed and receiving approval from the warden, Rose came to Eglin Prison Camp, Monday, May 19, 1997. For approximately two hours, I shared with Rose my opinion and views concerning my 36 months at Eglin. In a nutshell, other than being away from my family, friends, church, and loss of income, this was the best vacation I had ever had—also the longest. Having always been a workaholic who wouldn't take a vacation, it was like a vacation.

In the interview, I complimented the excellent medical and dental staff, as well as sharing that I had maintained a good rapport with the officers and employees.

I also had maintained a good relationship with the inmates.

On Sunday, May 25, 1997, my interview was published on the front page of the Metro section of the Birmingham News. The story was accurate and well written, but by Wednesday, May 28, several of the inmates from Alabama who were subscribers of the paper received their copy and became upset at some of my comments concerning medical care. They felt that they had not received good medical service and disliked several of the officers.

It was quite obvious that they didn't understand that I was giving my opinion and views of how I had been treated. I was not speaking on behalf of the inmates.

By Friday, May 30, 1997, unbeknown to me, several inmates allegedly were making threats and plans to cause me bodily harm. The compound snitches made the captain aware of these threats.

Around 2:00 p.m., Friday, May 30, one of the officers came to the barbershop where I was working and informed me that the captain wanted to see me in his office. I was just finishing up with one of the inmate's hair, and the officer told me to report to the captain when I finished. Before I could finish, another officer came to the barbershop and informed me that I was being paged to report to the captain's office immediately. The officer stayed with me until I packed up the barber tools, and we walked to the captain's office together.

As I entered control, where the captain's office is located, the captain met me and informed me that I was being transferred.

"Why?" I asked. "For your personal safety," he responded. Then the captain went into more detail and shared with me about the alleged threats. The captain could not be more specific other than to share with me that some of the inmates were "out to get me" for my remarks.

I informed the captain that I did not want to be transferred, and I would be willing to sign a release that would exempt the prison from any liability in case the threats became a reality. "I am not concerned about threats from a few irate inmates," I said. The captain let me know that the decision had been made and that was it.

"Is this retaliation for my comments to the newspaper about being on a vacation?" I asked.

"No," he responded, "we permitted the interview. This, is about our obligation to keep you safe while incarcerated."

As our conversation ended, I was asked to go into the restroom and change into a different set of clothes that had been brought in by another officer. After stripping, being searched, and dressing in the other set of clothes, I was escorted to a van by a different officer. Bureau of Prison policy dictates an inmate being transferred should be cuffed and shackled, but it is up to the individual officer to make the call. I was permitted to travel without this "prison jewelry.

As the officer drove the van away from Eglin, I asked,

"Where am I being transferred to?"

"Jackson County Correctional Center at Marianna, Florida," he responded.

As we traveled the 1-1/2-hour trip to Marianna, Florida., my thoughts were that this was retaliation for the newspaper article. Even though my remarks were complimentary and truthful, I wondered if someone higher up was upset because I had shared with the taxpayers that a prison camp was like being on a vacation.

Upon arrival at Jackson County Correctional Center (fancy name for county jail), I was escorted inside the facility. Having heard so many horror stories about the various county jails from the inmates who had spent time in them waiting to be transferred to prison, I was pleasantly surprised at the cleanliness of the facility and overall pleasant demeanor of the officers.

Having arrived at the facility around 5:00 p.m., I was placed in a holding cell with a black male in his 50's. We were brought a covered tray and upon removing the top, I discovered our meal consisted of greasy turnip greens, greasy pinto beans, macaroni and cheese, cornbread, and a glass of grape Kool-aid Having looked over the meal, I chose to eat the cornbread and drink the Kool-aid. The inmate in the cell with me gulped down his food and asked if he could have what I was not going to eat. I learned later from one of the regular county inmates that this man was mentally ill and was always being arrested for some charge or another. This was his home.

After about 30 minutes, I was removed from the cell and taken to the processing desk. This being the 30th of May, it was Jessica's birthday, and I was supposed to call her at 7:00 p.m. and wish her a happy birthday. I explained the situation to the officer processing me, and he informed me that once he finished with all the paper work, taking my picture, and fingerprinting me, he would let me place a call to my granddaughter.

Around 7:00 p.m., I was permitted to place a collect call to Jessica to wish her a happy birthday and shared with her that I would be spending next May 30th with her as she celebrated her 15th birthday. I did not share with my "tiger Lou" that I had been placed in a county jail. I was not permitted to call Mary until the next day.

Having finished my conversation with Jessica, I was taken to a section of the jail designated for federal inmates. This cell had 8 beds, one stainless steel lavatory, and one commode. The four bottom bunks were concrete and the top bunks were metal. The inmates were given a mattress about 4" thick. Needless to say, the mattress was of little comfort on the concrete bed.

There were four other inmates in the cell with me. One was a mass murderer who had been sentenced to life and was on his way to the Atlanta, Georgia, Penitentiary. Another one was a kingpin drug dealer being transferred to Tallahassee, Florida. The third inmate was serving time for growing marijuana and was being transferred to Talladega, Alabama, my hometown. The fourth inmate was a black male in his 40's who had lost one of his legs in a motorcycle accident. This was his 8th time in prison. He had become addicted to drugs, and each time he was released on supervised release, he would get back on drugs and fail his urine test, and his probation would be revoked, and he would be sent back to prison. I remained in Jackson County Correctional Facility for 13 days and then was transferred to Tallahassee, Florida, Prison.

Upon arrival at the Tallahassee facility, after processing, I was assigned to a two-man cell. My cellmate was a 19-year-old, black male who had been arrested for selling crack cocaine but had not been to court, and the government would not set him a bond The prosecutor was trying to force him to turn in the people who were supplying him with the crack. The prosecutor supposedly told him that if he didn't cooperate and plead guilty, if he was found guilty at trial, he would be sentenced to 15-25 years.

After a couple of days at Tallahassee, I was waiting in line to make a call to Mary. The inmate ahead of me looked to be about 15 years of age. As we waited our turn for the phone, we made small talk about the prison system in general and the differences in the facilities

"How old are you?" I asked the young man. "24." He responded. "How long have you been in?" "Eight years." The young man continued that he had joined the Costa Nova, a Mafia group when he was sixteen years of age, and shortly thereafter, the federal government indicted the members of the organization. Everyone was tried together, found guilty, and sentenced to life plus 30 years plus 20 years. The group had been charged with loan sharking, racketeering, murder, money laundering of drug money, and numerous other charges.

After a week at Tallahassee, I was awakened one morning around 3:00 a.m. and was informed that me and 10 other inmates and myself were being transferred but was not told where to. We were not permitted to make any phone calls to let our families know we were being transferred. We were taken to a holding cell in another part of the prison, handcuffed, with waist chains and leg irons placed on us. Around 7:30 a.m., we were taken to a waiting Greyhound bus outside the prison and told we were going to Tampa, Florida, to catch a plane that would fly us back to Atlanta, Georgia.

This is the craziest thing I have ever heard, I thought. From Tallahassee, Florida, it was only a few hours to Atlanta but was about 7 hours to Tampa and then would be flown to Atlanta.

After 7 hours we arrived at Tampa, Florida, airport. For the next 3 hours, we remained on the bus chained and shackled, waiting for the plane to come in. Finally, we were informed that the plane had engine problems, and we would not be flying. We were transferred back to Tallahassee. For 17 hours, 11 inmates were chained and shackled and transported on a $100,000 bus with three armed guards. I wonder what this cost the taxpayers.

If you have never tried to eat or go to the restroom while your hands are cuffed and chained to your waist and leg irons, coupled by being on a moving bus rocking and swaying as you travel about 65 mph, it is an unexplainable messy experience.

Upon our arrival back at Tallahassee prison, I was placed back in the same cell where I remained for the next 7 days.

On July 1, 1997, I was awakened along with 20 other inmates around 4:00 am. and told we were being transferred. Around noon, we were cuffed and shackled once again, loaded on a bus and transported to the Tallahassee airport. The trip to the airport took about 30 minutes.

Upon arrival at the airport, we were loaded into a 727, along with more than 100 other inmates, which included 35 women, young and old. We were all flown to Atlanta, Georgia, where we were placed on another bus and transported to the "big house," the Atlanta Penitentiary. I had heard a lot of wild tales about this facility from the various inmates who had served time, but this was my first experience behind the gray walls of the facility allegedly where rape, fights, and murder are common occurrences.

As the bus pulled into the enclosed tunnel (like a dungeon or underground corridor), there were approximately 15-20 guards waiting to welcome us. As our names were called, we exited the bus, still chained and shackled, and were lined up against the wall.

The first thought that crossed my mind was that we were going to be shot. The long, dark corridor of the Atlanta Penitentiary reminded me of scenes out a horror movie. For the next hour or so, the 100-plus inmates were processed into the facility. Of all my 37 months in prison, this was the first time I had really felt uneasy. The thought of the bunkmates whom I would be assigned to "cell" with and how many per cell was scary. Having already been told by other inmates who had been here, I was aware that most of the cells had 4-6 inmates in a two-man cell. With only two bunks placed in a 10'10' cell, this meant that somebody had to sleep on the floor.

With all the paperwork completed, and having been served supper—two bologna sandwiches and a cup of diluted grape soda—with my set of different prison clothes, I was escorted down the corridors of the Atlanta Penitentiary. As the guard escorted me down the corridors, the different inmates already in the cells were hollering and cursing the guards as we walked by. At the end of a long corridor, I was placed in a two-man cell with a white male in his late 50's. I learned from him that he had won an appeal and was on his way back to court in Oklahoma. Shortly after becoming acquainted and getting the top bunk ready to sleep on, the cell door was opened, and a guard brought a Mexican in along with a mattress. He was to sleep on the floor. Fortunately, he was only in the cell until about 3:00 a.m. the next morning, at which time he was removed and allegedly transferred to Texas.

For the next 7 days, just the two of us occupied the cell. During this time, we were fed three times a day but just barely enough to survive. The food was the worst of any facility I had been in. Cold, greasy eggs with cold, greasy potatoes were served twice during this stay for breakfast, and the other days we were served one box of dry cereal. For the noon meal, we would get bologna sandwiches with watered-down grape drink. For the night meal, we were served greasy pork, beef, or bad-tasting fish, usually with potatoes and a piece of white bread. Even though most of the food was not what I would have preferred or prepared if I had not been in prison, I still gave thanks for the food. I am sure there were millions of people in the world who would have loved to have had this much food to eat.

The food was not the worst part of my stay in Atlanta. Due to a female officer being attacked by one of the inmates prior to my arrival, all the inmates were locked down 22-1/2 hours a day. "Lock-down" only permitted the inmates to be out of the cell 1-1/2 hours per day and not at all on the weekend. During this 1-1/2 hours, we had to shower, change our laundry and linen, and make phone calls if there were any phones available. There were only 8 telephones for the hundreds of inmates. One of the times that I was out of my cell, I noticed the floor was glossy from waxing, but under the clear wax, I could see what looked like bloodstains on the floor. I asked one of the long-term trustees if this was blood, and he informed me it was and could be found over several areas of the prison. He said it was from inmates fighting and stabbing each other. When the blood would spill on the floor, it would dry, and it was almost impossible to get it off the concrete floor.

A couple of nights after my arrival at Atlanta, I heard one of the young prisoners screaming and hollering for the guards. This went on for several hours into the late night. The way sound carried in the corridors it was impossible to know just where the sound was coming from or what was being said, but the next day one of the trustees indicated it was a 19-year-old who had been giving the guards a hard time so they placed him in the cell with three prisoners who were in for life and had been in for several years. According to the trustee, the three "lifers" had taken terms raping and sodomizing the young man. The trustee said this was not unusual for the guards to do this to any prisoner who gave them a hard time.

As the week came to an end and I was made aware of some of the horrible things that went on, I was glad that we were being kept locked down and especially glad that I had been placed in a cell with a family man. The good Lord was still looking out for me.

On July 7, after one week of the nightmare, I was notified by one of the guards that I was being transferred to Birmingham, Alabama, for my court appearance of July 10. Upon being taken out of my cell and transferred to another holding area, I was ordered to strip, then searched, and given another set of clothes for traveling. Upon dressing, I was turned over to two marshals who handcuffed and shackled me along with 3 other men and placed us into a van. For the first time, I really felt good about being cuffed and chained. I knew I was almost home.

Upon our arrival at the Jefferson County Jail in Birmingham, the cuffs and chains were removed, and the deputies began processing us.

More personal questions, picture taking, fingerprinting, strip searched and then a set of striped pants and shirt. I really looked like a convict now. After dressing in my new clothes, we were placed in a holding cell. From where we were, I could see the bulletin board, and it indicated that there were almost 1400 prisoners in the jail. I asked one of the guys with us who was a regular visitor to the jail how many was the jail built for. He indicated around 650-700. I knew this meant 3-4 per cell. When the officer called me up to the front desk to finish processing me in, I asked him where would I be assigned to sleep.

"Probably floor 5." he responded

"Is this good or bad?" I asked.

"This is where the "homos" and crazies are. All the other cells and floors are packed."

"I realize I don't have a say in the matter, but I sure wish I could be placed somewhere else," I responded.

The officer was a super nice man, and he smiled and asked me to have a seat on the bench across from the processing desk, and he would see what could be worked out. While I waited, I reminded God that so far he had done a great job of looking after me, and I was too close to home for Him to let me be placed in a cell with a bunch of perverts and drug-crazy people.

After a short time, the deputy called me back up to the desk and said that he had found me a cell on the protective custody floor. I was further informed that I would be in a cell by myself and that there were only three other inmates in this section. One was an ex-policeman charged with drug conspiracy, another was serving time for money-laundering, and the third one was being held pending charges for home invasion and murder. I soon learned that I would have a TV set, good food, and would not be locked down but for a few hours a day plus at night time. God had come across again.

Before I was taken to my cell, I was escorted to the medical station and informed that I had to have an AIDS test. I informed the nurse that I had just been tested a few weeks ago at Eglin, but she informed me that all inmates being incarcerated in the county jail had to have the test. I had been stuck so many times, I was beginning to feel like a pin cushion. This being completed, I was given some bed linen and taken to my cell. I quickly became acquainted with the three other prisoners. After a few hours, I soon learned about "home invasion" and how it went down. According to Tony, several gang members would go to a known drug dealer's home, knock on the door, and pretend to be an insurance salesman or some professional person. Once the unsuspecting drag dealer would open the door and usually invite the person in, the other gang members would come out of their hiding at the edge of the house and burst into the house. They would tie up the drug dealer and any family members at home and then proceed to carry out the drugs, money, or valuables they wanted. On more than one occasion, they would kill the people. If they chose not to kill one of their victims, they felt secure because they felt the drug dealer could not report them to the police. I learned Tony had gotten saved since coming to jail and had agreed to cooperate with the police and help solve numerous killings and burglaries in and around Birmingham.

On July 10th, I was cuffed and chained by two marshals, placed in a van with two other prisoners, and transported to the federal building for my final appearance before Honorable Judge U.W. Clemons.

As I entered the courtroom, 20 pounds lighter in baggy prison clothes and steel shackles on my feet, I noticed that several of my relatives and friends, including my wife, sister, son and daughter-in-law, Ann Gaither, a cousin, reporter Cheryl Marsh of the Daily Home and reporter Rose Livingston of the Birmingham News were there. When the Honorable Judge U.W. Clemons entered the courtroom, my attorneys, Rod Giddens and Steven Salter and I approached the bench for the verdict. After comments from the prosecution and response from my attorneys, Judge Clemons sentenced me to 41 months which meant time served. Four days later on July 14, I was released from Birmingham County Jail, and my wife and brother was there to take me home. This was my first taste of freedom in 37-1/2 months. It sure was a great feeling to walk out of the jail without chains and shackles and in civilian clothes—my clothes.

My second taste of freedom became a reality when Mary, Charles, and I stopped off at the Cracker Barrel in Leeds, Alabama Having promised Cheryl Marsh of the Daily Home that I would call her upon my release from jail, I placed a call to her at the paper in Talladega, and when she found out that I was in Leeds, she informed me her and photographer Jim Smothers wanted to drive the 35 miles and interview me at the restaurant. I agreed to her request.

Cheryl and Jim arrived at the Cracker Barrel about the time we were finishing our meal of chicken, pinto beans, potatoes, cornbread, a big glass of real milk, and a chocolate dessert.' It was a great feeling to be reunited with my family and friends. The food was great, too!

After the interview, Mary, Charles and I headed for Talladega. Upon arrival at home, I was humbled to see so many relatives, friends, neighbors, and news media there to welcome me home.

Among the first people I saw was my mother, Ruby, my mother-in-law, Nell Chandler, Delane, Becky, Jessica, and the list is endless. Then I moved among the crowd, shaking hands and greeting everyone. Around midnight, Mary and I were finally alone after more than 37-1/2 months.

The next day, Rev. Harvey Bowlin, pastor of Trinity Lighthouse, invited me to be a guest on his weekly TV show, and also invited Mary and me to sing and speak at his church.

On the Sunday following my release from jail on Monday, a special homecoming service was held, and my friends, Max and Joan Morris, Paul and Linda Wesson, and Dr. and Mrs. Yung Chul Han, Overseer of the Church of God in Korea and president of the university, were there along with Pastor and Mrs. Lee Brasher, all the church members, and my family to welcome me home. Needless to say, I was overwhelmed. At the close of the service, the ladies of the church had prepared a meal second to none. The fellowship was great.

My mother and dad purchased a 1969 Plymouth Fury III in 1969 and only had 64,187 miles on the speedometer when I returned home. Since mother no longer drives, I spent the next few weeks driving mother wherever she needed to go, and on Wednesdays, we ate dinner at our long-time friends' Ernest and Mary Gooden's restaurant. Without a doubt, they serve the best barbeque in the world. They also had visited me at Eglin

Undecided on what I wanted to do for employment, I decided to take a few weeks and work on my books and spend time with Mother. Mary had returned to work after a few days off. As mother and I would go to the different stores shopping, people would come up to me and welcome me home and usually would ask two questions. The first was "Are you going to run for mayor again?" The second was, "What are you doing?" meaning "Where are you working?" I would answer, "I don't know whether I will run for mayor again or not," and "All I am doing right now is 'driving Ms. Ruby.'"

Just prior to my release from prison, Detective Ken Sisk, one of the officers who was involved in my investigation, resigned his position with the city police department, Chief of Police Mike Hamlin submitted his letter of resignation, and District Attorney Robert Rumsey resigned his office. In view of the D.A.'s sudden decision to resign and not having heard from the Attorney General concerning my earlier request for an investigation into the death of Jamie Grace, I wrote the following letter:

September 24. 1997

Honorable Bill Pryor

Attorney General

Alabama State House

II South Union Street

Montgomery, Alabama 36130

Dear Mr. Prior:

On September 16, 1996, 1 wrote a letter to then Attorney General Jeff Sessions requesting he reopen the investigation into the death of Ms.

Jamie Grace, the former director of Talladega County United Narcotics Operations (UNO). who operated under the direction of Talladega County District Attorney Robert Rumsey.

On September 26, 1996, I received a letter from then Chief Investigator. Edward F. McFadden, acknowledging receipt of my letter to Mr. Sessions. In this letter, Mr. McFadden assured me that he would look into the request and be back in touch with me.

On October 2 and October 14, 1996, 1 wrote 10 Mr. McFadden, supplying him with additional information that I felt was pertinent surrounding the alleged suicide of Ms. Grace.

On February 4, 1997, after you had been appointed Attorney

General. I contacted you by letter and shared my concern about the death of Ms. Grace and brought you up to date on my request.

As of this date. I have received no response from Mr. McFadden, you. or anyone from your office in relation to where you are with the investigation.

Mr. Pryor. I realize you are a very busy man and apparently working short-handed. but if Jamie Grace had been an influential white woman, every law enforcement officer in the state would have been assigned to investigate her death.

As stated in my letter to Mr. Sessions on September 16, 1996, 1 strongly believe that one or more persons connected with the DA.'s office was involved in the murder and coverup of Jamie.

Now that Mr. Rumsey has announced his retirement and two of his former employees have left. the politics should no longer present a problem for you, if this is the case.

Mr. Pryor. if you have no intention of following up on my request due to my being a former federal inmate, at least have the courtesy to respond. The citizens of Talladega who feel as I do, that Jamie Grace was murdered and her murder covered up by informing the people that it was suicide, deserve an answer from your office.

Thank you for permitting me to share my concern and frustration with you.

Sincerely,

Larry Barton

Enclosure

EPILOGUE

As the weeks turned to months and everything began to fall back in place, I continued to spend every spare moment working on my manuscript. After I completed the manuscript, REFLECTION OF AIDS, and sent it to my publisher, I continued working on my manuscript, FROM POLITICS TO PRISON.

As I began to finalize the manuscript, I realized there were still several individuals who had been friends with the late Jamie Grace that I had not been able to contact prior to my going to prison. I immediately started working to locate these individuals. I was still trying to find out information that would prove Jamie did not commit suicide.

The names—Greg, Carol, and Leon had been mentioned numerous times, but other than Leon Thomas, I did not know for sure who the other individuals were.

One day I was talking with a friend of mine and the subject of Jamie came up, and I inquired of my friend if she knew Greg and Carol. I hit the jackpot. Not only did this friend know both of these individuals but provided me with last names and phone numbers

I first tried contacting Leon Thomas, the Talladega city detective who allegedly had found Jamie Grace dead. After several attempts, I finally reached him by phone and shared with him that I would like to talk with him about the unanswered questions that were bugging me. Leon agreed to meet me at my place of employment the next morning. He never showed up or contacted me to explain why. I made no further effort to contact him.

Next I contacted Carol (not her real name and explained to her what I already knew and asked her if she would be willing to share with me what she knew about the last days of Jamie. Carol shared with me that Jamie had been a personal friend and had shared much with her, but she felt Jamie had shared in confidence about things, and Carol did not want to betray this confidence. I asked Carol if there were an investigation into the death of Jamie, would she share her information with a grand jury? Her reply was yes, she would not have any choice.

Finally, I was able to make contact with Greg. When I shared with Greg who I was and what information I needed, Greg knew me and was most helpful. He confirmed much of what I already knew, but one piece of information was new. Greg said that Jamie had approached him several weeks prior to her death about the possibility of his installing a security system either in the room where the safe that held confiscated drugs and money was housed or either on the vault itself. Greg went on to explain that he was very capable of installing this type equipment, but he referred Jamie to a company in Anniston, Alabama, that specializes in this type work.

Using the name and number of the company in Anniston, I contacted the owner and informed him who I was and asked him if he remembered a person by the name of Jamie Grace contacting him about installing a security system in the D.A.'s office. The owner did not recall the name immediately because of the length of time and the number of calls he receives. He did say that he would be more than willing to go back to 1991 or 1992 and look at his records if he were requested to do so by an investigator or a grand jury.

In February, 1998, Alabama Governor Fob James appointed Attorney Jonathan Adams to fill the unexpired term of D.A. Robert Rumsey who had suddenly announced his resignation.

Since I had not received any response from Alabama Attorney General Pryor concerning my request to re-open the investigation surrounding the death of Jamie

Grace, and based on information and material in my possession concerning other matters, I decided to make one last effort to try and learn the truth. The following is a copy of my letter to the Honorable Jonathan Adams, Talladega County District Attorney.

Larry Barton

Post Office Box 588

Talladega, Alabama 35161

March 5, 1998

Honorable Jonathan Adams

District Attorney

Post Office Box 572

Talladega, Alabama 35161

Dear Mr. Adams;

As a resident of Talladega County I am making a request for you to present to a grand jury evidence concerning the death of Jamie Grace and other possible thefts from the Office of the District Attorney. I have tapes and other evidence to present to a grand jury. Autopsy reports are also available relative to Jamie's death.

I have waited until you have settled into your job before making this request. I believe the time is right for these matters to be investigated.

Sincerely,

Larry Barton

As FROM POLITICS TO PRISON goes to press, I have not received an answer from D.A. Adams.

The citizens of Talladega may never learn the truth about the death of my friend, Jamie Grace, but I will continue to seek answers and maybe someday, someone on his or her deathbed will confess to what really happened.

In the meantime, Mary and I are receiving invitations to visit churches throughout the U.S. as well as overseas to sing and share the message of how God blessed and looked after Mary and me while I was incarcerated.

As you finish reading FROM POLITICS TO PRISON, I trust you that you have been informed, but above all, blessed and realize that God can sustain and protect in any situation. Mary and I desire your prayers.

After several weeks of being free, mother and I were spending quality time together. I was taking her shopping and various places she wanted to visit.Everywhere we went, I was bombarded with questions concerning the death of Jamie grace.Although it had been several years, people were still perplexed and had their opinion as to how she had died. If she was dead.

Do you believe she killed herself? Do you think clarence haynes covered it up?He was the corner. You know he was having an affair with rumsey detective the surrett woman.Is it possible that the white policeman that raped her came back and killed her?Did they examine her to see if she was raped? There was no autopsy.Some of the police didn't like it because she got that position over dem.Reckon they kilt her?I heard it was a powerful drug dealer involved with her. Every opinion conceivable was being tossed around. Everyone knew for a fact what had taken place.The blacks had their opinion and the whites had theirs. Would the truth ever be revealed?Maybe Jamie had left a note if she had decided to take her life. But at the end of the day, very few believed that jamied committed suicide. Or dead.Had any of her family viewed the body?Who had seen the body since it was a closed casket?

My birthday was a few days away.April 17, 1998.This would be my first birthday back home since July 1994. Three years.No word from d.a. Jonathan adams in response to my letter requesting the death of jamie be investigated. Mary, mother, and I decided to go to stampede restaurant in town and share lunch.

We would have been better off having gone out of town.Friends I had not seen since being incarcerated, came to our table welcoming me back home and yes, expressing their opinion about how I had been set up.Then, they wanted to express their views about Jamie. Our thirty-minute lunch turned into two-plus hours.

The more questions people asked or shared with me their thoughts; the more memorics of this event began coming back to my remembrance.Thoughts I had placed on a back burner. I had kept busy at eglin working in the supply room, or later in the barber shop.I was also helping out with planning the music for Sunday chapel service.I was trying to teach myself how to play the trumpet.

The more each one shared, thoughts kept recuring in my mind. Jamie's gun was missing. Where had the gun come from that was in her bed?Had ann placed it there after killing her?Question galore. Had beautiful Jamie grace committed suicide.Some do not believe she is dead.They contend she is in protective custody.There was no evidence or proof of the variety of any of the rumors.I still held to my belief based on what Jamie and Sandra had shared with me when all this was taking place.

After lunch I took mother and Mary home and decided to take a quick nap. During my nap, I dreamed I was in my cube, laying on my back on my prison half bed, looking at the thumb-size roach bugs manuver their way across the ceiling.Jamie was on my mind.Sleep was scarce during late hours as my thoughts would wander back to Ann and Dennis and the money that had been stolen.Jamie had indicated ann had stolen thousands of dollars. I recalled something my long-time friend, sally mitchel had shared with me.Sally had worked in the d.a.'s office forever.She had warned Robert that Ann could not be trusted.Sally was of the opinion that Robert was on ann's radar.It was rumored that she had been screwing several talladega, police officers, detective eugene jacks, as well as Dennis surrett and clarence haynes. Was Robert rumsey her next trophy, or had she already scored with him?Was this why Ann had already been given so much authority?

''I told Robert that Ann was no good.She's a thief, a whore that makes everyone that she has sex with, believe they are the only one.She uses them.I have known and worked with and for robert many years and have never known him to be unfaithful to his wife, but since Ann has come into his life, I'm beginning to wonder.He has turned everything over to her.She's going to destroy him.She is an egotistical, sex-starved control freak. She is like a spoiled brat and a smart ass and doesn't care who she has to step on or destroy to be in control.Dennis is like a male dog following a female dog around that's in heat.Dennis is an excellent detective, but Ann will destroy him and his marriage. Ann is using Dennis because of his status," sally said she had told Robert." "she will destroy you robert rumsey."

Not sure what caused me to snap out of my sleep unless it was sally calling rumsey's name, but my thoughts returned to the animosity that had come into play when d.a. Robert rumsey held a press conference and announced Jamie was being appointed to head up united narcotics office.

As mayor and since Jamie was a city employee, Robert had requested my support. The resentment was very obvious, especially from captain willard e. Pee wee hurst. As a ranking officer, he felt he was equally qualified, but robert had his mind made up. I supported his decision. I recalled how upset capt hurst was when the d.a. Announced that Dennis surrett would be appointed to take jamie's position as chief detective. Is it possible the captain could have been a part of this sorid event? Was he still upset Jamie had reported him trying to rape her several months earlier? Is it possible pee wee came back, raped her then killed her? No autopsy had been performed, so there was no evidence indicating whether she had been raped or not. Who had made the decision not to perform an autopsy? Over and over thoughts rolled through my mind like a movie that continued showing over and over. It had to stop. It was on my mind day and night.

More thoughts began swirling in my thoughts. I recalled how impressed I had been the first time I met Jamie. She was first class and presented a resume that none of the men could come close to. Jamie proved her trustworthiness, honesty, and loyalty. Over the next several months and until her death, whatever Jamie needed or suggested Jamie received.

My mind suddenly changes channels, as Ann surrett flashed back in my thoughts. The more I thought of her and her fiasco, the more I had a hatred in my heart. Ann was still sand in my craw. I was still upset by the way she and a few others had manipulated the judicial system for their benefit in their successful effort to remove me from office.'"they could not defeat me at the polls, so they came up with a law that allegedly is seldom used to make my case conform to this law.,' I thought. But I guess overall, the fiasco that had been played, by judge feilding was still leaving a bitter taste in my spirit. He completely lied to the people of talladega county people that trusted him and kept voting for him. "Should he change his name to judge judas.?, I wondered. 'Had he partaken of the fruit of ann? After all, despite all the rumors and allegations of who had tasted the fruit, the tree still looked alive and blossoming.Maybe the tree had just been pruned, but not cut down and just needed an arborist.Anyone can cut off a little limb, but it takes a master arborist to come in and provide the tender care and treatment needed to thrive.Was the judge fielding a master arborist? Jerry fielding had been a man i respected and felt was above reproach.After allegedly playing footsie with Ann white surrett, my opinion changed.I had heard rumors, but i did not believe them.I did now.

I was receiving numerous calls about job offers.I knew i was fortunate and blessed to have so many caring friends that knew i had done wrong.Even if i had been guilty of stealing fifty-nine hundred seventy-five dollars, there was no way a sentence of five years was justified. Rapists, child molesters, or murderers rarely receive this type of sentence.They could not control, so they trumped up a law.

I was not sure what path i wished to pursue.Three years of incarceration can mess with the mind of a person. No real responsibilities other than a few hours a day cutting grass or helping keep the military golf greens in excellent shape or cutting the inmate's hair. As an ex-mayor, i was confined to the base.

I finally accepted a sales position with roebuck chrysler in birmingham, alabama.I received a guaranteed salary and medical benefits.I gained top salesman status in my first month.One thousand dollar bonus."this beats .29 cents an hour cutting hair in prison", i chuckled to myself.

I soon learned the manager was not being honest with the prices we were given to work with.He had fake invoices so when we gave a customer what we thought was a good deal, in reality, we were being dishonest with them. I turned in my resignation telling the owner i was not going to deceive the customers. He told me that it was just the automobile game.I told him not for me. "there are men serving time in prison for fraud," i told him." i immedi- ately quit.The dollars i had made, i had saved them and immediately went to the bank and paid off our loans.

Dutton and hill went above and beyond to let mary pay interest on the car and house loans for the time i was incarcerated. No way was i going to default.I was becoming more agitated., restless, and irritated. House and car payments were going to have to begin.I had given my word that as soon as i returned home from incarceration, and went to work, i would resume making payments. Bankers at two different banks had put our payments on hold or what was called a single payment loan when i went to prison.Joe williams., joel elliott. And johnny before going to prison i had never been unemployed. I was a work a hollic.I was becoming concerned and agitated and the idleness gave me too much time to recount how i had arrived at this point in life.

I knew for a fact i had not stolen any money.As mayor i did not have access to checks nor any authority to write or sign a check much less the ones that had been written and given to jerry jackson. Jerry would always come by city hall in the afternoon and pick up his check that had been placed in a sealed envelope.I had been accused of cashing the checks and pocketing the money.However, when the checks were examined for fingerprints, only one check had my thumbprint on it.

Jerry had called me and shared he was running late and asked if i would pick up his check for him.The clerk had written the check and gotten it signed but had not placed it in an envelope.Not thinking, she handed me the check and i returned to my office.About an hour or so later, jerry came by my office and i handed it to him.That is the only way my thumbprint could have possibly gotten on the check.

Since steve giddens, a new da had been elected, i decided to request he reopens the case. I had numerous items i could share with the d.a., including a taped conversation between jamie and sandra surrett the ex-wife of d an investigator dennis surrett. I remembered jerry had brought me the tape that jamie instructed him to do. I took my tape machine and inserted the tape and for almost an hour i listened in awe. I remembered the tape being brought to me, but soon realized i had not listened to it.The conversation was about the plot to kill jamie. I then listened to the taped conversation between their brother of jamie and myself.He was a very powerful man in the washington d c. Circles but lived in texas.He and i had talked during the time jamie had first died.He had been fired up at that time, but for whatever the reason, had backed off to help get an investigation open.

I decided to call him and let him know i was still concerned about the unexplained death of jamie. I was convinced that, if jamie was dead, she did not kill herself.I remembered what he had shared when jamie first died.Dialing his number, after several rings he answered.

As i shared the reason for my call, he responded and said, "mr mayor, jamie thought the world of you and would do anything you asked even to risk her life. "you are one of a few electred officials that jamie loved," he commented.She shared with me that she was convinced that investigators in the da. Office was out to harm her including murder.She was 'crazy' about mr. Rumsey but knew ann had him convinced that she was indispensible.Jamie indicated that there could be over a half million dollars in money and drugs that the two detectives had absconded with.Jamie shared everything with me including the police captain trying to rape her.She said several of the officers and a couple of detectives would try to get her to have sex with them, but that was not her priority.Jamie was a very private person and some thought she was a lesbian. To my knowledge, there was one man she loved, but something happened, and they broke up.After this, she began experiencing some emotional and health issues and was under an allusion that there was a conspiracy to undermine every-thing she tried to do.

Even though i was no longer the mayor, he still referred to me as mayor.Mr. Mayor, i loved my sister and was proud of her accomplishments.She loved her family and they loved her. Jamie and i contributed financially to their welfare.They depended on us, but i would be naive to think she could never have been placed in a compromising situation. She was tough but she was also human. So much time has elapsed since her death.I think it would be wise for all concerned to just cherish her qualities, accomplishments, and memories.I would not want a from n investigation to uncover a mistake jamie could have made. On behalf of the family and myself, thanks for all you did for her. We are going to miss her.

December 31, 1998, the headline of the daily home was talladega water board may face an ethics probe. The article had been written by reporter jason landers. The article allegeding the possibility of wrongdoing. Talladega mayor charles osborne was indicating close to two hundred thousand dollars had been spent illegally.

Rumors had been running rampant for several months that several board members had misused the money, possibly spending it for personal use. Attorney steve giddens had just been elected talladega county district attorney, but would not be sworn in until january 18, 1999. He committed to investigate once in office.

Another week passes and even though i was being offered a job i was unsettled. Jamie's death was still gnawing at my mind. I could not let it go. Although jamie's brother wanted to move on, i was not eager to do so. I had lost thirty-seven months out of my life…. Three years away from my wife and ninety-year-of-age mother. No, i was not prepared to walk away from it…. Not yet anyway. A lot of praying and job seeking was ongoing. This was a priority.

Out of the clear blue sky, i received a phone call from jackie, a young man i had known his entire life inquiring if our house was for sale. Mary and i had discussed the possibility, but right out of prison, all we had done was discuss it between ourself. Our family members were not aware of our interests.

I informed jackie that we had talked about building a house but no decision had been made. "We have to sell this house before we could make a decision," i responded.

"If you decide to sell, my wife and i will buy your house," jackie responded.

"God has already found a buyer before we put it up for sale," i thought.

Around february 2, 2001, after a ten-month grand jury investigation, according to a daiy home article, two water and sewer board members were indicted. The sixteen felony charges included using their positions for personal gain. This indictment could bring additional charges, according to the prosecutor.

Jim armstrong, son of council member james armstrong, jim was indicted on three charges including knowingly or intentionally using his official office or position for personal gain. Armstrong, who resigned from the board in 1998, is accused of using his office to boost sales at his b and sports.

Howard ''rip" williams faces four counts of using his office for personal gain, one count of conspiracy to use his office for personal gain, one count of aiding and abetting armstrong, and seven counts of perjury.

Charges against williams stem from spending on heaters at brecon springs park. This one hundred seventy thousand dollar project was a violation of its charter. Williams is also accused of misusing a board nextel cell phone. More than twelve thousand minutes were used in one fiscal year. Perjury charges against williams involve statements made to the department of examiners or the grand jury.

If convicted, they could be sentenced to two to twenty years.

As i read the news article, my thoughts returned to the day that councilwoman edythe sims, had questioned me about who jerry jackson was. A few weeks later, edythe sims passed away.

Several weeks later, after the death of jamie, not completely sure of who kept the jerry jackson issue alive, an investigation was suggested. The council was informed an investigation could not begin until someone filed a formal request.

Not sure who made the suggestion, but 'rip' signed a formal complaint stating he did not know who jerry jackson was. It is my understanding 'rip' never officially requests an investigation. Once the document was signed, it wound up being the responsibility of detective ken sisk to initiate an investigation.

At the end of the investigation, i was eventually indicted, tried, found guilty, and sentenced to serve thirty-seven-plus months, before my sentence was overturned.

February 08, 2001, jim armstrong and howard "rip" williams, two former talladega water board members pled guilty to ethics and perjury charges. The charges had been reduced to laundering water board funds into their own pockets partly through a babe ruth league.

Armstrong and williams agreed to make restitution and testify against other water board-related cases that might be brought. Armstrong was ordered to pay twenty-two thousand dollars in restitution. Williams was ordered to pay ten thousand five hundred forty-nine dollars. Neither one received any jail time.

Having learned of the sentences, my thoughts turned back to my sentence. I had been found guilty of less than six thousand dollars in illegal expenditure and sentenced to fifty-one months. Ann surrett had been found guilty of stealing more than one hundred thousand and served less than two years. Judge jerry fielding was the judge in all the cases.

On sunday, march 31, 2002, i purchased a copy of the birmingham news and started pouring over the want ads one after the other bingo. I had not worked as a barber for more than twenty years. My eyes are like a laser focused in on a small ad. Wanted a barber to work at the cahaba heights barber shop. Guaranteed six hundred fifty dollars a week. Jefferson county barber license required contact tom pilkington.

My spirit dropped. I was a barber. A good barber, but i did not have a jefferson county barber license and to get one i had to be a graduate of a licensed barber college.

On monday, april 1, 2002, i drove to birmingham to meet the owner of the barbershop

"God, i need a job. Are you listening? I want this job.' i was quietly praying ".

Having met tom, he asked how long had it been since i barbered. When i said probably twenty years, he responded no problem. Like riding a bicycle, it will come back quickly. He agreed to hire me that day.

I immediately contacted the barber board chairman don matthews and learned the criteria for obtaining a license to barber in jefferson county was told i would have to have a minimum of 1000 hours. I shared with

Don, i have a suggestion. Is there a policy or rules that prohibits taking a refresher course combined with do

 Don that i had more than 1000 hours of barbering experience and was it possible a refresher course would be cumention or verification proving i am more than qualified? I would gladly pay the fee. A week later, i received a jefferson county barber license.

The next day, i called john hill. He had been promoted to vice president of citizens bank. John had also been elected as a city council member. John had been instrumental in working out a plan, when i went to prison, for mary to keep the house. We had paid off the car loan and the house payment was brought current. When john answered the phone, i said ''john, mary, and i would like to build a house on our dellwood property. We need some money.

''How much do you need,'' john asked.

''Around one hundred fifty thousand dollars,'' i responded.

''Let me know when you need it,'' john said.

I immediately called jackie. When he answered the phone, i asked if was interested in buying our house.

"How much do you want for it," i told him, jackie made a counterproposal. Mary and i accepted, with the understanding he would let us pay him rent and live there until we could build our house.

For the next three months, i stayed busy barbering and keeping an eye on our house being built. Everything was great. God was good.

In 2011, my rights had been restored and the urge to run for mayor again was strong i love politics, and my supporters were encouraging me to run again. I had reservations as to where i could win a fourth time; especially since i had served prison time.

I decided to 'throw my hat in the ring. The most that could happen would be i would lose. I was pumped up. Ann and dennis surrett, ken sisk, and some of the other police officers thought it was funny and i was crazy. ''He will get hell beat out of him," some said.

In 2011, i faced three opponents for mayor. Saundra bellamy, harvey bowlin, and bobbye trammell, on election night, i received forty-one percent of the vote. I was short about 300 votes winning. There would be a runoff between a church of god pastor and myself.

For the next three weeks, i campaigned hard. My enemies campaigned just as hard. Every lie known was being told. If i was put back in office, i would steal more money. I would hire jerry jackson, my finance director. I would turn all the inmates loose. Lies lies lies, i kept smiling, shaking hands, and asking for votes.

On election night when all the votes were tabulated, i had won by fifty-three percent of the vote. My opponent was not only a pastor, but owned the t.v. Statio, and had previously served as talladega county revenue commissioner. I was thrilled. I had won my fourth term.

While i was in prison, senator jim preuitt, reverand horace patterson, and eddie tucker, along with several barton haters wanted the form of government changed. They could not defeat me at the polls, so they were successful in getting a constitutional amendment passed changing from mayor council to city manager. This took the authority away from the mayor and gave it to a city manager.

During my fourth term, even though not having the power i previously possessed, i still promoted talladega. I spent time researching through the minutes searching for any information concerning jamie grace and dennis and ann surrett.

Around the middle of the year, i learned that ''pee wee" hurst, the police captain that allegedly tried to undermine jamie and attempted to rape her, was experiencing some serious health issues. The rumors where he was losing his mind. Citizens started circulating that he was reaping what he had sown. On october 06, 2012, willard e. ''Pee wee" hurst passed away. He was 57 years of age.

Before and after the funeral rumors were rampant. What part did he play in jamie's death? Did he go to her apartment, rape her then kill her? Did he use a confiscated weapon to shoot her? Were he and surrett involved sexually and she conspired to get him to kill jamie? Did he lose his mind"?

January 02, 2013, graveside service was held for my long-time personal friend sally mitchell. She had been the administrative assistant to two district attorneys for thirty-two years. Sally was instrumental in helping expose crooked ann white surrett. It was her opinion that ann had stolen more than one-half million dollars in money and drugs. She tried to convince everyone that it was jamie.

Friday march 01, 2013, my mother willie ruby hartley barton passed away in her sleep. Mother was 101 years of age. She had lived a long life and for the most part, had been blessed with excellent health. Mother was a devout christian and had been a singer and sunday school teacher. She also served as a pianist at times. She was hoping to live until jesus raptured the saints.

In 2015 i qualified to run for mayor. If elected, this would be my fifth term to serve. My opponents were vann caldwel, constable, and jerry cooper sr. A retired postal office employee. I would be facing two good men but felt that i could win a fifth term.

Three weeks before election day, i had just parked my car in the parking lot at cahaba heights barber shop. It was aug 8th 2015. I had been working there for several years. As i took hold of the door handle to exit my car, the door swung open and a figure dressed in a trench coat, from head to foot, started hitting me repeatedly in my face, legs, and knees with a tire thumper.

This instrument is about three feet in length with a letter strap affixed on the smaller end of an odd-shaped object. On the larger end, it has iron or steel encased in rawhide covering. This gadget is used by truck drivers to check tires to make sure they are aired up.

I eventually was able to grab what i thought was a sawed-off ball bat holding on to it as i turned in my seat. With my feet and legs outside the car, i started kicking the hooded figure in his balls. Holding on to the instrument, i was able to exit my car. Standing straight up, the assailant grabbed hold of my barber jacket pulling me forward. His action caused the two of us to fall to the pavement, with me on top. I immediately roll to my right removing myself from him. The ball kicking and the falling on his back with 200 pounds on top, took the fight out of him. He stood up and walked to the end of the building.

Fortunately, several men were standing across the street getting ready to go on a trail bike ride and had called the police. By the time the assailant reached the building, the police arrived. He had ridden a bicycle several miles from his residence to the barber shop.

When the assailant's rain gear was removed, i realized the man, apparently attempting to kill me was benny green, a long-time friend. He had been helping me put up campaign signs. He and his wife charlotte and mary and i had been friends for twenty years. It was not unusual for us to eat at a restaurant a couple of times a week. During football season, mary and i were at their house every saturday night watching the alabama ball game. Benny always grilled a steak and charlotte prepared a salad and baked potatoes and rolls.

Benny and charlotte owned a convenience store and charlotte owned a package store. I had a t.v. Talk show and benny or charlotte served as a co-host. What was wrong with benny? I had no idea. He and i had never had a crossword or disagreement. I had no idea what had caused him to try and kill me.

The police arrested benny and charged him with one count of first-degree assault. He was placed under a one hundred fifty thousand dollar bond. When questioned benny alleged that charlotte and i were sexually involved. Claimed he had pictures or videos of us having sex. I laughed at this. I was impotent and had been for many years. Only mary and i were aware of this. Mary was upset about the accusation, but amused at the thought of my sexual ability. My attorney requested a copy of any items benny had, but he never responded.

I continued campaigning with my face black and blue and rumors floating. Everyone had their version of what had happened. On election night, innuendos. Rumors, allegations of an unfounded sexual tryst, mistakes, and outright lies cost me the election. The final vote count was barton, one thousand thirty-seven, caldwell 197, and cooper two thousand.

"i feel good; i'm at ease with everything. When a person stays in office as long as i have, it's obvious i'm going to make enemies. The citizens wanted change. I respect their wishes.', i said to the news reporter during an interview. Only one other person has been elected more times than me. Dr james l hardwick was elected five times and had the form of government not been changed, he would still be the mayor. His enemies hated him and were unable to defeat him at the polls, they were successful in changing the form of government from a part-time mayor to full-time. Dr. Hardwick would have had to close his medical practice to be mayor.

I contacted monica kemp the owner of cavalier barber shop. This is the shop i opened in the late 60's. I had sold the shop to eddie kemp. Monica was his daughter and had learned the barber trade. She now owned the shop. As we talked, we practically solved all the world problems. And in the end, it was agreed that her shop did not have enough customers to justify my working for her full-time. I agreed to work a couple of days a week with monica. I had already decided to go back to birmingham and work in the barber shop. I knew i could return anytime i wanted. I had built a tremendous customer base

Several days had passed before i called faye pray, a beautiful first-class barber. We had worked together for almost fourteen years at cahaba plaza. Barber shop. She had a personality and a smile that could put electricity in a lamp. As we talked, i learned she had opened up her barber shop and was needing a part-time barber. She offered me a job, working thursday thru saturday. Bingo. I had the best of two worlds. I was working with two of the best barbers in the world. My anxiety, frustration, and restlessness were subsiding. I was disappointed i had gotten defeated for mayor, but happy to be back doing what i enjoyed doing.

Benny green's court date had finally come due on a divorce filing. He had filed for a divorce on incompatibility. He had told everyone he had all the evidence including pictures of charlotte and me having sex. I knew it was impossible unless he had gotten a professional to manipulate pictures.

When the trial began, charlotte's neice kim youngblood keating, who had become a very close friend to benny, took the witness stand. She testified that i had caused benny and charlotte to divorce. When questioned by the attorney for charlotte, about what had been done to break up the marriage, kim responded, ''he goes to her house every saturday night and she fixes supper for him.'' the judge and others in the courtroom had to control their laughter. Benny was in the courtroom too but refused to take the witness stand. I couldn't help but wonder where were all the pictures of charlotte and me having sex.

On august 30, 2017, benny jack green was back in court. He had decided to plead guilty and was there to be sentenced. Jefferson county circuit judge clyde jones sentenced benny to serve a five-year sentence. He immediately suspended the sentence placing him on probation. The judge then sentenced him to another 36 months of supervised probation to commence once he completes his five-year sentence.

Everything was going great. I was staying busy and making more money than ever in my life. Back on top of the world. My time incarcerated was becoming a blur of the past. God was good.

Tragedy strikes……. Again. I was injured in a freak car accident.

My car, a 1988 mercury grand marquis was parked in the driveway with the nose of the car on the incline. The big wide heavy door was difficult to open and remain open. The weight forced the door to swing back shut if not physically held.

As i exited the driver's door, i had not cleared the opening before the door swung back hitting me and slamming me up against the car, and forcing me to fall head first onto the concrete.As i lay on the hard concrete, i was awake but paralyzed.Mary was not home but fortunately, a person in the area had witnessed what had happened and called911.

In short order a paramedic group responded.I was in severe pain but unable to tell where the pain was coming from.I lay there helpless. Nothing would move except my eyeballs. They followed the medics.

As they were checking my pulse. Heartbeat and asking questions all i could do was lay there on my back with my eyes locked on the one standing directly over me

Can you hear me?Can you hear me?I could hear but could not move. Only my eyes stayed fixed on the paramedic

I heard one voice say. Put a neck collar on him.I was in excruciating pain all over.I am passing out.I am back.My back is killing me neck pain is unbearable.Nothing is moving.

Get the backboard and straps.Get over here. Give me a hand.Orders are being spouted. Give me a hand.I can hear. Can't move.Pain. Eyes fixed i am gone

Larry. Larry mr barton, can you wake up?Larry. Come on larry wake up.

This is mary your wife. Can you hear me

I could hear but sounded like a faint call

Larry wake up darling. This is mary.

Not sure how long i was unresponsive but i could hear several voices.

Mr barton this is dr okar. Can you understand me?

Larry, can you talk with the dr

My eyes slowly open. I am looking upward. A smooth olive skinhandsome young man is standing to the left side of my bed looking down into my eyes i could hear voices sounding like delane i heard mary calling my name was i dead i was not hurting i was not hot so i must not be in hell i did not see any angels or bands playing so i must not be in heaven.I felt like i was floating.

Dont remember what my remarks were but everyone thought it funny. They were laughing uncontrollable was i at a comedy club i did not see a comedian

Mr barton this is dr ocar. I have been taking care of you for the past few hours you are in the hospital.

Did i have twins?

Laughter

I feel like i have been in a fight. Who won? I asked

The car door, dr. Ocar responded,

More laughter

Not sure how long dr ocar stood beside my bed talking in a very respective manner. His voice had a calming voice

'I have just put your neck, back, and hip back together", he commented

''Sounds good to me i.I did not know it had been separated.,' i mumbled.

"i have good and bad news. Which do you want me to share first," dr ocar asked

''I can handle it,give it to me," i responded

''The good news is you are alive, dr okar said"

"the bad news is you will be paralyzed for the remainder of your life. You will be confined to bed and will have to be hand fed, diapered, and use a urinal or a bed pan. You may have to have a catheter if your kidneys do not start back working. You will have to be shaved and bathed in your bed.You are lucky to be alive, "dr ocar commented.

'Who is this man and what is he talking about wearing diapers? What kind of crazy dream am i having? Where am i and where is mary.?' i thought

"not sure how long you will be in the hospital, but i have put you back together. Nursing care will be needed once you leave the hospital but until you have the necessary help and hospital bed you will need to stay in a nursing facility," this voice kept talking. I could hear but my eyesight was blury like there were two of these people talking. I could hear several voices that seemed to be in another room. Larry is waking up. He is beginning to respond to the doctor. Praise the lord. Thank you, jesus.

Slowly i was coming back to a form of realization that this man had been talking about me. I was still feeling light-headed and in a daze. I recall asking the dr. What had he done to me and him saying i kept you alive. "Why wasn't i alive? Why did he think i was dead? People that die see jesus or say they are in hell. I ain't seen nothing, so i must still be alive. I still did not recall what had happened.

As dr. Ocar started sharing, i interrupted him and said", "i'm in pain but i can't move.". Asking the nurse to give me some type of shot, he started explaining all he had done.

''Your neck was a mess, i had to insert screws into several places to hold your head in place on your neck and shoulder'. He began saying. ."people say i'm screwey in the head, so now it is true.' i responded receiving a big laugh from everyone in the room

''Then i started on your back. I had to put your back together with pins, screws, and small plastic tubing or rods. These rods will not bend so you will not have the flexibility to bend. You may be able to bend at the waist a little, however, time will not increase the flexibility. Metal and plastic tubing is not going to give. I'm not going to provide you with false hope. I never deceive my patients.'

As dr. Ocar continued sharing, i could feel anger, animosity, and bitterness began seeping into my mind. The realization of what had happened to me was coming back in focus. I was becoming bitter at god for permitting this to happen "god, mary, and i pay tithes, support the church and help so many in need. Now you let this happen. Now i will no longer be able to work and pay tithes.I don't understand you" i was thinking in my thoughts. I was becoming more bitter by the minute. The pity party was being planned.

Snapping back into the issue at hand, dr. Ocar said, "i did not operate on your hip. A female physician from u.a.b. Was brought in to assist.The bones were so fragmented, she had to tear out all the bones and replace them with a new hip.Hopefully, her procedure will be successful", dr. Ocar concluded.

The next morning, i was in lots of pain, but most of the fuzziness had left my mind.I was evaluating all the information dr. Doctor ocar had shared.At first, i thought maybe everything had been a nightmare, but it did not take long to realize it was real.The pain in my groin was severe from where a catheter had been inserted.This was my first experience with a 'miniature hose rammed inside my penis. I did not like it; one little iota.The only positive thing was all i had to do was just lay in my bed and when the urge hit to empty my bladder, all i had to do was just lay there and let it flow. The urine flowed into the catheter 'and inside a long tube that emptied into a large plastic bag.When it was filled, someone would switch bags and i could just pea and pea and pea.Drink and pea.Pea and drink. This might not be too bad after all, ''i thought and smiled.

Looking down at my hands and arms, there were tubes fastened to the end of needles sticking from my body.The tubes were attached to a bottle of clear-looking substance. This bottle was hanging from a metal roll-around cross-looking gadget.I soon learned this was saline, used due to dehydration.Saline is a mixture of sodium chloride and water.

 A bowel movement urge became dominant.I press the call button on my bed to let someone know i needed to go to the bathroom.Answering the call, i was informed i would be using a bedpan.This was a first for me. I was too young to recall my first butt wiping and diaper change, but don't believe it was as demeaning and embarrassing as it was this day. I'm not into a man sticking a gadget, called catheter, in my penis or wiping my butt; still not. This is for babies that just lay there smiling and goo gooing and do doing.

I had never been depressed in my life. Not even while in the army overseas, during the dangerous berlin buildup, nor while incarcerated.I have always been strong enough to roll with the punches and shake off negativisms.Not this time.

I have been done wrong several times in the workplace, but always been able to shake it off.I have been defeated in various dirty political contests and survived, but this physical condition i found myself in was slowly destroying me. It was on my mind twenty-four-seven primarily because i could not get away from it.Other than being able to move my right hand, arm, mouth and verbally communicate, i was paralyzed.I still had my hearing and eyesight.I was shut down. Not for a few hours, days, or weeks, but for the remainder of my life.

''This has to be a mistake.People get hurt every day and have operations to correct the problem. People have kidneys, hearts, eyes, and other replacements and live a productive life. Military personnel lose limbs in combat and have successful operations, and live a productive life.How can a doctor tell me i will be worthless, cripple, a burden, a freak, invalid, paralyzed, and helpless for the rest of my life.It just isn't fair. Not much left to live for, "i was thinking."If i knew there was not a hell, and i could get my hands on a weapon or extra pills, i would remove myself from society.My income will be cut off, the medical expense will be out the roof.All i will be is like a whatnot sitting on a shelf, except i will be a, 'what a nut lying in a bed'.Eat, pee in bed, dodo in bed, shave and bathe in bed. What a life to look forward to. Mary has worked all her life and just when she can get a break and enjoy life together, this happens.Now she will be tied down with a two hundred pounds of bones covered with skin.Way to go barton. ''My thoughts flooded my mind.

I have never run across anyone i could not communicate with.No matter the status in life, skin color, religious or political affiliation, i could hang in there.I've even had conversations with god.I was good at expressing my disdain when upset.I've heard folks say you are not supposed to become upset or question god about anything.If this is true, then i'm in serious trouble.

''God, it's time you and i have a sit-down.I'm not saying you caused my accident, but it's obvious you made no effort to stop it.You could have kept that car door from closing and knocking me down. But you didn't.You could have kept me from getting all broken up. But you didn't. God it looks like every time things are going great, you stop it, or it sure appears like it," i was saying to god wherever he was.

I was on a roll…. Having a pity party …. Letting god know just how upset i was at him. Bitterness was not an accurate word to express my hurt and anger.

"god, i've never asked you for any favors nor consideration in my life.I've always worked, paid my bills, tried to do the right thing about everybody, paid tithes, and supported your ministers, and missionaries, and this is where i have wound up.Broken bones, helplessness, a burden to mary and delane.A wore-out old man."i was tearing into god, while tears like rain was flowing down my face as i had my self-righteous pity party. I went to sleep while giving god my opinion.

The next afternoon, mary drove back from talladega to spend some time. She was still employed so there was no need for her to stay away from her job.I had been placed in a room across from the nurse's station and they were on duty around the clock.My anger had subsided, a little, but i was still having negative thoughts about my entire ordeal

As mary entered the room coming straight to my side, apparently, she could see from the redness and swelling in my eyes, i had been crying."Well darling, there is no need in me hanging around in the shape i'm in.Just get the doctor to give me a shot and you can take the insurance money, pay off everyone we owe and get you a good healthy young man," i said.

''I don't want no other man," she said, as she came over and kissed me.'' i married you for better or worse, thru sickness and health, until death do you depart.I heard what the doctor said, and i appreciate all he has done, but he is not the final authority.God is not finished with you yet," she said.

Tears start back again as mary removes from her purse, a small glass vial containing a liquid.It was her vial of anointing oil she carries wherever she goes.She receives calls often requesting prayer. She is a prayer warrior.Since we have been married, she has spent a lot of time in prayer.Removing the top from the vial, she starts anointing me from the top of my head to the bottom of my feet and from side to side, while all the time praying.

''Lord, as i anoint larry, i ask you to comfort him and ease the pain.I have tried to serve you and never question you.Why things happen in life will always be a mystery, but you never make a mistake.You tell us in all things give thanks, not for all things. Romans 8;28 reminds us that all things work together, for the good of those that love you and are called for your purpose. God, you know larry and i love you. Touch larry and heal his broken bones that they may be good as new.Give me the strength and ability to be able to help take care of him as he faces this time in life. Lord, larry was dedicated to you, by his parents when just an infant.He still belongs to you.I thank you for every blessing.In jesus name i pray.

Did i jump up out of my bed and start dancing?Were all needles removed from my arms and hands?Was i healed?No.But in a couple of days, feeling returned to my feet and i could wiggle my toes.My right hand and arm returned to normal.A few days later feeling began returning to my legs, then my torso.Every day there were slight improvements.

As the days came and went, my kidneys began functioning on their own and the catheter was removed. I was glad to get it out and it slid out much easier than forcing it in. Inserting a miniature hose pipe thru an opening the size of the eye of a needle is painful. After spending several months at u.a.b. And spain rehab, i was able to transfer to attalla nursing home for physical therapy.After almost one year in rehab, i was able to return home.I continued to improve daily.I am blessed to have aides that assist me around the clock.They have all been a blessing for mary and me.Without them, i would have been forced to remain at attalla nursing and health care facility or some other healthcare facility.

From the time mary anointed me with oil, and prayed until now, god has blessed us with a sit-to-stand lift that permits mary to lift me out of bed, place me on the bedside commode, and transfers me to my motorized wheelchair.God has blessed us with a handicapped-accessible, one-owner dodge van that i use for doctor appointments, church, or going out to eat. This is a miracle story itself.

Before my motorized wheelchair and van, once i returned home from the nursing home, periodically i had to visit the doctor for checkups, or dental appointments. This required one of my aides to manually roll me down the steps in my wheelchair, physically manhandle my 250 pounds by lifting me from my chair, and forcefully put me in the front seat of his suv. His vehicle was not conducive to my situation. I knew a van was needed, but i knew mary and i were not financially able to purchase a van a new one was cost-prohibited. One completely equipped would cost upwards to seventy-five thousand dollars and an old used one would cost upwards of twenty thousand. I would just have to keep struggling. Of course, i could call an ambulance but this would cost about one thousand dollars round trip. Prayer time again. Pray for a van mary.

A few weeks later, one of my aides, amanda, was talking with a friend of hers on her cell phone when i heard her say "i do.' how much do you want for it? Amanda is a cna and has worked for several families over the years. She knows everyone. She is also an excellent pianist as well as a semi-pro-gospel singer.

Turning to me she asked, " do you want to buy a van? "'i sure do," i responded.

While keeping the lady on the phone, amanda said my friend's husband just died and she is going to sell his van. He paid close to seventy thousand dollars for it and she will sell it for twenty-five thousand.

"Amanda, mary, and i couldn't buy it if it was a hundred dollars. Asked her what's the least she will take for it," i responded

"Tell him to make an offer, " the lady said. I told amanda i would let her know in a day or so.

Prayer time.

This time i was saying a silent prayer.I knew mary was praying too, but wondered if she was wearing out her welcome.God knew mary and i needed the van and this sounded too real to believe.

Amanda had said she would contact some friends and see if they would contribute.She believed we could raise the money.I knew mary and i could not afford it.

I picked up the phone receiver.Only god and i knew what was going on in my thoughts. The phone rings several times and a lady's voice said, "hello, this is erika, may i help you," a soft velvet voice asked.

Andi responded."Hello miss erika, this is larry barton and i want to know how much money can i borrow on my signature."?

Erika was a beautiful african-american lady who is a branch manager at regions bank in talladega.This is the same bank i served as vice president for twelve years.

Erika said, " let me check out something, hold on."after several minutes, erika said, "i can let you have fifteen thousand on your signature.More on a real estate loan'." "thanks, you are a very special lady and friend," i said.

I immediately called the lady with the van and shared with her that fifteen thousand dollars was all i could borrow.

"larry, i have been praying about your situation i have just purchased a car for my grand-daughter and paid fifteen thousand for it.I have decided to let you have the van for fifteen thousand and pay her car loan off.

God is still good.

Has god healed me you may ask?Considering where i was to where i am now. What do you think?

EPILOGUE

The citizens and i may never learn the truth about jamie.If she is dead, who killed her?If she is still alive, where is she?Was she placed in protective custody?Is it possible for her and her only true love back together, marry, and live on a foreign island?I have my opinion and i will continue searching for the truth.

I have enjoyed writing this book, and trust you enjoy reading it.Keep mary and me in your thoughts and prayers.Never take your life for granted. Be thankful and thank god for every blessing.